As Free and as Just as Possible

Blackwell Public Philosophy

Edited by Michael Boylan, Marymount University

In a world of 24-hour news cycles and increasingly specialized knowledge, the Blackwell Public Philosophy series takes seriously the idea that there is a need and demand for engaging and thoughtful discussion of topics of broad public importance. Philosophy itself is historically grounded in the public square, bringing people together to try to understand the various issues that shape their lives and give them meaning. This "love of wisdom" – the essence of philosophy – lies at the heart of the series. Written in an accessible, jargon-free manner by internationally renowned authors, each book is an invitation to the world beyond newsflashes and soundbites and into public wisdom.

1. *Permission to Steal: Revealing the Roots of Corporate Scandal* by Lisa H. Newton
2. *Doubting Darwin? Creationist Designs on Evolution* by Sahotra Sarkar
3. *The Extinction of Desire: A Tale of Enlightenment* by Michael Boylan
4. *Torture and the Ticking Bomb* by Bob Brecher
5. *In Defense of Dolphins: The New Moral Frontier* by Thomas I. White
6. *Terrorism and Counter-Terrorism: Ethics and Liberal Democracy* by Seumas Miller
7. *Who Owns You? The Corporate Gold Rush to Patent Your Genes* by David Koepsell
8. *Animalkind: What We Owe to Animals* by Jean Kazez
9. *In the Name of God: The Evolutionary Origins of Religious Ethics and Violence* by John Teehan
10. *The Secular Outlook: In Defense of Moral and Political Secularism* by Paul Cliteur
11. *Freedom of Religion and the Secular State* by Russell Blackford
12. *As Free and as Just as Possible: The Theory of Marxian Liberalism*
13. *Life, Liberty, and the Pursuit of Dao* by Sam Crane

Forthcoming:
Evil On-Line: Explorations of Evil and Wickedness on the Web by Dean Cocking and Jeroen van den Hoven

For further information about individual titles in the series, supplementary material, and regular updates, visit www.blackwellpublishing.com/ publicphilosophy

As Free and as Just as Possible

The Theory of Marxian Liberalism

Jeffrey Reiman

WILEY Blackwell

This edition first published 2014
© 2014 John Wiley & Sons Inc

Registered Office
John Wiley & Sons Ltd, The Atrium, Southern Gate, Chichester, West Sussex, PO19 8SQ, UK

Editorial Offices
350 Main Street, Malden, MA 02148-5020, USA
9600 Garsington Road, Oxford, OX4 2DQ, UK
The Atrium, Southern Gate, Chichester, West Sussex, PO19 8SQ, UK

For details of our global editorial offices, for customer services, and for information about how to apply for permission to reuse the copyright material in this book please see our website at www.wiley.com/wiley-blackwell.

The right of Jeffrey Reiman to be identified as the author of this work has been asserted in accordance with the UK Copyright, Designs and Patents Act 1988.

Wiley also publishes its books in a variety of electronic formats. Some content that appears in print may not be available in electronic books.

Designations used by companies to distinguish their products are often claimed as trademarks. All brand names and product names used in this book are trade names, service marks, trademarks or registered trademarks of their respective owners. The publisher is not associated with any product or vendor mentioned in this book.

Limit of Liability/Disclaimer of Warranty: While the publisher and author have used their best efforts in preparing this book, they make no representations or warranties with respect to the accuracy or completeness of the contents of this book and specifically disclaim any implied warranties of merchantability or fitness for a particular purpose. It is sold on the understanding that the publisher is not engaged in rendering professional services and neither the publisher nor the author shall be liable for damages arising herefrom. If professional advice or other expert assistance is required, the services of a competent professional should be sought.

Library of Congress Cataloging-in-Publication Data
Reiman, Jeffrey H.
   As free and as just as possible : the theory of Marxian liberalism / Jeffrey Reiman.
      p. cm. – (Blackwell public philosophy; 12)
   Includes bibliographical references and index.
   ISBN 978-0-470-67412-3 (hardback : alk. paper)   ISBN 978-1-118-72038-7 (paperback)
   1. Liberalism–Philosophy.   2. Philosophy, Marxist.   3. Rawls, John, 1921-2002.   I. Title.
   JC574.R445 2012
   335.401–dc23
                                        2011044951

A catalogue record for this book is available from the British Library.

Cover image: Snow Fence © Brendan Hunter / iStockphoto

Set in 10.5/13.5 pt Palatino by Toppan Best-set Premedia Limited
Printed in Malaysia by Ho Printing (M) Sdn Bhd

1   2014

For Sue

Contents

Contents

List of Abbreviations

ASU   Robert Nozick, *Anarchy, State, and Utopia* (New York: Basic Books, 1974)

C   Karl Marx, *Capital* (New York: International Publishers, 1967; originally published: volume 1, 1867, volume 2, 1893, volume 3, 1894)

Essay   John Locke, *An Essay Concerning Human Understanding* (New York: Oxford University Press, 1975; originally published 1690)

JF   John Rawls, *Justice as Fairness: A Restatement*, ed. Erin Kelly (Cambridge, MA: Harvard University Press, 2001)

Letter   John Locke, *A Letter Concerning Toleration* (Indianapolis: Hackett, 1983; originally published 1689)

LHPP   John Rawls, *Lectures on the History of Political Philosophy* (Cambridge, MA: Harvard University Press, 2007).

MER   Robert C. Tucker, ed., *The Marx–Engels Reader*, 2nd edition (New York: Norton, 1978)

MM   Immanuel Kant, *The Metaphysics of Morals* (Cambridge: Cambridge University Press, 1996; the two parts of *The Metaphysics of Morals*, "The Doctrine of Right" and "The

Doctrine of Virtue," were originally published separately in 1797)

PL   John Rawls, *Political Liberalism* (New York: Columbia University Press, 1996)

RJE   G. A. Cohen, *Rescuing Justice and Equality* (Cambridge, MA: Harvard University Press, 2008)

ST   John Locke, *The Second Treatise of Government*, in John Locke, *Two Treatises of Government* (London: Dent & Sons, 1975; this is a reprint of the first state of the first edition of Locke's *Two Treatises of Government* originally published in 1690)

TJ   John Rawls, *A Theory of Justice*, rev. edn. (Cambridge, MA: Harvard University Press, 1999)

Preface

It was from Karl Marx that I learned to admire capitalism and to fear socialism. In both the *Communist Manifesto* and in *Capital*, Marx wrote about the enormous productivity unleashed by capitalism, as well as of capitalism's power to liberate people from older more repressive social systems. For Marx, capitalism's productivity would provide the means for freeing human beings from unwanted toil, which he thought would be achieved in communism. Capitalism's dissolution of the bonds of feudalism, and its promotion of individual liberty, paved the way for freeing human beings from domination by other human beings, which Marx believed communism would also bring. At the same time, Marx thought that capitalism was an unfair and brutal system. For Marx, capitalists' ownership of the means of production (factories, machines, natural resources) gave them power over the rest of society, because it gave them control over the opportunities for earning a living. And this power was exercised for profit rather than for satisfying human needs. No one who has seen the news recently will find this hard to believe.

Marx thought that the remedy for capitalism was socialism: replacing private ownership of means of production with public ownership. But, as I said, I also learned from Marx to fear socialism. States are already dangerously powerful, with their police forces and armies. If ownership of the means of production is as potent a mechanism of power over people as Marx thought, then it is simply too great – too easy to misuse, too tempting to abuse, too likely to corrupt the powerful – to place it in the control of the state. And in Russia, Eastern Europe and China, history has shown that the danger is real. Whatever good they have done, socialist states have not been hospitable to freedom.

But, not only does Marx's belief that ownership of means of production is a mechanism of power over people suggest that socialism will be dangerous to freedom, it suggests as well that capitalism's relatively decentralized ownership of means of production supports the individual freedom that has generally characterized capitalist societies. This might work in the way that James Madison thought that the large number of independent religious sects in America worked to protect religious freedom.

What, then, is to be done? I think that the time is ripe for a philosophical theory of justice that combines Marx's insights – about capitalism, and about the conditions of freedom and the mechanisms of coercion – with the liberalism that socialist states have lacked. Marxian Liberalism is such a theory of justice. It aims to satisfy the lovers of individual freedom, and the fans of free enterprise, while realizing some of the egalitarian values dear to socialists – but in a form less likely to lead to tyranny. The liberal ideas that Marxian Liberalism combines with Marx's insights are drawn from the classic work of John Locke, and the recent work of John Rawls, said by some to be the John Stuart Mill of the twentieth century. Marxian Liberalism starts by bringing together the Lockean idea that people have a natural right not to be coerced, with the Marxian idea that private ownership is coercive. From there, it develops a theory of justice that calls for a highly egalitarian form of capitalism combined with a strictly liberal state, and holds that this combination makes for a society that is as free and as just as possible.

Because *As Free and as Just as Possible: The Theory of Marxian Liberalism* is published in a series on public philosophy, I have written it for the educated layperson, though I hope that professional philosophers find it interesting as well. I have tried to put forth my ideas and arguments in widely accessible non-technical language. Where technical terms are necessary, I define them in plain English.

Though some background in philosophy will help in reading this book, I have tried to write it so that such a background is not necessary.

While working on the book, I encountered the late G. A. Cohen's *Rescuing Justice and Equality*, a profound full-scale critique of Rawls's theory of justice. Since Cohen is a philosopher with Marxist sympathies who objects to some of the very features of Rawls's theory that are crucial to Marxian Liberalism, I had to respond to his objections. Consequently, I engage with Cohen's views at many points throughout *As Free and as Just as Possible*. I think that I am able to defend the features of Rawls's theory that play a role in Marxian Liberalism against Cohen's objections. And I think that Marxian Liberalism is a better theory as a result. I am grateful to Cohen for this, and feel all the more deeply the great loss his untimely death is for philosophy.

I believed some combination of liberal and Marxian beliefs long before I thought of them as a doctrine with a name of its own. For this reason, I have occasionally been able to make use of previous articles of mine here. Parts of Section 2.1 are from my "The Marxian Critique of Criminal Justice," *Criminal Justice Ethics* 6, no. 1 (Winter/Spring 1987), pp. 30–50 (copyrighted material reprinted by permission of The Institute for Criminal Justice Ethics). Section 2.2 draws on my "Is Racial Profiling Just? Making Criminal Justice Policy in the Original Position," *The Journal of Ethics* 15, no. 1–2 (Winter 2011), pp. 3–19. Section 4.3 uses material from my "Exploitation, Force, and the Moral Assessment of Capitalism: Thoughts on Roemer and Cohen," *Philosophy & Public Affairs* 16, no. 1 (Winter 1987), pp. 3–41. Material from my "The Labor Theory of the Difference Principle," *Philosophy & Public Affairs* 12, no. 2 (Spring 1983), pp. 133–159, turns up in Sections 5.1 through 5.4, and Section 6.5. Finally, some of what I say in Sections 2.4, 2.5, and 7.4 is derived from my entry "Marx, Karl," in Hugh Lafollette, ed., *The International Encyclopedia of Ethics* (Boston, MA: Wiley-Blackwell, 2013). I thank these publications for supporting my work, and for permitting the use of these writings in the present book.

Other thanks are due as well. Though he will surely disagree with Marxian Liberalism, Jan Narveson (whose work is dealt with at a number of points in this book) deserves thanks for being a perfect philosophical pen pal: always ready to argue about the issues and always in a friendly manner. I am grateful to my old friend, Arthur Lothstein, for inviting me to speak at C.W. Post University and give the core ideas in this book their first public airing. I thank Joe Rees, an excellent former undergraduate philosophy student of mine (now pursuing his doctorate at Georgetown University), who read a draft of this book and gave me lots of helpful and challenging comments. Joe also tried to convey to me the questions that his generation of young philosophers might have about my project, and I have tried to respond to those questions in my text. I am grateful to two graduate students: John Fantuzzo, who did most of the historical and legal research reported in Section 6.2; and Brian Brinker, who filled in some of the rest.

I thank Michael Boylan, Marymount University philosopher, and editor of the Blackwell Public Philosophy Series, for inviting me to contribute to that series, for warmly encouraging me along the way, and for reading and commenting extensively on an early draft of the book. I thank Jeff Dean, my editor at Wiley-Blackwell, for his candid advice and friendly support of my project. I am grateful to Jack Messenger for ably copyediting the manuscript, and to Joanna Pyke for skillfully guiding my project from manuscript to book. I thank both of them for accommodating my unpredictable work schedule. And I thank (once again) American University, where I have taught for more than forty years, for providing me with a tolerant and welcoming intellectual environment in which I have been free to follow my philosophical impulses where they led. I am especially grateful to my colleagues in the Department of Philosophy and Religion at American for their warmth and interest and their deep commitment to philosophical inquiry.

Finally, I have had the great good fortune to spend my life with a wonderful, brainy, funny, passionate woman, a professor and an author in her own right, with three books to her name. She stimulates my mind and brightens my days. She is part of everything I do. For this reason, this book is dedicated to her, the other Marxian Liberal, my wife and partner, Sue Headlee.

I

Overview of the Argument for Marxian Liberalism

Marxian Liberalism is a theory of social justice that results from combining certain liberal beliefs, most importantly, that people have a natural right to liberty understood as a right to be free from unwanted coercion, with some Marxian beliefs, most importantly, that private property is coercive. Because Marxian Liberalism aims to protect people from both the normal forms of coercion and the subtler structural coercion of private property, it calls for a society that is *as free as possible*. Because it defines justice historically, as what can be required of people in light of their changing human nature, it calls for a society that is *as just as possible*.

A crucial result of combining the right to liberty with the belief that private property is coercive is that *on liberal grounds*, to be justified, a right to private property must be consented to by all affected by it, which means by all present and future humans. Consequently, consent must be *theoretical*, not a matter of asking actual people to sign on the dotted line, and I shall explain why theoretical consent is satisfactory in this context (see Section 3.3). To seek theoretical

As Free and as Just as Possible: The Theory of Marxian Liberalism, First Edition. Jeffrey Reiman.
© 2014 Jeffrey Reiman. Published 2014 by John Wiley & Sons, Ltd.

consent is to appeal to what, in the philosophical tradition, is called a *social contract*. To determine what sort of right to private property would receive this theoretical consent, I deploy an imaginary contracting situation modeled on John Rawls's original position and veil of ignorance, but with a special difference: The knowledge that the parties in this original position possess includes certain liberal and certain Marxian beliefs. I contend that the parties in this Marxian-Liberal original position will agree to a right to property limited by a strongly egalitarian requirement, namely, Rawls's *difference principle*. (I lay out Rawls's theory of justice in Section 2.2.)

Marxian Liberalism should not be confused with Left-Libertarianism. (I reserve the term "libertarian" *tout court* for the generally rightist view that the natural right to liberty entails a right to property limited only by other people's like rights to liberty and property, and thus which justifies a virtually unlimited free market capitalist economic system.) Left-Libertarians start from two independent moral principles, first, that individual human beings own themselves and, second, that all humans own the world.[1] Marxian Liberalism makes neither claim, though possession of the right to liberty effectively amounts to individual self-ownership.[2] For reasons that will emerge in what follows, I believe that ownership and its rights should be derivative in a theory of justice rather than foundational. The authors of a recent defense of Left-Libertarianism hold that "Left-libertarianism seems promising because it recognizes both strong individual rights of liberty . . . and also grounds a strong demand for some kind of material equality."[3] Marxian

---

[1] Peter Vallentyne, Hillel Steiner, and Michael Otsuka, "Why Left-Libertarianism Is Not Incoherent, Indeterminate, or Irrelevant: A Reply to Fried," *Philosophy & Public Affairs* 33, no. 2 (2005): 201; on the independence of the two basic principles, see pp. 208–210.

[2] Locke appears to infer self-ownership from the right to liberty, and uses it as part of his argument for the right to own property for consumption (*ST*, v:27). Kant rejects self-ownership, holding that only things, and not persons, can be owned. He argues directly from the right to liberty to the right to property (*MM*, 41, 56). See Sections 4.1 and 4.2, below.

[3] Vallentyne et al., "Why Left-Libertarianism Is Not Incoherent," 201.

Liberalism seems promising for the same reasons, plus it has the virtue of being simpler, since it starts with one moral principle – the right to liberty – rather than two.

Marxian Liberalism takes justice to be a historical notion, one whose requirements change over history. This is not a form of historical relativism. Justice has a timeless meaning: *It calls for the maximum provision for the interests of others that can reasonably be morally required of people given human nature.* However, since Marxism sees human nature as changing in history, the content of justice changes historically. For the most part, I shall consider what justice requires now and for the foreseeable future. Along the way, I will speculate about what, given Marx's view of where history (and thus human nature) is headed, justice will require in the future.

Readers familiar with G. A. Cohen's important book, *Rescuing Justice and Equality (RJE)*, will be struck by the fact that the definition given of justice in the previous paragraph includes reference to historically changeable facts about human nature; whereas Cohen, in his attempt to rescue justice from John Rawls, argues that fundamental moral principles are independent of facts. Cohen may be right about fundamental moral principles in general (though I shall press an alternative view in Section 3.2), but he is missing something important about justice in particular.

Rawls appeals to facts (about human nature, among other things) in identifying the principles of justice with what people would choose in the original position, knowing facts about human psychology (*TJ*, 399). But Cohen argues that Rawls has misidentified "the question 'What is justice?' with the question 'What principles should we adopt to regulate our affairs?'" (*RJE*, 269, see also 267, 350–351). Cohen recognizes that rules to regulate our affairs are rules that we can require actual people to live up to, and he grants such rules do properly take account of facts about human nature (*RJE*, 308–309, 342–343, *et alia*). But he thinks that such rules follow from justice; they are not equivalent to justice. This is a mistake.

Justice is a special kind of value that spells out what can be required of people. Thus, by Cohen's own argument, it must take account of facts about human nature. Both Immanuel Kant and John Stuart Mill, for example, held it to be distinctive of justice that it can be required, even coerced, from people. Kant held that what distinguishes justice (his word is *Recht*, usually translated as "right," but equivalent to "justice") from other aspects of morality, such as virtue, is precisely that justice can be coerced. Actually, Kant held it to be a tautology that justice could be forced (*MM*, 25). And Mill wrote that "the idea of legal constraint is . . . the generating idea of the notion of justice."[4] This does not mean that justice must be forced, or that it is always wise to force it. It is however what we are entitled to require, that is, at very least, what we may insist upon from our fellows, regardless of how we make this insistence stick. Thus, I include in the definition of justice both that it can be required, and that it must be reasonable in light of facts about human nature.

As to the fundamental moral principles that Cohen says are fact free, and thus which we cannot require of people, they are commonly called *ideals*. And they are normally distinguished from duties, that is, requirements. Extreme heroism and extreme generosity are ideals, but not duties. We are praised if we live up to them, but not blamed if we fail to. Blameworthiness depends on facts about human nature.[5] Thus, justice is not an ideal. It can be required and so it depends on facts about human nature. Does this mean that the notion of *ideal justice* is a contradiction in terms? Not quite. It certainly means that ideal justice is not justice now, in that it is not now required. It is what would be required if human nature were ideal, or at least as good as could be expected, or what will be required when human nature improves. This is why, as we shall see in Section 5.5, Marxian Liberalism can accept Cohen's (fundamental, fact-free, thus) ideal justice as what corresponds to the

---

[4]John Stuart Mill, *Utilitarianism* (Indianapolis: Hackett, 1979), 47.
[5]Interestingly, Cohen recognizes that the question of blameworthiness (which is related to, though not identical to, that of what is our duty) depends on facts about human nature (*RJE*, 140n55).

improved human nature that Marxists believe humans will one day have.

Turn now to the notion that private property is coercive. As we shall see, Marx meant something quite specific and controversial by this idea. He was referring particularly to private ownership of means of production by a handful of capitalists. At this point, however, we can make use of a more general and less controversial version of the claim: Private property (whether of means of production or not) is coercive in the following ways: It is a constraint on other people's freedom. It excludes others from the free use of something in the world. Also, a right to private property is an enforceable right, thus it is backed up by coercion. Moreover, the exclusion of others from using something may be a tool of coercion itself. If, say, one person owns what another needs to survive, the owner will be able to coerce the nonowner to do his bidding. And where – as is now just about everywhere the case – virtually everything is owned by someone, owners will surely own what nonowners need to survive. Thus they will be able to coerce them.

A right to liberty is also an enforceable right, so it justifies coercion that is necessary to protect people's liberty. Beyond that, however, the right prohibits any other coercion except that which people consent to. If it seems odd to think that people would ever genuinely consent to coercion, note that we do it all the time, and it is often quite a rational thing to do. For example, when I sign a contract to rent an apartment, I subject myself to coercion by the state in the event that I refuse to pay my rent. This enables me to offer a guarantee to the landlord that my mere promise to pay could never have provided. Consequently, that I consent to coercion adds to my ability to realize my own purposes. Likewise, though private property may be coercive, it may still be rational to agree to it if it adds to people's ability to act on their purposes.

It is part of Marxian Liberalism that private property (subject to certain constraints that will be specified in due course) does – at least in the current historical era – enhance people's ability to act on their purposes. Indeed, Marxian Liberalism holds that a capitalist system allowing private ownership of means of production (likewise subject to certain constraints) enhances people's ability to act on their purposes, and thus would be rational for people to consent to. But this poses a difficult theoretical problem. Those who may be coerced by private property include all present and future humans. Not only my neighbors, but people on the other side of the world (who may travel here or want to invest here) will be subject to coercion because of my property. And not only my contemporaries, but people who do not live now but who will live in the future may likewise be subject to coercion because of my property. Consequently, for a system of private property to be morally legitimate it must be consented to by *everyone who lives now or who will live in the foreseeable future*!

Needless to say, such consent would be impossible to get if we think of it as a matter of asking actual people to say whether they consent or do not. We can't ask all actual people whether they consent, and we surely can't ask future people if they do. Moreover, a right to private property that depends on getting the actual consent of every new person who turns up would be pointless. A right is a guarantee of free action. But a guarantee of free action is only valuable to an actor if she knows that she has the guarantee before she acts on it. The various benefits that a right to property may be thought to bring with it, for example, the incentive to improve bare natural resources, depend on knowing before I invest in such improvement that I will be able to benefit from the improvement. Consequently, a right to property that depends on the consent of every new person who appears in the world is as good as no right at all.

If property is to be morally legitimate, consent to it must be *theoretical*, that is, a matter of what it would be rational for people to consent to, not a matter of asking actual people to sign on the dotted line. Thus, rights to private property will have to be the object of a theoretical social contract, just the sort of contract that philosophers from Hobbes and Locke to Kant and Rawls have appealed to, to justify the existence of the state or to determine the principles of justice to which a state must conform.

I will set about to determine what sort of right to private property would receive the theoretical consent of everyone affected by it.[6] Notice that the question is not simply whether the right to property would be theoretically consented to or not. The question is *what sort of right* to private property – with what built-in limits if any – would be consented to. To address this question, I will deploy an imaginary contracting situation modeled on John Rawls's *original position*. Though the contracting situation is modeled on Rawls's social contract theory of justice, the contractarianism that underlies Marxian Liberalism is Lockean rather than Rawlsian. As in Locke's theory, Marxian Liberalism's appeal to the social contract is morally required by the prior existence of the natural right to liberty, rather than, as in Rawls, an exercise aimed at determining all moral rights from scratch.

Rawls's original position is the philosopher's equivalent of what a scientist would call a "thought experiment." Thought experiments – where inferences are made about the behavior of entities under imaginary or idealized, or even physically impossible, conditions – have been used successfully by scientists from Galileo (who imagined balls rolling down frictionless planes, which is impossible) to Einstein (who imagined observers traveling at the speed of light, which he thought was impossible). Such thought experiments have been crucial to the undeniable progress of modern science.

In the Rawlsian thought experiment, we imagine a group of individuals who represent us, and who are to choose unanimously the principles of justice to govern their shared existence. The parties in this imagined original position are taken to be rational individuals who have knowledge of general matters (e.g., history, psychology,

---

[6]This assumes that, even if human nature changes, the kinds of basic interests that people have regarding property will remain the same. So, for example, if people become more altruistic, they will still have an interest in having secure possessions even if only to give them away. Charity is not possible without something like ownership.

economics), but are otherwise behind a *veil of ignorance* that denies them knowledge of their specific identity and situation. Since they do not know facts about their own situations, they cannot tailor principles to their individual interests. None can insist on principles that advance his or her interests at the expense of those of others. Accordingly, they choose under fair conditions, and we are entitled to believe that the principles it would be rational for them to choose are just: they serve the interests of all alike, and justify no exploitation or coercion of anyone simply for the benefit of others.

The original position that I shall make use of is like this, but with a special difference: The general knowledge that the parties have in this original position includes certain Marxian and liberal factual beliefs. (The qualification "factual" is important here, since it makes clear that the Marxian and liberal beliefs in the Marxian-Liberal original position do not alter the fact that Marxian Liberalism is based on a single moral principle – the natural right to liberty.) It is possible that we would reach a point in history at which these Marxian and liberal factual beliefs became part of what is widely recognized as general knowledge – in the way that certain beliefs about how markets lead to efficiency, or about how freedom of the press improves government performance, are part of general knowledge today. In that case, they would be part of the general knowledge possessed by the parties in Rawls's original position.[7] To get to the Marxian-Liberal original position with the least violence to

---

[7] In Rawls's *Political Liberalism* (PL), he puts forth his theory of justice as a freestanding political conception, meaning that it is not based upon any of the comprehensive philosophical or moral or religious views that different citizens may hold. He contends that this is necessary if a conception of justice is to garner willing morally grounded allegiance from the citizens of a free society, since people in free societies characteristically hold differing and incompatible comprehensive doctrines. Marxian Liberalism is, to be sure, a comprehensive doctrine. But, if we might genuinely believe that its underlying beliefs could become general knowledge one day, then it – or at least significant parts of it – could become a freestanding political conception. To those readers, then, who are drawn to Marxian Liberalism but distressed that it is not a freestanding conception of political justice, I say: Be patient.

Rawls's version, then, we need only assume that this point in history has been reached, and so I shall. With such general knowledge, I will argue that the parties in the Marxian-Liberal original position will find it rational to agree to a right to property limited by a strongly egalitarian requirement, namely, Rawls's *difference principle*.

The difference principle holds that inequality in an economic distribution must be the least inequality necessary to maximize the life-time share of the worst-off parties in the distribution (*TJ*, 266). Rawls says that "the difference principle is a strongly egalitarian conception in the sense that unless there is a distribution that makes both [the more advantaged and the less advantaged] persons better off . . . , an equal distribution is to be preferred" (*TJ*, 65–66). It is also strongly egalitarian because reducing inequality beyond what the difference principle allows would require reducing the share of the worst-off party. Thus, the difference principle calls for the greatest amount of equality possible without making the poor even poorer. I will argue that the Marxian-Liberal original position provides a deduction of the difference principle, something that Rawls aimed for but did not think he accomplished in *A Theory of Justice*.[8]

In putting forth the difference principle, Marxian Liberalism joins Rawls in holding that inequality is just if it works to maximize the share of the worst-off group. And it joins Rawls as well in holding that inequality does this mainly when greater-than-equal rewards serve as incentives that encourage more productive activity, thereby increasing the size of the pie for everyone. As a justification for inequality, however, this idea has been attacked from the right (by libertarian philosopher Jan Narveson) and from the left (by

---

[8]"One should note that acceptance of [the principles of justice in the original position] is not conjectured as a psychological law or probability. Ideally anyway, I should like to show that their acknowledgment is the only choice consistent with the full description of the original position. The argument aims eventually to be strictly deductive. . . . Unhappily the reasoning I shall give will fall far short of this, since it is highly intuitive throughout" (*TJ*, 104–105).

egalitarian philosopher G. A. Cohen). I shall show that Marxian Liberalism's use of the difference principle can – with respect to the current historical era – be defended against these attacks; and – with respect to the future – can absorb them.

I shall contend as well that parties in the Marxian-Liberal original position will agree to the existence of a state whose authority is limited to defending the natural right to liberty by protecting the basic liberties, assuring that the economy conforms to the difference principle, and prohibiting unwanted coercion not needed to perform these two functions.

Before trying to join them, it will be useful to make some general remarks about liberalism and Marxism as they will be understood here. I take *liberalism* to be the general doctrine that sane adult human beings should be free *in the sense of free from coercion that would block their ability to act on the choices they make*. This qualification is important for a number of reasons. First of all, it shows that the freedom crucial to liberalism is political or social freedom, the absence of coercion, the space that humans give each other to act as they see fit. This is the freedom that is called *liberty*.

Liberty is not the freedom at issue in the famous philosophical debates about free will versus determinism. *Free will* is a matter of whether people can be said really to make choices which are not determined by psychological or physical forces outside of their control. But whether or not people can be said to make choices that are free in this way, they can be either free to act on the choices they make, or blocked by others from so acting. They can have or lack liberty. In spite of thinking that human beings' choices were fully determined by natural causes, philosophers such as Thomas Hobbes and Benedict Spinoza believed in the importance of liberty. This is the freedom that liberalism aims to protect.

The qualification ("free *in the sense of free from coercion that would block their ability to act on the choices they make*") is important in another respect. It shows that liberty is the ordinary freedom of ordinary people. It is not an ideal of perfect freedom, such as one might have who acts with perfect rationality or perfect information about the alternatives before her, or who acts with full awareness of the motives that arise from her particular psychology or from the culture in which she has been reared. To be sure, a liberal society will be one in which information will flow freely, ideological and traditional beliefs will be subject to lively questioning, and reflection on the influence of psychology and culture will be encouraged. Nonetheless, because it aims to protect the ordinary freedom of ordinary people, it leaves it up to individuals how they make use of this information and participate in this questioning and reflection. Accordingly, liberalism cannot be used to justify "re-educating" people to make them more free, nor can it be used to justify – in Rousseau's ominous words – forcing people to be free.

This is not to say that liberalism defends every exercise of liberty or every human's right to exercise liberty. As already noted, liberalism licenses the use of coercion to prevent acts that constrain other people's ability to act on their equal right to liberty. Moreover, insane people and children will have to be constrained in their ability to act on their choices because they fall below the ordinary ability to identify their purposes and thus may act, unknowingly, against their purposes. Their liberty will be restricted, not because they cannot exercise it, but because it is not really a value for them.

Important for us, here, is that liberalism holds that we have a general right to be free from unwanted coercion that is not tied to a particular view of what constitutes coercion. In this regard, it is different from *libertarianism*, which defines coercion very narrowly as primarily physical aggression (see, for example, *ASU*, 32). I say "primarily" here because libertarians generally include as coercion fraud, since deception functions to undermine and subvert people's ordinary choices.[9] And some libertarians include psychological coercion in its grosser forms as coercion as well.

---

[9]Nozick's prohibition on physical aggression is based on the Kantian prohibition against using other persons for one's ends without their consent; but that will rule out fraud as well since it is a means of using others without their consent. And Narveson's prohibition on coercion is based on a presumed agreement between individuals; and that will rule out fraud since it presupposes that individuals are bound to honor their agreements.

Overview of the Argument

By contrast, liberalism is in principle open to recognizing, and thus adapting itself to, new forms of coercion. This is one way to understand the difference between what liberalism meant in the nineteenth century and what it came to mean in the twentieth. That difference is quite striking, and the cause of no small amount of confusion. Nineteenth-century liberals defended the idea of a minimal state – sometimes called the "nightwatchman state" – that does little more than protect people from domestic and international threats of violence to their bodies and property. By contrast, twentieth-century liberals have called for a larger and more active state that, in addition to protecting against domestic and international violence, protects people against poverty and unemployment and racism and sexism. We can understand this development as a change in the understanding of what is coercive. Where nineteenth-century liberals were effectively libertarian in their narrow understanding of coercion, twentieth-century liberals came to see a wider range of conditions as coercive. Interestingly, this means that both nineteenth- and twentieth-century liberals are genuine liberals, that is, genuinely interested in protecting liberty. Where they differ is over what the threat is that needs protecting against.

Among the liberal beliefs that I shall take to be general knowledge in the Marxian-Liberal original position are that people have an interest in the liberty protected by the right to liberty. That is, they have an interest in protecting and expanding their ability to act on their choices. Also part of their general knowledge is that private property is a necessary support of individual liberty; and that a state is necessary (for the foreseeable future at least) to protect both liberty and property. The Marxian beliefs that I shall take to be general knowledge in the Marxian-Liberal original position are a set of beliefs which together amount to a *theory of the conditions of liberty*.

It is common, however, to think of Marxism as an enemy of liberty. I believe that this comes from taking Marxism as equivalent to communism, and thus as equivalent to the profoundly illiberal – and now mostly failed – attempts to establish communist societies in the twentieth century. But, even a cursory look at Marx's works shows that it is a mistake to identify Marxism with the oppressive communist regimes in Russia and Eastern Europe. Marx's work is about a lot more than communism or socialism. Of the thousands and thousands of pages that Marx and his collaborator Friedrich Engels wrote, only a small number are devoted to discussing socialism or communism. By far the greatest number are devoted to analyzing capitalism, and after that, to Marx's theory of history, called "historical materialism." That Marx has little to say about socialism and communism should be no surprise. When Marx wrote, there was no communist state nor had there ever been one. The examples of socialism that existed were few and small and short-lived.

By and large, Marx reached socialism and communism by putting a negative sign next to the feature of capitalism that he took to be the source of its unjust and oppressive nature, namely, private ownership of the means of production. By "means of production," Marx meant factories and machines and raw materials. Since property in means of production gave its owners control over the opportunities for gainful employment, it gave them leverage over the great majority of humanity who did not own means of production. Those people would have to work for the owners – the capitalists – in order to gain a living, which is to say, in order to live at all. Here is the special coerciveness that Marx saw in private ownership of means of production.

Rather than Marx's recommendation of socialism or communism as the remedy for capitalism showing him to be an enemy of liberty, Marx made this recommendation precisely because of his commitment to liberty. I shall discuss Marx's theory in greater detail shortly (Section 2.1). Here I want to point out that Marx opposed private ownership precisely because he took it to thwart liberty. Peter Stillman, for example, writes that "it is clear that Marx criticizes capitalist private property precisely because it limits individuality, individual development and freedom."[10] Though Marx thought

---

[10]Peter G. Stillman, "Property, Freedom and Individuality in Hegel's and Marx's Political Thought," in *NOMOS XXII: Property*, eds. J. R. Pennock and J. W. Chapman (New York: New York University Press, 1980), 153.

that individual liberty (or, as he called it, "personal freedom") had social conditions, he clearly endorsed its value. In *The German Ideology*, for example, he (along with Engels) wrote: "Only in community [with others has each] individual the means of cultivating his gifts in all directions; only in the community, therefore, is personal freedom possible" (*MER*, 197). And Marx recognized the importance of liberal individual rights. In "On the Jewish Question," he wrote: "Political emancipation [exemplified by the liberal rights granted in the French *Declaration of the Rights of Man and the Citizen*, and in the American Revolutionary-era state constitutions of Pennsylvania and New Hampshire] certainly represents a great progress" (*MER*, 35, 40–44). Even if liberalism sometimes serves capitalism ideologically by hiding its coerciveness, that does not imply that liberalism is wholly false or regressive. Ideology must be in some measure progressive to work as ideology. Otherwise, it could not put a positive face on existing injustice.

It was because he took private ownership of means of production to be coercive, that Marx sought to abolish it. Abolishing private ownership of means of production could be done in two ways, by replacing private ownership with public (that is, state) ownership, and by replacing private ownership with direct (that is, stateless) ownership by the workers. Marx and Engels thought that communism would start with state ownership and become direct ownership as the state withered away.[11] Presumably, these phases correspond to the two principles of economic distribution that Marx discusses in *Critique of the Gotha Program* (*MER*, 530–531; see Sections 2.5, 6.5, below).[12] Later writers have called the first phase *socialism* and the higher phase *communism* (see, for example, *LHPP*, 359, 366). Using this nomenclature, we can say that the states that

[11] "When, in the course of development, class distinctions have disappeared, and all production has been concentrated in the hands of a vast association of the whole nation, the public power will lose its political character. Political power, properly so called, is merely the organized power of one class for oppressing another" (Karl Marx and Friedrich Engels, *Manifesto of the Communist Party*, Chapter 2, *MER*, 490).
[12] See note 22, below, and accompanying text.

have called themselves communist are (or were) socialist states aspiring to communism.

The feasibility of both socialism and communism was a completely speculative matter in Marx's time. They represented ways of saying *no* to capitalism, not ways of organizing society on a large scale that had been shown to be satisfactory and workable over time. Indeed, there are good Marxian grounds for doubting that socialist or communist states could be liberating at all. If ownership of means of production is the main source of coercive power in a society, Marxists above all should be wary of placing that ownership in the hands of any single institution, much less the state with its police and its armies.

Interestingly, there are good Marxian grounds for believing that capitalist states will better preserve liberty than socialist or communist states: Private, and thus (compared to socialism and communism) relatively decentralized, ownership of means of production is the material basis for the freedoms that have generally characterized capitalist societies and that have been generally absent from communist and socialist ones. Much the way Madison thought that a multiplicity of different religious groups – each with a strong interest in preventing any other from dominating it – would work to protect religious freedom from the state,[13] the existence of a multiplicity of competing centers of economic power works to protect individual liberty from the state. For this reason, we cannot assume that granting ownership of means of production to a modern liberal democratic state will protect against the abuse of the enormous coercive power that that would represent. On Marxian grounds, the liberal democratic states that we know are as free as

[13]"Freedom of religion . . . arises from that multiplicity of sects, which pervades America, and which is the best and only security for religious liberty in any society. For where there is such a variety of sects, there cannot be a majority of any one sect to oppress and persecute the rest." James Madison, spoken at the Virginia convention to ratify the Constitution, June 12, 1788. See *The Founders' Constitution*, vol. 5, Amendment I (Religion), Document 49, http://press-pubs.uchicago.edu/founders/documents/amendI_religions49.html.

they are because of capitalism's relatively decentralized ownership of property.

Crucial for us are two points: First, that Marx's recommendation of socialism and communism is based on the threat to liberty that he perceived in capitalists' ownership of the means of production. And second, that that recommendation is separable from the critique of capitalism that led Marx to it. The second point means that, though the failure of the communist states in Russia and Eastern Europe shows that establishing a truly liberating socialism or communism – at least in the current historical era – is doubtful in the extreme, that in no way refutes Marx's diagnosis of capitalism. It simply leaves that diagnosis in need of a remedy. Marxian Liberalism aims to be such a remedy.

As such a remedy, Marxian Liberalism recommends a kind of liberal Marxism. That is, a Marxism in which control over their lives by free men and women takes precedence over the particular way in which production is organized. Where Marx does discuss socialism or communism, his emphasis is often less on the way production will be organized, than on the fact that it will be consciously controlled by the workers themselves. For example, anticipating communism in *Capital*, Marx wrote: "The life-process of society, which is based on the process of material production, does not strip off its mystical veil until it is treated as production by freely associated men" (*C*, I, 80).

Note that this view leaves open the question of how free people will organize the "the life-process of society" that they consciously control. I shall contend that – for Marxian, liberal, and historical reasons – in the present and for the foreseeable future, free people will adopt a form of capitalism subject to certain important constraints needed to preserve and maximize liberty.

This will be the outcome of the Marxian-Liberal original position for reasons such as the following. First of all, among the Marxian beliefs that inform the knowledge of the parties in the Marxian-Liberal original position, I include the belief that increasing material productivity is crucial to increasing people's liberty. Marx wrote that freedom in the realm of productive labor consists of "associated producers . . . rationally regulating their interchange with Nature, bringing it under common control, instead of being ruled by it as by the blind forces of Nature; and achieving this *with the least expenditure of energy*" (C, III, 820; my emphasis). Marx saw freedom as resulting from increasing human beings' control over nature so that they are able to satisfy their wants with the least expenditure of human energy. Increasing humans' control over nature so that wants are satisfied with the least expenditure of their energy amounts to increasing the material productivity of labor. As their wants are more fully and more easily satisfied, the scope of people's ability to act successfully on their choices grows apace.

But material productivity does not only contribute to freedom by increasing our ability to satisfy our wants. Marx held that increasing material productivity also brings freedom by reducing required labor (C, III, 820). It brings about conditions under which more and more of people's labor can be done because they want to do it, rather than because they must. Thus, labor itself becomes increasingly an object of choice rather than compulsion.

Marx acknowledged the unprecedented power of capitalism to increase material productivity in the *Communist Manifesto*, where, with Engels, he wrote that capitalism,

> during its rule of scarce one hundred years, has created more massive and more colossal productive forces than have all the preceding generations together. Subjection of Nature's forces to man, machinery, application of chemistry to industry and agriculture, steam-navigation, railways, electric telegraphs, clearing of whole continents for cultivation, canalization of rivers, whole populations conjured out of the ground – what earlier century had even a presentiment that such productive forces slumbered in the lap of social labour? (*MER*, 477)[14]

---

[14] Writes Nagel, "What capitalism produces is wonderful." Thomas Nagel, *Equality and Partiality* (Oxford: Oxford University Press, 1991), 93.

17

And Marx took capitalism to be progressive precisely because its enormous productivity made possible a freer society: "It is one of the civilizing aspects of capital that it enforces [the extraction of] surplus-labour in a manner and under conditions which are more advantageous to the development of the productive forces, social relations, and the creation of the elements for a new and higher form than under the preceding forms of slavery and serfdom, etc." (*C*, III, 819).

What Marx saw in the nineteenth century has only speeded up in the twentieth. International economist Nariman Behravesh writes:

> Worldwide real per capita GDP [gross domestic product] rose about fivefold in the last [the twentieth] century – no other century has come even close. Other measures of human development also improved dramatically, including longevity, infant death rates, the incidence of diseases and accidental deaths, the workweek, the quality of living conditions, the level of education, racial and sexual equality, and the environment. Unfortunately, not everyone in the world has benefited from these very positive trends.[15]

As for the cause of these improvements, Behravesh writes:

> Notwithstanding their flaws, free markets have provided far and away the most successful means of delivering sustained improvement in our lives. Command-and-control systems have neither provided the incentives nor been flexible enough to respond to rapid changes in market conditions and technologies.[16]

Though not everyone has benefited from these improvements, and income inequality has not consistently narrowed, poverty levels have fallen:

[15]Nariman Behravesh, *Spin-Free Economics: A No-Nonsense Guide to Today's Global Economic Debates* (New York: McGraw-Hill, 2009), 13.
[16]Behravesh, *Spin-Free Economics*, 14.

In 1900, roughly half of American households earned incomes that would have classified them as poor by today's standards. In the early twenty-first century, about 10 to 15 percent of households fall into this category, which is a vast improvement, but still too high.[17]

Bear in mind that poverty statistics are about income. Such statistics do not necessarily reflect people's actual material standard of living, which is a matter of what they can buy with their income. In this respect, poor people in America today are considerably better off materially than poor people were even a few decades ago. For example, the US Department of Energy reports that, in 2009, 82 percent of households below the poverty line had air conditioning. As of 2001, virtually everyone in the United States had a refrigerator (99.9 percent of households), a cooking appliance (99.7 percent), and a color TV (98.9 percent). And even in the lowest income bracket, households earning less than $15,000 a year, 25 percent had a large-screen TV, 64 percent had cable or satellite TV, 54 percent had a stereo, 57 percent had a clothes washer, 45 percent had a clothes dryer, and 75 percent had a microwave oven.[18]

The stagnant economies that characterized the Soviet Union and its Warsaw Pact allies in Eastern Europe give us powerful historical evidence that socialism or communism cannot duplicate capitalism's ability to increase material productivity. The adoption of capitalism by the People's Republic of China is testimony that even communists have recognized this fact. The enormous increase in growth and in people's standard of living that

---

[17]Behravesh, *Spin-Free Economics*, 15.

[18]Department of Energy, Energy Information Administration, Residential Energy Consumption Survey, RECS 2009 – Release date: August 19, 2011, at: http://www.eia.gov/consumption/residential/reports/air_conditioning09.cfm (accessed November 7, 2011); and "The Effect of Income on Appliances in US Households" based on information from the 2001 Residential Energy Consumption Survey (RECS), conducted by the Energy Information Administration. Released: January 1, 2004. Available at: http://www.eia.gov/emeu/recs/appliances/appliances.html (accessed November 7, 2011).

China's opening to capitalism has brought with it confirms the fact.[19]

From the failure of communism in Russia and the countries of Eastern Europe, there is yet another lesson to be learned. Communism did succeed in bringing those countries, Russia especially, into the industrial era. What it could not do is make the next great leap forward to a modern technological and computerized economy. Top-down command economies could mobilize the labor needed to produce iron and steel and fuel, to build roads and railways, and to work on factory assembly lines. They could not mobilize the labor needed for a modern technological and computerized economy, however, for the simple reason that people who do that kind of labor need and insist on more autonomy than did earlier industrial laborers. Modern technological and computerized economy is inherently in conflict with top-down command organization. Communism was not able to give up this type of organization in the face of the growing demands of its most advanced workers for more autonomy.

These facts explain how, in spite of the remarkable growth that communism was able to achieve in its early years, it was not able finally to compete with late capitalist societies in keeping the loyalty and commitment of its workers. And that tells us something else important about capitalism. Marx criticized capitalism for treating the worker as an appendage to a machine and thus stunting and crippling him. However, this applied to the early form of industrial capitalism that Marx saw in the nineteenth century. Later capitalism, by contrast, does not seem to stunt and cripple the worker. Predictions of capitalism deskilling workers, reducing them to ever simpler and more easily replaceable cogs in the productive machine,[20] have not been borne out in the advanced capitalist states.

[19] "By some estimates, the recent rapid economic growth in China and India has pulled nearly half a billion people out of poverty" (Behravesh, *Spin-Free Economics*, 15).

[20] See, for example, Harry Braverman, *Labor and Monopoly Capital: The Degradation of Work in the Twentieth Century* (New York: Monthly Review Press, 1976).

Instead, we see demand for more autonomous workers, with broader educations, who are able to respond to changing circumstances and new challenges. These are the workers whose allegiance communism was not able to win. In spite of his criticisms of early capitalism, Marx foresaw this aspect of advanced capitalism. In *Capital*, he wrote:

> Modern Industry . . . compels society . . . to replace the detail-worker of today, crippled by life-long repetition of one and the same trivial occupation . . . , by the fully developed individual, fit for a variety of labours, ready to face any change of production, and to whom the different social functions he performs, are but so many modes of giving free scope to his own natural and acquired powers. (C, I, 488)

In short, the dehumanizing effects of labor under capitalism that Marx passionately criticized are not an objection to the advanced capitalism currently emerging around the globe.

The upshot of all this is the following: History and Marxian theory give us reasons for fearing that socialist and communist societies will be oppressive (at least in the current historical era and for the foreseeable future), and for believing that, in spite of their problems, capitalist societies will preserve individual liberty. And advanced capitalist societies will reduce the alienating and dehumanizing aspects of labor that characterized earlier phases of capitalist production. History also gives us reasons for doubting that socialist and communist societies can match capitalism's productivity, and thus its ability to produce the material conditions of freedom. I shall not try to prove all of these claims. Rather I take them as part of general knowledge and thus part of the knowledge possessed by parties in the Marxian-Liberal original position. For such reasons, *on Marxian grounds*, Marxian Liberalism will support the formation of a capitalist society – subject, I shall contend, to the requirements of the difference principle, as well as to limitations intended to protect individual liberty and political equality.

Note, here, that by a capitalist society, I do not mean a society in which every transaction is capitalist. Nor do I mean a society characterized by every feature of capitalism. It should be clear, for example, that the capitalist society that Marxian Liberalism supports is one in which the state will do many things to keep inequalities within the range permitted by the difference principle, which, as we shall see, may even include acting to assure that ownership of productive resources is widely spread out in society. Likewise, it will act to prevent concentrations of economic wealth from getting so great that they undermine the right of all citizens to a roughly equal chance to influence political decisions.

Thus, I define capitalism for purposes of this book rather loosely. It represents a society in which most productive resources are privately owned by individuals or groups. It is an economic system in which competition for profit is the primary aim of the owners of productive resources, and in which workers can be laid off or fired if economic conditions warrant. Such a view of capitalism is compatible with extensive government involvement in the economy, with taxation and other policies aimed at redistribution, and with a substantial public sector. It is even arguably compatible with some redistributive schemes that others may identify as socialist, or at least as "market socialism," though not if this requires state ownership of productive resources or a largely planned economy.[21]

Marxian Liberalism takes justice to be a historical standard. Like Marx himself, Marxian Liberalism looks forward to a time when technology will produce all the goods that people need and want (when "the springs of cooperative wealth flow more abundantly"), and people will labor for the pleasure of it (when "labour has become . . . life's prime want"). At that point, the difference principle would give way to the so-called "communist" principle: "From each according to his ability, to each according to his needs" (*MER*, 531). The difference principle leads to the communist principle, when historical conditions are ripe, because the communist principle is a principle of complete equality. It is more than merely a

---

[21] See, for example, the interesting proposals in John E. Roemer, *A Future for Socialism* (Cambridge, MA: Harvard University Press, 1994), some of which might be compatible with what Marxian Liberalism takes to be a capitalist society.

call for equal shares (which would still be a form of the difference principle, if inequalities were no longer needed to maximize the worst-off shares). The equality called for by the communist principle is not equality of shares, but, rather, the equality of each person as the standard of what he or she gives and gets. This principle announces the end of private property's coerciveness because it makes what workers receive depend on what they need, rather than on the labor they give. Thus, under this principle, no one is forced to work in order to live.[22] Until the historical conditions of the communist principle arrive, however, capitalism constrained by the difference principle – and subject to political constraints needed to protect liberty – would make for the least possible coercion in the economy, and the greatest possible freedom.

In light of these last remarks, it might well be wondered why the doctrine here defended is called "Marxian Liberalism" rather than "Liberal Marxism." Though the latter label would not be wholly false, the former is chosen to highlight the idea that the theory here defended is a normative one, a theory of justice, an idea about how society should be organized. Moreover, it is a liberal theory of justice, one that holds that society should be organized to protect and promote individual liberty. Liberalism is modified by the adjective "Marxian," rather than vice versa, because Marxian theory informs this liberalism's conception of the conditions that must be achieved to protect and promote liberty. Marxian Liberalism is a form of liberalism, not of Marxism.

As I indicated above, what Marxian Liberalism mainly draws from Marxism is a set of beliefs that, together, can be called *a theory of the conditions of liberty*. That theory identifies private ownership of means of production as coercive; it does so by showing that private ownership of means of production exemplifies a mechanism of social coercion the recognition of which is one of Marx's great discoveries. I call this mechanism *structural coercion*: the way patterns of social behavior work to constrain people's choices beyond

[22] This is why Marx thought the state would no longer be necessary in communism.

23

the limits of nature or morality. Beyond the normal use of force to protect persons and property, structural coercion works without overt violence. For this reason, it tends to be invisible. The invisibility of structural coercion is the core of *ideology* in capitalism. By "ideology" is meant a set of beliefs whose overall effect is to hide the moral failings of a society. The invisibility of structural coercion functions ideologically because it hides the coerciveness of private ownership of means of production. Its result is that transactions in capitalism appear free because they are free of overt violence. Libertarian defenses of capitalism characteristically fall prey to this ideology. Seeing no special power in great property-holdings, they think that all that is necessary for justice is that transactions be free of violence or fraud.

As we shall see (in Chapter 4), some philosophers before Marx saw that property limited liberty, but they did not see it as coercive. I contend that it was Marx's *dereified* view of social phenomena that enabled him to see structural coercion for what it is. Marx saw that social institutions were nothing but patterns of human behavior. This idea had its roots in modern political philosophy. Hobbes, for example, saw that the commonwealth was the organization of people into a large artificial monster, which he called Leviathan. Marx extended this idea to apply as well to economic realities. Of capitalism, for example, he wrote, "capital is not a thing, but a social relation between persons" (C, I, 766). Because Marx saw both economic and political institutions as patterns of human behavior, he was able to go beyond the philosophers who saw that property was a *limitation* on liberty and see that those limitations were imposed by people on people. Thus they constituted *coercion*, rather than mere limitations.

Because structural coercion functions without overt violence and thus tends to be invisible, we need a way of measuring its presence. To do this, I will propose a *moral version of Marx's labor theory of value*. Unlike Marx's own labor theory of value, the moral version makes no claim to account for prices in capitalism. Nor, of course, does this view hold that there is some mystical substance called value produced by labor, or even (as Marx sometimes seems to hold) "congealed labor" that *has* value. Its claim, rather, is a moral one, namely, that what is morally significant about economic systems is that they constitute arrangements in which people work for one another. Crucial then to the moral evaluation of competing economic systems are the proportions in which people work for one another. And the measure of those proportions is the amounts of labor that people exchange in society.

Since private property is coercive, inequality in the proportions in which people labor for each other is evidence of subjugation mediated by the economic system, which, because it is imposed by people on people, I call *social subjugation*. In light of the moral version of the labor theory of value, I shall contend that the difference principle is a principle for reducing social subjugation in the economic system to the minimum compatible with realizing capitalism's liberatory potential.

This means that Marxian Liberalism does not follow traditional liberalism in dividing the question of liberty (as a matter of political justice) from that of the distribution of goods (as a matter of economic justice). For Marxian Liberalism, the distribution of goods is a measure of forced labor, and the problem of economic justice is thus as much a problem of protecting liberty as is the problem of political justice.

In addition to structural force and the moral version of the labor theory of value, the Marxian theory of the conditions of liberty includes, as we saw above, a conception of the *material* conditions of freedom, namely, that freedom comes, not only from the elimination of coercion imposed by human beings on one another, but equally from the growth in material productivity that brings workers a higher standard of living and thus a greater ability to act on their own choices, and that ultimately frees workers from unwanted toil. Since this means that liberty is constrained by both social and material factors, I shall call this aspect of the Marxian theory of the conditions of liberty *the fungibility of material and social subjugation*. In light of this notion, I shall argue that the difference principle is a principle for reducing social *and* material subjugation to the minimum possible, and thus for maximizing liberty overall.

In sum, *liberalism* indicates the goal of the theory, and *Marxism* characterizes the conditions for achieving that goal. Thus, the theory is called *Marxian Liberalism*.

My argument unfolds in the following order. Since Marxian Liberalism develops and alters elements of Marx's and Rawls's theories, it will help to have the basics set out for reference and comparison in what follows. Accordingly, in Chapter 2, "Marx and Rawls and Justice," I present the basics of Marx's theory of capitalism, and of Rawls's theory of justice. I shall also briefly discuss Rawls's own quite sympathetic view of Marxism, and suggest where Marxian Liberalism goes beyond Rawls's view. Since Marxian Liberalism is a theory of justice, I will also show in this chapter that, contrary to the view of some interpreters of Marxian theory, there is no antipathy between Marxism and justice. And I will explain how Marxian Liberalism interprets Marx's comments on justice in light of its *historical* conception of justice.

In Chapter 3, "The Natural Right to Liberty and the Need for a Social Contract," I present an interpretation of Locke's argument for the natural right to liberty stripped of Locke's appeal to religious beliefs and, thus, suited to the secular temper of our time. I shall show as well that this argument can be defended against the claim that it is Anglo- or Eurocentric. And I shall show that the right to liberty requires appeal to a social contract to justify a right to property.

In Chapter 4, "The Ambivalence of Property: Expression of Liberty and Threat to Liberty," I present Locke's and Kant's arguments from the right to liberty to a right to large and unequal property, and discuss as well libertarian philosopher Robert Nozick's latter-day version of Locke's argument, and libertarian philosopher Jan Narveson's version of Kant's argument. I shall show that Locke (implicitly) and Kant (explicitly) recognized that, in addition to expressing liberty, property also limits liberty. I shall contend that neither Locke nor Kant, neither Nozick nor Narveson, provides for adequate protection of liberty against the threat posed by property. I turn then to Marx's notion that private property is, not merely a limitation on liberty, but a form of structural coercion.

In Chapter 5, "The Labor Theory of the Difference Principle," I present the moral version of the labor theory of value and show how the difference principle works when it is thought of as primarily distributing labor-time. I shall show that, so understood, the difference principle can be seen more clearly to be a principle of reciprocal benefit than Rawls was able to show. And, I shall address the critique of the use of incentives in the difference principle that has been proposed by Narveson and Cohen.

In Chapter 6, "The Marxian-Liberal Original Position," I formulate a Marxian-Liberal version of Rawls's original position, in which the parties' general knowledge includes the Marxian theory of the conditions of liberty as well as some factual beliefs characteristically held by liberals. I shall argue that it will be rational for the parties in the Marxian-Liberal original position to agree to a principle protecting basic liberties, to a right to property subject to Rawls's difference principle understood in light of the moral version of the labor theory, to a principle prohibiting unwanted coercion not necessary to realize the first two principles – and to a limited state empowered to protect liberty and implement the difference principle. I shall show how, as historical conditions change, the difference principle will call for Marx's "socialist" principle of distribution, and eventually give way to Marx's "communist" principle of distribution.

In Chapter 7, "As Free and as Just as Possible: Capitalism for Marxists, Communism for Liberals," using the principles agreed to in the Marxian-Liberal original position, I sketch Marxian Liberalism's conception of the just society and the just state for the current historical period. I shall argue that what a number of writers, including Rawls, have called "property-owning democracy," and that Rawls defended as a way of realizing his two principles of justice, is, now and for the foreseeable future, the ideal society for Marxian Liberalism – as free and as just as possible.

In the Conclusion, I will reflect on what the merger of Marxism and liberalism tells us about the doctrines of Marxism and liberalism as formulated by Marx and Rawls.

Overview of the Argument

Note that, though I point to anticipations of Marxian views about property in traditional liberal philosophers such as Kant, and to endorsement of individual liberty by Marx, I am more interested in the theory that results from combining liberal and Marxian elements, than in fidelity to the sources. I do not claim that the view presented here is the only one that could count as Marxian Liberalism. That would be unlikely in any event, since both Marxism and liberalism mean different things to different people. Accordingly, I will exercise a fair amount of selectivity in choosing, and philosophical license in interpreting, the elements of Marxian Liberalism as I join them together. I hope that the theory that results is interesting enough to justify this approach.

2

Marx and Rawls and Justice

Since Marxian Liberalism develops and alters elements of Marx's and Rawls's theories, it will help to have the basics set out for reference and comparison in what follows. That is the main job of this chapter. In the first two sections, I will present the basics of Marx's theory of capitalism and its ideology, and of Rawls's theory of justice, as these will be understood here. In Section 2.3, "Rawls on Marx," I shall discuss Rawls's own quite sympathetic view of Marxism, and indicate some points at which Marxian Liberalism goes beyond Rawls's view. In Section 2.4, "Marx and Justice," I take up the claim of some writers that there is an intrinsic antipathy between Marxism and justice, and present Rawls's view of the matter. In Section 2.5, "Marxian Liberalism's Historical Conception of Justice," I give Marxian Liberalism's view of the matter, and present its understanding of the historical nature of justice.

As Free and as Just as Possible: The Theory of Marxian Liberalism, First Edition. Jeffrey Reiman.
© 2014 Jeffrey Reiman. Published 2014 by John Wiley & Sons, Ltd.

2.1 Marx's Theory of Capitalism and Its Ideology

Marx says that capitalism is a system of "forced labour – no matter how much it may seem to result from free contractual agreement" (*C*, III, 819). Here is both the truth that Marx asserts about capitalism and the ideology that shrouds that truth.

For Marx, the value of any commodity is equivalent to the average amount of labor-time necessary to produce it.[1] Under capitalism, the worker's ability to labor – Marx calls this *labor-power* – is sold to the capitalist in return for a wage. Because labor-power is also a commodity, its value is also equivalent to the average amount of labor-time necessary to produce it. *Producing labor-power* means producing the goods needed to maintain a functioning worker. The value of labor-power then is equivalent to the labor-time that on average goes into producing the goods (food, clothing, shelter, and so on) necessary to maintain a functioning worker at the prevailing standard of living, which Marx understood to differ among countries depending on their respective histories (*C*, I, 171). The worker receives this in the form of a wage, that is, in the form of the money necessary to purchase these goods.

---

[1] Note that Marx does not hold that the value of a commodity is equivalent to the *actual* amount of labor-time that goes into producing it. On that view, commodities would be more valuable the more inefficiently they were produced. Instead, recognizing that a commodity will command a price no higher than that for which commodities like it are selling, Marx takes the commodity's value to be determined by the average or socially necessary labor-time it takes to produce commodities of its kind. See *C*, I, 189. Furthermore, although Marx claims that value is equivalent to average labor-time, he assumes that values and market prices coincide only for the purposes of the argument of volume I of *Capital* about the fundamental nature of capitalism. In the subsequent volumes, Marx shows at length the mechanisms in capitalism that lead prices to diverge from values. Even after these common misinterpretations of the theory are eliminated, it must be admitted that Marx's labor theory of value has come in for so much criticism in recent years that many, even many Marxists, have given it up for dead.

The capitalist obtains the money she pays as a wage by selling what the worker produces during the time for which he is employed. If the worker produced an amount of value equivalent only to his wage, there would be nothing left over for the capitalist and no reason for her to hire the worker in the first place. Labor-power, however, has the unique capacity to produce more value than its own value (C, I, 193–194). The worker can work longer than the labor-time equivalent of the value of the wage he receives. The amount of labor-time that the worker works to produce value equivalent to his wage Marx calls *necessary labor.* The additional labor-time that the worker works beyond this Marx calls *surplus labor,* and the value it produces he calls *surplus value.* The surplus value belongs to the capitalist and is the source of her profit (C, I, 184–186). That is, when the capitalist sells the product made by the worker, the capitalist gives some of the money she gets back to the worker as a wage (this corresponds to the value that the worker put into the product during his necessary labor-time), and the capitalist keeps the rest as profit (this corresponds to the surplus labor-time that the worker put in after his necessary labor-time).

Profit, then, rests on the extraction of unpaid surplus labor from the worker. To see this, one need only recognize that, though *all* products in the economy are produced by labor, only a *portion* of those products come back to the worker as wage-goods. This *portion* is what workers get paid with for producing *all* the products in the economy. The remainder belongs to their bosses and is effectively uncompensated. The wage-goods only compensate the necessary labor-time to which they are equivalent in value. What workers produce beyond this goes to the capitalist gratis. Thus, writes Marx, "The secret of the self-expansion of capital [that is, the secret of profit] resolves itself into having the disposal of a definite quantity of other people's unpaid labour" (C, I, 534).

For Marx, however, capitalism is not only a system in which unpaid labor is extracted from workers, it is also a system in which workers are *forced* to provide this unpaid labor. Workers are not merely shortchanged; they are enslaved. Capitalism is "a coercive relation" (*C*, I, 309). The coercion, however, is not of the direct sort that characterized slavery or feudal serfdom. It is, rather, an indirect force built into the very fact that capitalists own the means of production and laborers do not. Means of production are things such as factories and machines and land and resources – things that are necessary for productive labor. Lacking ownership of means of production, workers lack their own access to the means of producing a livelihood. *By this very fact*, workers are compelled to sell their labor to capitalists for a wage because the alternative is (depending on conditions) either painful or fatal: relative pauperization or absolute starvation.

This compulsion is not contradicted by the fact that the terms upon which workers work for capitalists result from free contractual agreements. Indeed, the compulsion works *through* free agreements. Because the agreements are free, each side must offer the other a reason for agreeing. If workers offered capitalists only as much labor as went into the wage-goods they will get back in return from the capitalists, the capitalists would have no reason to purchase their labor. It follows that, no matter how free the wage contract is, as long as it occurs in a context in which a few own all the means of production, those who do not own means of production will be compelled to give up some of their labor without compensation to those who do. Thus, Marx describes the wage-worker as a "man who is compelled to sell himself of his own free will" (*C*, I, 766). The compulsion of the worker operates through the structure of property relations: "The dull compulsion of economic relations completes the subjection of the labourer to the capitalist. Direct force, outside economic conditions, is of course still used, but only exceptionally" (*C*, I, 737).

As I shall point out later (Section 4.3), this is the core of one of Marx's most important discoveries: the nature and possibility of structural coercion that functions without the need for overt force. It is the very existence of the social structure that includes the roles of capitalist and worker – defined by ownership and nonownership of means of production, respectively – that coerces the worker to work without compensation. Because the workers do not own means of production, they can only get a chance to work at all, which is to say a chance to earn a living at all, which is to say a chance to live at all, if they work on what the capitalists own. For that they will have to give the capitalist something in return. And since all they own is their labor, that's all they can give. Overt force is only needed or threatened to maintain this structure of social roles, which is to say, the state uses force to protect private property. But, once the structure of social roles is in place, all that is necessary is that individuals choose, from among the alternatives available to them in their roles, the course of action that best serves their self-interest, and the extraction of unpaid surplus labor is enforced without further need for overt force except in unusual circumstances.

Interestingly, the state can protect this structure while acting neutrally, that is, by using force to protect both capitalists and workers alike in the freedom to exercise their rights of property over what they happen to own. Capitalists happen to own the means of production, and workers happen to own the muscles in their arms. Capitalism, then, naturally appears as a system of free exchanges between people with equal rights (over unequal amounts of property). This brings us to the phenomenon of ideology.

Ideology, for Marx, means beliefs that people hold that are in some way false so that they deceive people about what is wrong with their society. This can happen even if many or most of the beliefs in ideology are true. The crucial falsehood of capitalist ideology is the denial of capitalism's coerciveness. With this covered over, beliefs, say about how the market works, can be true and yet function ideologically. So, for example, much of what is found in classical or neoclassical economic theory – say, as found in the writings of Milton Friedman – is true about the way markets function to lower prices and rationally allocate productive resources. Combined, however, with the false belief that the system is free, this amounts to ideology because it makes the whole system appear to be just because freely chosen, and thus a morally unproblematic way of serving the public good.

As its etymology suggests, *ideology* refers to a science of ideas, where science can be taken in the ordinary sense as the study of causal connections. In the context of Marx's theory, ideology then means ideas caused by the mode of production, that are false in a way that hides what is morally questionable about the society. Thus understood, for Marxism, the study of ideology denotes the study of how the mode of production gives rise to people's false beliefs about society. In *The German Ideology*, Marx writes:

> If in all ideology men and their circumstances appear upside down as in a *camera obscura*, this phenomenon arises just as much from their historical life-process as the inversion of objects on the retina does from their physical life-process. . . .
> The phantoms formed in the human brain are also, necessarily, sublimates of their material life-process, which is empirically verifiable and bound to material premises. (*MER*, 154)

As this statement makes clear, the study of ideology requires that both the existence and the falsity of ideological beliefs be given a *materialist* explanation.

To understand this requirement, consider that Marxian materialism is the conjunction of two distinct claims, an ontological claim and a social scientific one. The *ontological* claim is that what exists is material, that is, physical objects in space. Mind and spirit, in any immaterial sense, are chimera. ("From the start the 'spirit' is afflicted with the curse of being 'burdened' with matter, which here makes its appearance in the form of agitated layers of air, sounds, in short, of language" [*MER*, 158]). The *social scientific* claim is that the way in which a society is organized for the production of the material conditions of its existence and reproduction ("the mode of production") plays the chief (though by no means the only) causal role in determining the nature and occurrence of social events. ("The mode of production of material life conditions the social, political and intellectual life process in general.")[2]

[2]Marx, "Preface to *A Contribution to a Critique of Political Economy*," *MER*, 4.

According to this social scientific claim, the belief that societies are shaped primarily by their members' attitudes, or that history is shaped by the progressive development of knowledge or ideals, is false. Rather, it is primarily the organization of production that shapes people's attitudes, and the progressive development of modes of production that shapes history. ("That is to say, we do not set out from what men say, imagine, conceive, nor from men as narrated, thought of, conceived, in order to arrive at men in the flesh. We set out from real, active men, and on the basis of their real life-process we demonstrate the development of the ideological reflexes and echoes of this life-process" [*MER*, 154]; "it is not the consciousness of men that determines their being, but, on the contrary, their social being that determines their consciousness" [*MER*, 4]).

Of the two claims, the social scientific is more restrictive than the ontological. The ontological claim requires only that we attribute ideology to material realities, be they brains or agitated layers of air or modes of production. The social scientific claim requires that among these material realities, priority be given to the mode of production as the primary cause of ideological beliefs. This means that the *main* source of false ideology is to be found not in the perceiving subject but in the perceived objects. It is not a "subjective illusion," the result of erroneous perception by individuals of their material conditions, but an "objective illusion," the result of more or less accurate perception of those conditions.[3]

Viewing ideology this way has the added benefit of leaving the door open just wide enough so that the theory of ideology does not

[3]"It is not the subject who deceives himself, but reality which deceives him." Maurice Godelier, "Structure and Contradiction in Capital," in Robin Blackburn, ed., *Ideology in Social Science* (Glasgow: Fontana/Collins, 1977), 337. Rawls says of Marx's doctrine of ideology that ideology consists of illusions and delusions, which correspond roughly to what I am calling objective and subjective illusions, and he suggests "being taken in by the surface appearances" is an illusion, and that religion – which Marx notoriously took to be "the opiate of the masses" – is a delusion (*LHPP*, 359–362).

exclude the possibility of all true beliefs – and thus of the very science upon which it is based. A materialist theory of ideology, then, must show that the falsity in ideology is an *objective illusion* arising primarily from more or less accurate perception of the organization of material production, rather than from some subjective error.[4] Bear in mind that this is a matter of placing primary emphasis on objective factors, not of absolutely excluding subjective ones.

We can fix the idea of an "objective illusion" by considering a very common example of one, namely, the illusion that the sun goes around the earth. Any illusion, any erroneous belief that an individual holds, can be *stated* as a subjective error – but not every erroneous belief arises primarily *because* of a subjective error. A person who believes that the sun rises above a stationary horizon in the morning makes a mistake. Since the earth rotates around its axis, what actually happens is that the horizon tips down before the sun. But, note that this sort of mistake differs crucially from, say, the mistake that a color-blind person makes in believing that the light is green when it is red, or the mistake a person balancing his checkbook makes in believing that a number is 4 when it is 2. In these latter cases, the mistaken beliefs arise in the individuals primarily as the result of a defective perceptual faculty or misuse of a sound one. These are *subjective* illusions. In such cases, correcting the defect in the perceptual faculty (or in its use) should undo the mistake. The mistaken belief that the sun goes around the earth, by contrast, arises as a result of a sound perceptual faculty properly

[4]Examples of theories of ideology that trace its distortions to subjective illusions are the attempt by some members of the Frankfurt School to explain the appeal to German laborers of fascism by means of a Freudian account of the persistence of irrational authoritarian attitudes, and the attempt of some sociologists to trace ideology to an existential need to reify a mythic worldview as protection against the terrors of meaninglessness. For the former, see Martin Jay, *The Dialectical Imagination: A History of the Frankfurt School and the Institute for Social Research, 1923–1950* (Boston: Little, Brown, 1973). For the latter, see Peter Berger and Thomas Luckmann, *The Social Construction of Reality* (New York: Doubleday, 1966).

exercised. This is an *objective* illusion. Neither healthier vision nor looking more carefully will enable an individual to correct this mistake and see that what occurs at dawn is not the sun rising above the horizon, but the horizon tipping down.

The ideology of capitalism is the illusion that capitalism is uncoercive. This illusion is a mistake of the same type as the illusion that the sun goes around the earth. What corresponds in capitalism to the movement of the sun seen from the earth is the free exchange of wages and labor-power between capitalists and workers. That the sphere of exchange is the objective basis of ideology is recognized in effect by Marx, when he writes that in this sphere, freedom rules "because both buyer and seller of a commodity, say of labour-power, are constrained only by their free will" (*C*, I, 176). *The normal perception of what goes on in exchange gives rise to the ideological illusion that capitalism is uncoercive.* This is not because the freedom in exchange is an illusion. The fact is that, for Marx, capitalism works only because the moment of exchange, through which the circuit of capital continually passes, is truly free:

> For the conversion of his money into capital, therefore, the owner of money must meet in the market with the free labourer, free in the double sense, that as a free man he can dispose of his labour-power as his own commodity, and that on the other hand, he has no other commodity for sale, is short of everything necessary for the realization of his labour-power. (*C*, I, 169)

That the second of these senses of freedom is the worker's "freedom from" ownership of means of production (which effectively forces him to sell his labor-power to the capitalist) does not deny the reality of freedom in the first sense (without which we would have slavery or serfdom rather than capitalism).

In exchange, the power that capitalists have over workers recedes from view. We can distinguish two sorts of power: (1) the power to withhold one's commodity until offered something preferable, and (2) the power to command obedience and back this up with violent force. In the sphere of exchange, the second kind of power is suspended and all that remains is the first kind. This power is a power that all parties to the exchange have equally. Thus, the unequal power of capitalist and worker appears as their equal power to withhold from exchange what they happen to own, and their social inequality takes the mysterious form of a difference between the things that they happen to own. To use the famous words of Marx's analysis of the fetishism of commodities, a "social relation between men assumes, in their eyes, the fantastic form of a relation between things" (C, I, 72).

If this accurate perception of what goes on in exchange is to explain how capitalism appears uncoercive, we need to understand how the sphere of exchange – which is only part of capitalism – should be the source of beliefs about the whole of capitalism. Why should the experience of freedom in exchange, rather than, say, the experience of taking orders on the production line, determine the beliefs that members of capitalist societies come naturally to have? How is the representation of exchange *generalized* into a view of capitalism as a whole?

Marx offers a clue to the answer to this question when he says that the fetishism of commodities results because "the producers do not come into contact with each other until they exchange" (C, I, 73). Free exchange transactions are the salient points of social contact for economic actors in capitalism. They punctuate capitalist social relations. Every social interaction between individuals playing roles in the capitalist mode of production begins with such a transaction (say, the signing of a wage contract exchanging labor-power for money) and can be ended with such a transaction (say, the dissolution of the wage contract). Each of these beginnings and endings is characterized by the absence of either party having the power to command the other's obedience and use violence to get it. Each party knows that he can enter or withdraw from any capitalist social interaction without being subject to the command or the overt force of the other. What constraint either one feels seems to be only a matter of what he happens to own, which appears as a feature of his own good or bad fortune rather than a condition coercively imposed by the other. Like the apparently unmoving horizon against which we observe the sun, free exchanges appear to be the baseline from which all capitalist transactions arise and at which they cease. Thus, *all* capitalist social interactions, *not just the exchanges themselves*, appear as voluntary undertakings (or as the product of voluntary undertakings) between equal people who happen to own different things.

Exchange accurately perceived and then generalized is what leads workers in capitalist societies to believe that they are free, although they take orders most of their waking lives. Thus, ideologically false beliefs about capitalism result from accurate perception of exchange, when the rest of capitalism is, by default, assumed to be more of the same.

2.2 Rawls's Theory of Justice as Fairness

John Rawls has famously developed a theory of justice which he calls *justice as fairness*. "Justice as fairness," he writes, "generalizes and carries to a higher level of abstraction the traditional conception of the social contract" (*TJ*, 3). The notion of the social contract, used by philosophers such as John Locke and Thomas Hobbes, aims to determine the conditions of legitimate political authority by asking what, if any, form of state would people in a nonpolitical condition find it rational to agree to. In the traditional doctrine, the nonpolitical condition in which people make this agreement is called the *state of nature*. In Rawls's theory, the state of nature is replaced by the *original position*, and the issue is no longer what form of state people would agree to, but what basic principles of justice to govern their treatment of each other would they agree to. Where the state of nature might conceivably have existed, the original position is a purely imaginary situation.

The "parties" in the original position, as Rawls calls them, are imagined to be rational in the economic sense of being able to determine the most effective means to their ends. However, though they know they have ends of their own, a *veil of ignorance* prevents them from knowing their identities or the specific content of their ends.

The parties in the original position "know they have some rational plan of life, they do not know the details of this plan, the particular ends and interests which it is calculated to promote" (*TJ*, 123). Thus, the end they have in the original position is that of promoting their ability to live according to whatever ends they turn out to have.

Moreover, they are imagined to be "mutually disinterested" in that their judgment of what is most rational for them to agree to is measured only by how it promotes their own ability to live the life they turn out to want to live (*TJ*, 11–12). Mutually disinterested persons are not necessarily selfish. They aim to promote their own purposes, which may be charitable or even self-sacrificing. Crucially, however, their choices in the original position are not determined by envy (which would lead to them choosing to be worse off so that others would not have more than them) or by altruism (which would lead to them being indifferent between whether their purposes or others' purposes are satisfied). Mutual disinterestedness assures that what is agreed to in the original position will serve the interests of each and every individual. This helps to make the principles that emerge from the original position principles of justice, principles that do not justify the sacrifice of some for the benefit of others.

The parties in the original position have general knowledge: "It is taken for granted that [the parties in the original position] know the general facts about human society. They understand political affairs and the principles of economic theory; they know the basis of social organization and the laws of human psychology. Indeed, the parties are presumed to know whatever general facts affect the choice of the principles of justice" (*TJ*, 119). The veil of ignorance, however, deprives them of knowledge of their specific circumstances. The kinds of knowledge excluded (in addition to the content of their particular ends) are knowledge of their sex, race, age, level of abilities, social position, degree of wealth or what generation they are in, and so on. The point of this restriction is to make it impossible for the parties in the original position to tailor principles to their own circumstances.

Parties in the original position cannot gamble on where they will end up in the social order that will emerge from the principles they agree to. Though Rawls offers arguments to prove that gambling on the position one will end up in is not rational in the original position (e.g., *TJ*, 134–135; see also 149–150), I think he should have ruled gambling out in the very design of the original position. Rawls expressly designed his original position "to lead to a certain conception of justice," in particular to one that honors the inviolability of humans (*TJ*, 3), and thus provides a moral limit on what can be done to individuals for the common good. This is one reason that decisions in the original position must be unanimous. But gambling takes back what unanimity gives. If the rewards of some arrangement are great enough and the risk of a negative outcome small enough, a group of rational individuals who are permitted to gamble will find it rational to agree unanimously to that arrangement no matter how badly it treats a few – because their risk of ending up one of those few is so small. (Since we regularly take the small risk of death or grave injury just in order to drive across town, surely it would be rational to take a small risk of ending up a miserable slave for a large chance of being a rich master.) Nonetheless, some people will end up in such positions (just as some people win the lottery even though the odds against winning are so great), and thus "justice" will allow sacrificing those few for the benefit of the rest. But this is precisely what Rawls wanted to avoid. Whether by showing it is irrational or disallowing it from the outset, gambling must be prohibited if the original position is to issue in principles that do not justify the sacrifice of some for the benefit of others.

The overall result of these features of the original position is that the parties must choose principles thinking that they may turn out to be anyone in the society that will be governed by those principles. And this assures that the principles will be just, because it will only be rational for them to agree to principles that they could accept whoever they turn out to be. Rawls writes:

> In justice as fairness the original position of equality corresponds to the state of nature in the traditional theory of the social contract. . . .
> It is understood as a purely hypothetical situation characterized so as to lead to a certain conception of justice. Among the essential

features of this situation is that no one knows his place in society, his class position or social status, nor does anyone know his fortune in the distribution of natural assets and abilities, his intelligence, strength, and the like. . . . The principles of justice are chosen behind a veil of ignorance. This ensures that no one is advantaged or disadvantaged in the choice of principles by the outcome of natural chance or the contingency of social circumstances. (*TJ*, 11)

This exercise is a mental experiment, but it is aimed at determining what is reasonable for the actual people who will be governed by the principles of justice agreed to in the original position. This is hard to see because the abstractness of the thought experiment raises the suspicion that it is not relevant to actual people. But the abstractness is needed precisely to ask whether a practice is in the interest of every actual individual.

Consider that in any existing society, people with certain personal traits (say, intelligence, physical strength or beauty) are likely to have privileges that those who lack those traits do not have. And, likewise, in any existing society, people in certain socially generated positions (say, property-owners, managers, or political officials) normally have privileges that those in other positions do not have. Notice that the question of whether this distribution of privileges is in every actual person's interest is different from the question of whether any actual person is content with his or her position in the distribution. For example, the question whether it is in every actual person's interest that their society gives special rewards to the skilled is different from the question whether I, an unskilled worker, wish I were treated as a skilled worker. Just as it is different from the question whether you, a skilled worker, are content with your rewards.

Accordingly, if we want to ask whether this distribution of privileges is in the interest of every actual person, we must formulate our question in a way that distinguishes it from the question of whether people are happy with their position in the distribution. We might pose the question in this manner to actual people, but they may not be able to separate the two issues in their minds.

We could ask them to imagine that they are ignorant of their particular situations, but we cannot be certain that they can actually carry out this act of imagination so that their unavoidable knowledge of their particular situations does not inappropriately influence their answers. Moreover, we want to know whether the distribution is *truly* in everyone's interest, not merely if everyone *thinks* it is in their interest. Actual people may not be able to evaluate the distribution in this way; they might be influenced in their judgment by emotion or bias or idiosyncrasy. They may give answers that are shaped by what they are accustomed to, or what the society's educational and ideological institutions have convinced them is right or good.

These considerations combine to make the question of whether the distribution is in every actual person's interest a *theoretical* question rather than a matter of polling actual people. The theoretical question is: *Would it be rational for everyone to choose this social practice over other possible alternatives when they are ignorant of where they stand in that practice?* The abstractions built into the original position are aimed precisely at making it a way of asking this theoretical question. Since the theoretical question is about actual people, the original position is a way of asking whether any social practice is in the interest of every actual person affected by that practice. Writes Rawls,

> One should not be misled, then, by the somewhat unusual conditions which characterize the original position. The idea here is simply to make vivid to ourselves the restrictions that it seems reasonable to impose on arguments for principles of justice. . . . At any time we can enter the original position, so to speak, simply by following a certain procedure, namely, by arguing for principles of justice in accordance with these restrictions. (*TJ*, 16–17)

Of course, posing the question by arguing in this way is not infallible. We too may fail to answer the question correctly for the same reasons that we cannot be sure that polling actual people will yield the correct answer. The advantage of the original position is that it identifies clearly what the terms of the question are, and thus makes clear what sorts of considerations must be avoided. Nonetheless, we must recognize that any answer we propose to the question is only a *theory* of what is in every actual person's interest. The measure of its truth is, like that of all theories, that it can stand up to counterarguments in a wide-open forum.

Asking whether a social practice is reasonable to all its actual participants is a way of asking if the practice is just. This presupposes a particular understanding of justice. It takes justice to be a matter of the mutual reasonableness of institutions – or of the rules that govern them – to all the parties affected by those institutions, understood as separate individuals with distinct interests. This is a deontological conception of justice; indeed, as Rawls recognized, it is a Kantian conception (see *TJ*, 221–227). It does not prohibit the consideration of consequences, since it is, at least in part, by their consequences that rules are reasonable or not to individuals. It is deontological, rather, because it builds into the test of reasonableness the assumption that reasonableness is owed to each individual separately (which corresponds broadly to Kant's idea that every person should be treated as an end-in-himself). And that assumption cannot be justified by its consequences since it is an assumption about how consequences are to be counted in the first place.[5]

[5] It might seem that this claim would imply that even utilitarianism is a deontological theory since it too has a conception of how to count consequences, e.g., pleasure or pain of the same duration and intensity is to be counted alike no matter who (or what, i.e., humans or animals) has the pleasure or pain. But this conception can be explained by the claim that pleasure is good and pain is bad, that is, by reference to the nature of the consequences that are to count. If pleasure is good and pain bad, then it will be so wherever there is pleasure and pain, and thus equal duration and intensity of either will count the same wherever they occur. However, as soon as utilitarians start to qualify their counting, say, by looking at the consequences of rule-following rather than simple acts, I believe they do contaminate utilitarianism with smuggled-in deontological principles. But I am not complaining. There is hardly a better advertisement for deontological ethics than the efforts of twentieth-century utilitarians to make their theory look like a deontological one.

G. A. Cohen, as we saw earlier, held that fundamental moral principles are fact free,[6] and thus that the principles agreed to in the original position (with knowledge of certain facts) could not be fundamental moral principles. Cohen's argument for this was that whenever a moral principle relied on facts, it presupposed some more fundamental principle that (a) did not rely on facts and (b) spelled out why the less fundamental moral principle did rely on facts.[7] Though I shall suggest an alternative to this (in Section 3.2), there is a way that a Rawlsian could accept Cohen's view. A Rawlsian could accept it by granting that the original position presupposes the more fundamental moral notion that justice is what it would be mutually reasonable for people to require from one another.[8] This would be suitably fact-free for Cohen, and suitably impracticable. We will quickly want to know what these requirements are and they will be spelled out in what are rightly called "principles of justice," though those principles are not as fundamental as the notion of justice as mutual reasonableness.

Rawls's theory takes the basic social structure, "or more exactly, the way in which the major social institutions distribute fundamental rights and duties and determine the division of advantages from social cooperation," as the subject of justice (*TJ*, 6). By major institutions, Rawls understands "the political constitution and the principle economic and social arrangements. Thus the legal protection of freedom of thought and liberty of conscience, competitive markets, private property in the means of production, and the monogamous family are examples of major social institutions" (*TJ*, 6). The principles of justice, then, are to govern the design of the social positions into which people are born, which determine in advance the possibilities and limits that each person faces from the

---

[6] "The principles at the summit of our conviction are grounded in no facts whatsoever" (*RJE*, 229).
[7] Cohen writes: "*if* any facts support any principles, then there are fact-insensitive principles that account for that relationship of support" (*RJE*, 247).
[8] Perhaps this is itself a product of the still more fundamental Kantian principle that human beings are ends-in-themselves.

start: "Not only are they pervasive, but they affect men's initial chances in life; yet they cannot possibly be justified by an appeal to the notions of merit or desert" (*TJ*, 7) because they are in place when people are born. The principles of justice are not, then, principles to govern individual choices (other than the choice to play by the rules of just institutions, and the choice of which changes in those rules to vote for). They govern, rather, the conditions in which people make their choices.[9]

In Section 46 of *A Theory of Justice*, Rawls gives what he calls a final statement of the principles of justice that he contends would be the reasonable choice of parties in the original position:

FIRST PRINCIPLE

Each person is to have an equal right to the most extensive total system of equal basic liberties compatible with a similar system of liberty for all.

SECOND PRINCIPLE

Social and economic inequalities are to be arranged so that they are both:

(a) to the greatest benefit of the least advantaged . . . and
(b) attached to offices and positions open to all under conditions of fair equality of opportunity. (*TJ*, 266)

The requirement that social and economic inequalities satisfy criterion (a) of the Second Principle is called the "difference principle." The difference principle will play a central role in Marxian Liberalism.

Of these principles, Rawls holds notably, first, that they are in *lexical* order. Rawls uses "lexical" as a less cumbersome version of

---

[9] G. A. Cohen points out that this description does not fit the family, since the family is largely constituted by choices that people make (*RJE*, 116–140). I agree with Cohen on this, and with the implication he draws from it, namely, that principles of justice apply to individual choices, not only to the design of institutions (see Section 5.5).

"lexicographical," signifying the kind of order one finds in a dictionary, where all the words starting with "aa" precede the words starting with "ab," and so on. "This is an order which requires us to satisfy the first principle in the ordering before we can move on to the second, the second before we consider the third, and so on" (*TJ*, 38). Thus, the first principle of justice must be satisfied before we turn to satisfying the second. Or, equivalently, the first principle may not be compromised in order to satisfy the second. Rawls gives a number of reasons for this priority, but, in my view, the strongest is that people have a "higher-order interest in how their other interests are shaped and regulated by social institutions" (*TJ*, 475). I take this to mean that people's higher-order interest in living the life they want to live is an interest in being able to determine what interests they pursue and how they pursue them, and in being able to influence the determination of which interests their political order promotes. Later, we shall see that Marxian Liberalism holds that the protection of basic liberties is lexically prior to satisfying the difference principle, on related grounds (Section 6.4).

In applying the difference principle, Rawls assumes that improving the share of the least advantaged will normally have the effect of increasing the shares of those above them. If this does not happen by itself, then Rawls proposes an expanded form of the difference principle which he also characterizes as lexical. The *lexical difference principle* holds:

> in a basic structure with n relevant representatives, first maximize the welfare of the worst-off representative man; second, for equal welfare of the worst-off representative, maximize the welfare of the second worst-off representative man, and so on until the last case which is, for equal welfare of all the preceding $n - 1$ representatives, maximize the welfare of the best-off representative man. (*TJ*, 72)

In short, the difference principle should be understood as requiring maximizing the standard of living of the whole society starting from the bottom and going up. Rawls suggests that this might be accomplished through taxation (especially on inheritance), creation of public goods, and transfer payments (*TJ*, 245–247; see also *JF*, 160–161).

G. A. Cohen holds that this lexical version of the difference principle is different from the one stated a few paragraphs earlier (from *TJ*, 266), since that one holds "that inequalities are forbidden unless they render the worse off better off," while the lexical principle seems to allow additional inequalities, ones "that don't harm but also don't help the worst off" (*RJE*, 156–161, quotes at 157). This is a mistake. If the best-off person were to receive an additional benefit on the assumption that it does not harm the worst off (though it does not help them), that benefit could be redistributed to the worst off. If that is possible, then the first clause of the lexical difference principle has not been satisfied, because the welfare of the worst-off person has not been maximized. That means that, if the lexical principle is satisfied, then the only additional benefit that can be given to the best-off person is one which, were it taken from the best off, would lead to the worst off being even worse off. And for that, the additional benefit to the best off must be working to improve the share of the worst off. Thus the lexical version is identical to the simpler version stated earlier.[10]

Rawls holds further that, in a liberal democratic state, the first principle is a constitutional essential, while the second principle, though a matter of basic justice, is not appropriately part of the constitution (*PL*, 227–230). Furthermore, he contends that the two principles presuppose that the social structure can be thought of as consisting of two distinct spheres, the political and economic (*TJ*, 53) – a distinction which, we shall see, Marx critiques as ideological.

Rawls's argument for the two principles of justice is complex and it changed over the course of his life. I shall point out only what is

---

[10]I think that the mistake that Cohen is making here, and in which he is not alone, is in reading "then" in the lexical principle as signifying a temporal relationship of before and after, when it signifies a moral relation of primary and lesser urgency.

necessary for understanding how Marxian Liberalism carries forth and alters Rawls's theory. Before arguing that the two principles would be the most reasonable choice in the original position, Rawls argues for their intuitive acceptability. The intuitive appeal of the equal liberty principle is easy enough to see. It guarantees people's rights to freedom of expression and to freedom of religion, to participate as equals in the making of political decisions, to move about, to choose their occupation, and in general to live their lives as they see fit to the greatest degree compatible with a like right for everyone else. This principle is strikingly similar to the principle that Kant called the "Universal Principle of Right," which holds that "Any action is right if it can coexist with everyone's freedom in accordance with a universal law" (*MM*, 24).

Rawls holds that the first principle of equal liberty will call for limits on wealth if that wealth undermines the justice of the political system (*TJ*, 70). Moreover, Rawls contends that the first principle implies an equal right of citizens to determine the outcome of the political process:

> The principle of equal liberty, when applied to the political procedure . . . , I shall refer to as the principle of (equal) participation. It requires that all citizens are to have an equal right to take part in, and to determine the outcome of, the constitutional process that establishes the laws with which they are to comply. (*TJ*, 194)

This principle of participation is realized by a set of political liberties, such as the right of free speech, the right to vote, the right to freedom of assembly, and so on. But it is not enough that these liberties and rights be enshrined in law.

> The liberties protected by the principle of participation lose much of their value whenever those who have greater private means are permitted to use their advantages to control the course of public debate. For eventually these inequalities will enable those better situated to exercise a larger influence over the development of legislation. (*TJ*, 198)

Accordingly, Rawls distinguishes the legal existence of rights from their worth or value. He holds that governments must act to maintain the fair value of the political liberties:

> Compensating steps must, then, be taken to preserve the fair value for all of the equal political liberties. A variety of devices can be used. For example, in a society allowing private ownership of the means of production, property and wealth must be kept widely distributed and government monies provided on a regular basis to encourage free discussion. In addition, political parties must be made indepen-dent from private economic interests by allotting them sufficient tax revenues to play their part in the constitutional scheme. (*TJ*, 198)

Rawls emphasizes that "universal suffrage is an insufficient coun-terpoise" to the untoward influence of private money on elections, and suggests the need for public financing of elections as well as of political parties (*TJ*, 199). "The fair value of the political liberties ensures that citizens similarly gifted and motivated have roughly an equal chance of influencing the government's policy and of attaining positions of authority irrespective of their economic and social class" (*JF*, 46).

As for the difference principle, its intuitive appeal lies in the fact that it aims to moderate the effects on people's life prospects of contingent factors that are commonly held to be arbitrary from a moral point of view. Rawls identifies two such factors, namely: (1) the socioeconomic class into which one is born in the society, and (2) the natural gifts with which one is born – neither of which can people be said to deserve. The requirement of fair opportunity that accompanies the difference principle mitigates the effects of the first by providing, not only for formal equality (prohibition of discrimi-nation based on race or gender or the like), but for educational opportunities so that people of equal natural gifts get something like an equal starting point irrespective of whether they are born to rich families or poor. The requirement that inequalities work to maximize the share of the worst-off groups (the difference principle as such) mitigates the effects of the second factor by making the condition of greater rewards to the more-gifted be that those rewards work (normally as incentives to stimulate innovation and growth in productivity) to improve the shares of the less-gifted (*TJ*, 62–67). Rawls writes that the difference principle "represents, in effect, an agreement to regard the distribution of natural talents as in some respects a common asset. . . . The naturally advantaged are not to gain merely because they are more gifted. . . . No one deserves his greater natural capacity nor merits a more favorable starting place" (*TJ*, 87). The difference principle, he contends, "expresses a conception of reciprocity. It is a principle of mutual benefit" (*TJ*, 88).

Rawls then argues that the two principles of justice are a more reasonable choice for the parties in the original position than average utilitarianism (*JF*, 94–119, esp. 96). (Where classical utilitarianism aims simply to maximize aggregate satisfaction for all, average utilitarianism seeks to maximize aggregrate satisfaction divided by the number of people concerned.) Here Rawls appeals to the decision-theoretical idea of a "maximin" strategy. A maximin strategy is one in which a person who must make a choice between alternatives, not knowing how she will fare in either, chooses the alternative that makes the worst that could happen to her the best it could be (*TJ*, 132–133). (A maximiner always carries his umbrella when there is the slightest chance of rain.) A maximin strategy is rational when three conditions exist: (1) lack of knowledge of probabilities, (2) what can be guaranteed is largely satisfactory, and (3) the rejected alternatives have unacceptable outcomes (*TJ*, 134). Rawls argues that all three conditions obtain in the original position, and thus that the maximin strategy is the rational one to use there. This supports the two principles since they protect liberty and they guarantee that the worst-off position is the best it can be (*TJ*, 134–135), whereas average utilitarianism may allow sacrifices of liberty for greater economic gains, and it may allow that some be made miserable if enough others are benefited as a result (*TJ*, 139–144). A maximiner will choose Rawls's two principles over this because the first guarantees his liberty, and the second guarantees that the worst that can happen to him economically is that his worst-off share will be the greatest it can possibly be.

Rawls goes on to compare the two principles to a mixed conception of justice, in which the first principle of justice is combined with some guaranteed minimum level of economic well-being (*JF*, 119–130). In this comparison, the maximin strategy is no longer compelling, since the mixed conception no longer satisfies condition (3) above. It no longer holds the risk of unacceptable outcomes because it protects liberty and guarantees some economic minimum. Here, Rawls appeals to the fact that the difference principle is a principle of reciprocity or mutual benefit, in which gains to the better off are matched with maximum gains to the worse off (see, *JF*, 126–130). In my view, this works well against the mixed conception, but not against a free market conception of justice. As I argue below, in Section 5.2, since free market exchanges only take place when both parties think they will be benefited by the exchange, the market seems to embody reciprocity as well. I shall show, in Section 5.4, how interpreting the difference principle as exchanging labor makes good on Rawls's claim that it is a principle of reciprocity or mutual benefit, and shows why the free market is not.

2.3 Rawls on Marx

Throughout the development of his theory of justice, Rawls showed himself to be very sympathetic to Marxian objections to liberalism, and willing in important ways to adapt justice as fairness to meet those objections. With the recent publication of Rawls's *Lectures on the History of Political Philosophy* (*LHPP*), we can see more generally Rawls's sympathetic understanding of Marxian theory. In this section, I shall sketch out some aspects of this understanding that illuminate Marxian theory in a way that supports its linkage with liberalism, and I shall point to where Marxian Liberalism goes beyond Rawls's interpretation of Marxian theory. I start, however, by indicating two features of Rawls's theory that appear intended to head off Marxian objections.

Marxists characteristically criticize the rights in liberal capitalist societies as merely formal: they are on the books, but most people lack the means to exercise them (for example, they can exercise free speech among their pals, but only a few rich people own newspapers or television stations). We have already seen that Rawls insists that government must assure the fair value of the political liberties, that is, that people must have adequate means to participate in political life and to influence the outcome of political decisions (*TJ*, 198). This notion was already present in the original edition of *A Theory of Justice*.[11] And it is found in Rawls's last written work, *Justice as Fairness: A Restatement* (*JF*, 149), where he states explicitly that it responds to a Marxian objection to liberal rights (*JF*, 148).

In *Political Liberalism*, Rawls made clear that his first principle that guarantees basic liberties presupposed "a lexically prior principle requiring that citizens' basic needs be met" (*PL*, 7). This clarification was apparently in response to Rawls's reading of Rodney Peffer's *Marxism, Morality, and Social Justice*, which defends the need for such a requirement to make it possible for people to exercise their liberties.[12] It is yet another way of responding to the Marxian concern that liberal rights are only paper guarantees.

Turning to Rawls's views of Marxian theory, it is worth noting that Rawls takes quite seriously Marx's labor theory of value. Rawls contends that the theory is not concerned with the formation of prices (*LHPP*, 330). Its point rather is to show that capitalism is a system of exploitation even though it appears to be a system of free exchanges between independent (free, autonomous) agents. Rawls, following numerous Marxist economists, does not regard the labor theory "as sound or as essential," but he nonetheless sketches clearly how it is to do its job (*LHPP*, 331). Rawls writes that

> it is a fact about class societies that the total value added is not shared solely by those who produce it, but large shares are also received by people who either perform no labor at all, or else their shares are far

[11] John Rawls, A *Theory of Justice*, 1st edition (Cambridge, MA: Harvard University Press, 1971), 225.
[12] Rodney Peffer, *Marxism, Morality, and Social Justice* (Princeton: Princeton University Press, 1989), 14 (cited in *PL*, 7n7).

in excess of what their labor time would warrant. How this happens in a slave or feudal society is open to view. (*LHPP*, 329)

And elsewhere:

> Both lord and serf know . . . the rate of exploitation, as given by the ratio of the days serfs work for the lord to the days serfs work for themselves. . . . All this . . . is obvious also in slavery. But workers in capitalism [who receive a wage for a day's work comprised of both the necessary labor that produces the value equivalent to their wage-goods, and the surplus labor that produces the value that redounds to the capitalist as profit; see *LHPP*, 360] have no way of telling how many of their hours worked are necessary to sustain them, and how many are surplus labor for the benefit of the capitalist. . . . Thus, the distinctive feature of capitalism is that in it, as opposed to slavery and feudalism, the extraction of surplus or unpaid labor of workers is not open to view. (*LHPP*, 325–326)

Thus, concludes Rawls:

> The point of the labor theory of value is to penetrate beneath the surface appearances of the capitalist order and enable us to keep track of the expenditure of labor time and to discern the various institutional devices by which surplus or unpaid labor is extracted from the working class. (*LHPP*, 329)

To further "illustrate the aim of Marx's labor theory of value," Rawls proposes "to conjecture how Marx would have replied to the marginal productivity theory of distribution" (*LHPP*, 346). Of this theory, Rawls writes: "Very roughly, the idea is that each factor of production – labor, land, and capital – contributes its share in producing society's total output. In accordance with the precept, to each person according to that person's contribution, it is just that those who contribute their land and their capital should share in the output along with labor" (*LHPP*, 347). Rawls goes on to suggest that Marx would say that capitalist and landlord are getting paid, not for their productivity, but for the productivity of machines and land, which they get paid for because society grants them owner-ship of those scarce factors of production. Rawls's conjecture about Marx's reply here can be stated in much stronger terms: Marx would say that labor isn't just a special factor of production, it is *the* factor of production. Even the so-called product of land and machines is the product of the labor that cultivates and harvests the land, and that produces and operates the machines. That capitalists and land-lords own land and machines, without which workers cannot labor at all, gives the capitalists and landlords a socially constructed power to make workers pay for the opportunity of working. "Workers must, as it were, pay a fee – their surplus labor – for the use of those productive instruments" (*LHPP*, 330). Due to the social construction of ownership, this fee looks like the just due of the capitalist and the landlord for the use of their productive assets. Thus is hidden the fact that the "fee" is simply the unpaid labor of the workers that capitalists and landowners can extract because ownership gives them power over whether workers work at all.

In presenting Marxian Liberalism, I will show that the difference principle interpreted in light of the labor theory of value can be used to penetrate beneath the surface appearances of capitalism to enable us to keep track of the presence of unequal exchanges of labor-time that constitute social subjugation mediated by the economic system. And I shall go beyond Rawls and defend the use of the difference principle in light of the labor theory of value as a necessary means to evaluate the justice of any eco-nomic system. The real claim of the labor theory of value is a *moral* one, namely, that labor is the only natural cost that human beings pay in an economy. This fact, taken together with the fact that capitalism *forces* the worker to provide unpaid labor to the capitalist, is what enables us to use the difference principle, under-stood in terms of the labor theory, as a way of measuring the pres-ence of social subjugation mediated by the capitalist economy (see Section 6.1).

Rawls goes on to discuss what he contends is Marx's ideal, "a society of freely associated producers." Rawls contends that underlying this ideal is an implicit conception of justice, namely, that "all members of society – all freely associated producers – equally have a claim to have access to and use society's means of production and natural resources" (*LHPP*, 354). It is this conception that accounts for Marx's treatment of capitalism as unjust (even if he does not say this in so many words), "since private property in the means of production violates that claim" (*LHPP*, 355).

Rawls rightly notices two important aspects of Marx's ideal society. First, once society is governed by freely associated producers according to a conscious plan, ideology disappears. The life-process of society "strip[s] off its mystical veil." Instead of profits appearing as the rightful due of nonproducing owners, they appear as what they are: surplus labor, labor beyond what workers need for their daily sustenance, and which they can decide democratically how to allocate.

Second, Rawls notes that a society governed by freely associated producers requires "a certain material ground-work" which results only after "a long and painful process of development" (*C*, I, 80). Thus Rawls writes that "a society of freely associated producers cannot be realized under all historical circumstances, and must wait for capitalism to build up the means of production and the accompanying technological know-how" (*LHPP*, 355). Earlier, Rawls had observed: "It is the enormous achievement of capitalism to build up the means of production and to make possible the communist society of the future" (*LHPP*, 352).

In presenting Marxian Liberalism, I shall contend that for the foreseeable future the notion of a socialist or communist society governed by a conscious plan must be abandoned as unrealistic, and, in light of twentieth-century history, downright dangerous. Moreover, the length of time in which capitalism must do the work of building up the means of production so that a truly liberating society is possible, one in which people labor for the pleasure of it, is unknown and unknowable. Marxian Liberalism contends that the liberatory "communism" that is actually available to us is one in which a society of freely associated producers adopts capitalism as its form of economy, while constraining capitalism in ways needed to maximize its potential for liberating people from unwanted toil and to minimize its tendency to enforce social subjugation.

Contrary to what Rawls suggests, such a society will not violate the conception of justice according to which everyone in society has an equal claim on the society's means of production and resources. Since the freely associated members of society will freely choose to adopt such a constrained capitalism, they will be exercising their rightful claims to society's means of production by determining how best they ought to be exercised. They will do this freely both in the sense that it will be an open democratic decision, and in the sense that it will be done in the absence of ideological distortion. Moreover, they will always possess the right to reorder the system of production democratically, if it turns out not to serve their purposes. As I shall argue later, the result will be a capitalism that Marxists can accept, and a communism that liberals can accept.

2.4 Marx and Justice

A number of philosophers have held that Marx did not believe that capitalism was unjust, or that socialism and communism ought to be pursued because they were just. There are several reasons for such an interpretation, chief among which are the following interconnected considerations:

(*a*) Marx expressly says that capitalist appropriation of unpaid surplus labor is not an injustice to workers. In *Capital*, for example, he wrote:

> The circumstance, that on the one hand the daily sustenance of labor-power costs only half a day's labor, while on the other hand the very same labor-power can work during the whole day, that consequently the value which its use during one day creates, is double what he pays for that use, this circumstance is, without doubt, a piece of good

luck for the buyer, but by no means an injury [i.e., an injustice] to the seller. (*C*, I, 194).

(*b*) Underlying Marx's assertion that capitalist appropriation of unpaid surplus labor is no injustice to workers is Marx's view that justice is an ideological notion, essentially the principles of the prevailing economic system erected into a norm.[13] For example:

> The justice of the transactions between agents of production rests on the fact that these arise as natural consequences out of the production relationships. The juristic forms in which these economic transactions appear . . . cannot, being mere forms, determine [the] content [of these transactions]. They merely express it. This content is just whenever it corresponds, is appropriate to the mode of production. It is unjust whenever it contradicts that mode. Slavery on the basis of capitalist production is unjust; likewise fraud in the quality of commodities. (*C*, III, 339–340)

(*c*) As a piece of ideology, justice focuses on the distribution of goods and thus carries forth the ideological blindness to capitalism's coercive relations of production.[14] In his *Critique of the Gotha Program*, Marx wrote:

> it was in general a mistake to make a fuss about so-called *distribution* and put the principle stress on it.
> Any distribution whatever of the means of consumption is only a consequence of the distribution of the conditions of production them-

---

[13]Considerations *a* and *b*, together, form much of the basis of Allen Wood's argument against the idea that Marx criticizes capitalism as unjust. See Allen Wood, "The Marxian Critique of Justice," *Philosophy & Public Affairs* 1 (1971–1972), 244–282; and Allen Wood, "Marx on Right and Justice: A Reply to Husami," *Philosophy & Public Affairs* 8 (1978–1979), 267–295.

[14]See, for example, Iris Marion Young, "Toward a Critical Theory of Justice," *Social Theory and Practice* 7, no. 3 (1981), 279–302. See also Robert Paul Wolff, *Understanding Rawls* (Princeton: Princeton University Press, 1977), 207.

selves. The latter distribution, however, is a feature of the mode of production. . . . Vulgar socialism . . . has taken over from the bourgeois economists the consideration and treatment of distribution as independent of the mode of production and hence the presentation of socialism as turning principally on distribution. After the real relationship has long been made clear, why retrogress again? (*MER*, 531–532)[15]

(*d*) Communism is held to be an ideal beyond justice, because justice is the balancing of antagonisms, while communism is the overcoming of antagonisms.[16] As a standard for resolving conflict rather than eliminating its causes, justice promotes the notion that conflict between people is natural. Thus justice would have us accept as inevitable the alienation of humans from one another that characterizes capitalism. Marx suggests this in talking about rights and liberties, which are the crucial elements of justice. In "On the Jewish Question," Marx wrote:

> The right of property is . . . the right to enjoy one's fortune . . . without regard for other men. . . . This individual liberty . . . leads every man to see in other men, not the *realization*, but rather the *limitation* of his own liberty. (*MER*, 42).

Against these considerations, as Rawls notes (*LHPP*, 343, 345, 345n10), is the fact that Marx repeatedly condemns capitalism in terms such as "robbery" and "fraud" that clearly imply injustice. Marx held, for example, that laborers "became sellers of themselves only after they had been robbed of all their own means of production" (*C*, I, 715). More generally, of this "primitive accumulation" of capital that creates a free proletariat by robbing agricultural workers of the land that feudalism accorded them, Marx wrote:

[15]See also Karl Marx, *A Contribution to the Critique of Political Economy* (New York: International Publishers, 1970), 201–202.
[16]Robert C. Tucker, *The Marxian Revolutionary Idea* (New York: Norton, 1970), 42–53.

The spoliation of the church's property, the fraudulent alienation of the State domains, the robbery of the common lands, the usurpation of feudal and clan property, and its transformation into modern private property under circumstances of reckless terrorism, were just so many idyllic methods of primitive accumulation. They conquered the field for capitalist agriculture, made the soil part and parcel of capital, and created for the town industries the necessary supply of a "free" . . . proletariat. (*C*, I, 732–733)

Taking statements such as these together with those in which Marx seems to say that capitalism is not unjust, G. A. Cohen concluded that "Marx mistakenly thought that Marx did not believe that capitalism was unjust."[17] Rawls sides with philosophers like Cohen who hold that, though Marx did indeed think that justice often functioned ideologically to cover over and justify the wrongs of capitalism, he also thought at least implicitly, and perhaps unbeknownst to himself, that capitalism was unjust and a socialist or communist society ought to be pursued because it cured that injustice (*LHPP*, 336, 342–346). As we saw earlier, Rawls holds that Marx believed that justice included a right of all to access to the means of production (*LHPP*, 354). Moreover, Rawls contends that, rather than transcending principles of justice, the standard "From each according to his ability, to each according to his need" is a principle of justice affirming everyone's equal right to self-realization (*LHPP*, 343). To which we might also add that, in consideration of *(c)* above, Marx did not reject concern with unjust distribution as such, he rejected focus on the unjust distribution of goods rather than of means of production.

---

[17] See G. A. Cohen, "Review of Allen Wood's *Karl Marx*," *Mind* 92, no. 367 (July 1983), 440–445. See also, Norman Geras, "The Controversy about Marx and Justice," *New Left Review* 150 (1985), 47–85; and Jeffrey Reiman, "The Possibility of a Marxian Theory of Justice," *Canadian Journal of Philosophy, supplemental volume VII: Marx and Morality* (1981), 307–322.

2.5   Marxian Liberalism's Historical Conception of Justice

In this section, I start by defending Marxian Liberalism's conception of justice. Then, I go beyond Rawls's discussion of Marx's views on justice to give Marxian Liberalism's own defense of the use of justice in a Marxian context, and to spell out the historical nature of the principle of justice that Marxian Liberalism uses to interpret Marx's comments on justice.

Marxian Liberalism's conception of justice is, as might be expected, a combination of Rawlsian and Marxian views. From Rawls, it takes justice to have a timeless meaning: It calls for the maximum provision for the interests of others that can reasonably be morally required of people given human nature. This is based on Rawls's assertion that the problem of justice arises for people who stand in the "circumstances of justice," a notion that Rawls attributes to David Hume (*TJ*, 109n3). In his *A Treatise of Human Nature*, Hume had argued that justice was an artificial virtue that only arises among people who live in moderate abundance (so that cooperation is mutually beneficial), and who are neither totally selfish nor totally altruistic (so that they both care about how things are divided up and are able to live according to rules that serve the common good). Hume summed this up as: "*that 'tis only from the selfishness and confin'd generosity of men, along with the scanty provision that nature made for his wants, that justice derives its origin.*"[18] For Rawls this is embodied in the original position by treating the parties there as mutually disinterested, that is, as interested only in their own interests. But it carries over into the society whose principles are determined by agreement in the original position (see, for example, *TJ*, 248).

---

[18] David Hume, *A Treatise of Human Nature*, 2nd edition (Oxford: Oxford University Press, 1978, originally published 1739–1740), Book III, part ii, section 2, 495, emphasis in original.

Arguing that it will be rational for people in the original position to agree to inequalities when they make everyone better off than they would be with equality, Rawls writes:

> One might think that ideally individuals should want to serve one another. But since the parties are assumed to be mutually disinterested, their acceptance of these economic and institutional inequalities is only the recognition of the relations of opposition in which men stand in the circumstances of justice. They have no grounds for complaining of one another's motives. (*TJ*, 131)

I interpret this to mean that justice involves acceptance of human beings' "confin'd generosity," that is to say, acceptance of human nature as it is (see Section 5.5, below). And then justice is a matter of requiring the maximum provision for the interests of others that it is reasonable to require of people given their actual human nature.

From Marx, however, Marxian Liberalism takes the notion that human nature changes in history. The result of the combination of this idea with the Rawlsian one is that, while justice has a timeless meaning, what it requires changes historically. If, over the course of history, people become more altruistic, then what justice requires will change accordingly. I return to this idea at the close of this section.

I turn now to consider the legitimacy of appealing to justice in a Marxian context. From the standpoint of Marxian Liberalism, the issue here is not what Marx thought implicitly or explicitly about justice. What matters is whether promoting a principle of justice, as Marxian Liberalism plainly does, is something that is compatible with Marxism at all. On this issue, the most troubling objection is the one suggested by consideration (*d*), above, namely, that justice is inherently a conflictual notion, emphasizing as it does rights of individuals which are limits on and limited by the rights of other individuals. In response to this objection, I shall make two points.

First, Marxian Liberalism does affirm a conception of justice that endorses a right of individuals to liberty that is potentially threatened by other individuals. Moreover, in the form in which it endorses the difference principle, Marxian Liberalism affirms an individual right to property that is potentially threatened by other individuals. However, in neither case is this individualism ideological. It does not imply that humans are social atoms, or that they are naturally asocial. It's an evident fact that human beings are social creatures. They are born into families, they think in terms of a shared language, their aims are distinctively shaped by their cultures. No liberal need deny such things. The rights of individuals are a normative matter that does not conflict with these facts. The individualism of individual rights reflects the truth that human beings are physically separate beings, with their own muscles to work with, and their own nervous systems to suffer by. (Even if capitalism was the historical precondition of our recognizing this truth, that would not mean that it was simply capitalist ideology. Capitalism was also the historical precondition of Marxism, which hardly makes Marxism simply capitalist ideology.) That human beings are physically separate implies that individuals can be oppressed and exploited. A group cannot be oppressed without oppressing individuals, but individuals can be oppressed without oppressing the rest of the group – and the same is true of exploitation. If individuals are not protected against oppression and exploitation, then we have not eliminated these evils. This is why Marxian Liberalism insists on individual rights.

Second, nothing about the individual rights asserted by Marxian Liberalism causes people to be inclined to conflict, or to remain in alienated relations. (Indeed, I shall argue later that Marxian Liberalism leads to a society that is an affective community [Section 7.4; and Conclusion].) Rather than covering over the conflict-producing tendencies of capitalism and thus blocking movement toward an unalienated society, individual rights give us the standard for determining if a society is one in which people are alienated from one another. The sign that people in capitalism are alienated is not that people *have* rights, but that they must *insist* on their rights, even *fight* for them at law or in the streets. That

63

socialism or communism has overcome alienation will be known, not by the fact that rights have been transcended, but by the fact that people's rights are satisfied easily, spontaneously, perhaps such that people never need to appeal to justice, maybe never need even to think about it. That members of a happy family treat one another in kind and loving ways, and thus never have to appeal to justice, does not mean that they do not, or should not, have rights in justice. The same applies to the unalienated members of a communist society. Ending alienation is morally good in part, perhaps even ultimately, because it will mean that people's rights in justice are fulfilled, not because they have been transcended. Indeed, people can only be benevolent if they freely give of what they own – which, likewise, they can only do if they have rights.

In light of the historical nature of justice, Marxian Liberalism interprets Marx's apparently contradictory remarks about justice in a different way than G. A. Cohen does, a way that does not require that we believe that Marx was mistaken about his belief in justice. Rather, we note that in *The Phenomenology of Spirit*, a book which profoundly influenced Marx, Hegel gave a philosophical history of consciousness itself. In the course of that project, Hegel regularly shifted perspectives, sometimes speaking from the point of view of evolving consciousness itself, and sometimes looking backwards on that evolution from its anticipated endpoint. Marxian Liberalism takes Marx's comments on justice as reflecting much the same shift.

When Marx says that justice is only the current relations of production idealized, when he says that extraction of unpaid labor is no injustice to the worker, he speaks from the standpoint of historically evolving justice itself. These things are just in the current historical era. On the other hand, when Marx characterizes capitalist appropriation as robbery, when he puts forth the perfectly egalitarian communist principle of just distribution, he speaks from the anticipated endpoint of the history of modes of production. (I do not claim that Marx knew he was making this shift in standpoint, only that he does make it.)

What justice requires at this endpoint is a more perfect equality between human beings than what justice requires during the era of capitalism. But the latter is, nonetheless, *really* just – not simply "believed just" – because, given the historical evolution of human nature, it is the maximum provision for the interests of others that can reasonably be morally required of human beings given their nature during the capitalist era. Later, when "the springs of cooperative wealth flow more abundantly," and "labour has become . . . life's prime want," a higher, more perfectly egalitarian principle of justice is appropriate, the so-called "communist" principle: "From each according to his ability, to each according to his needs" (*MER*, 531). Between the capitalist standard and the communist, there is the socialist principle which calls for equal valuation of all workers' labor-time, which (as we shall see in Section 6.5) Marx criticizes as insufficiently egalitarian.

In other words, over history, justice increasingly requires equality between all human beings. This evolution is based on a change in human nature that makes people less interested in having more than their fellows. Such a change in human nature is presupposed by the Marxian view that conflicts of interest between human beings are rooted in the structure of the mode of production. As modes of production change, we can expect human nature to change in ways that make people's interests less conflictual. This will reduce and eventually eliminate the need for unequal incentives for productivity, and thus they will no longer be necessary to stimulate high productivity.

The increase in productivity set in motion by capitalism will itself be a main cause of the change in human nature. The more wealth there is around, the higher the general standard of living will be. Satisfaction of basic needs will increasingly be assured, with the consequence that people will no longer fear for their basic security and well-being. Without that fear, they will no longer need to defend what they have, and their natural benevolence will incline them toward sharing the less basic goods. When technology truly produces just about everything that people want, there will be little to gain from having more than others. The desire to do better than one's fellows will wilt, and generosity will flourish. In that world, people will labor for the pleasure of it, and they will be happy to see everyone prosper according to their needs.

Accordingly, we shall see that the difference principle successively requires the capitalist standard of justice, then the socialist, and finally gives way to the communist (Section 6.5). There is, of course, no telling how long this evolution will take, and predictions to date – including Marx's own – have generally been wildly optimistic. You and I, dear reader, will be lucky if we live to see capitalism made historically just by applying the difference principle to it to limit inequalities to those needed to increase productivity and maximize the share of the worst-off people.

3

The Natural Right to Liberty and the Need for a Social Contract

The right to liberty is a right of people to act on their choices. It is a *moral* right, because its claim on us derives from its inherent rightness, rather than from being part of people's actual moral beliefs, or of some actual legal code. I call it a *natural* right, because it does not require any act of consent or authorization by others to exist, nor is it derived from some more basic right. It's a *negative* right because it is a right to noninterference with one's ability to act as one sees fit, a right against unwanted coercion by others, rather than to some particular performance on the part of others. It's a right against *unwanted* coercion, because it is not a right against all coercion; it allows coercion that is necessary to protect against violations of liberty, and it allows coercion that people consent to. This right to liberty might be established in numerous ways, so Marxian Liberalism is not limited to the way in which I defend the right here. Nonetheless, since liberals and libertarians often appeal to Locke's views on rights to liberty and property, I will present a Lockean argument for the natural right to liberty in this

As Free and as Just as Possible: The Theory of Marxian Liberalism, First Edition. Jeffrey Reiman.
© 2014 Jeffrey Reiman. Published 2014 by John Wiley & Sons, Ltd.

chapter, and trace his defense of the right to property in the next. By a "Lockean argument," I mean an argument in the spirit of Locke, one that stays close to his words, but occasionally interprets them in ways that make the argument more acceptable in our more secular times. It is an argument that Locke might have made were he around today. In the same spirit, I shall point out how this argument should satisfy those who fear that talk of natural rights is Anglo- or Eurocentric.

It is commonly held that Locke bases his claim that all humans have an equal natural right to liberty on theological assumptions, namely, that God's human creatures are equal in His eyes and, because they are His creations, they are not to be harmed. For example, Jeremy Waldron argues this point in *God, Locke, and Equality: Christian Foundations of Locke's Political Thought*: "Locke's equality claims are not separable from the theological content that shapes and organizes them."[1] I do not deny that this is what Locke may

---

[1] Jeremy Waldron, *God, Locke, and Equality: Christian Foundations of Locke's Political Thought* (New York: Cambridge University Press, 2002), 82. For a defense of a secular reading of Locke's theory against Waldron's claim, see Jeffrey Reiman, "Towards a Secular Lockean Liberalism," *Review of Politics* 67, no. 3 (Summer, 2005), 473–493. Responding to my defense of a secular view of Locke's notion of equality, Waldron suggests that only a theological grounding "has what it takes" to override the many reasons we may have to treat others as less equal than ourselves, and doubts that a secular grounding of the sort I proposed "has what it takes to do this": see Jeremy Waldron, "Response to Critics," *Review of Politics* 67, no. 3 (Summer, 2005), 512. Interesting in this respect is that when, in his *Essay Concerning Human Understanding*, Locke takes up what determines the will, he says that, if the greatest future good were enough to determine the will, then "I do not see how [the will] could ever get loose from the infinite eternal joys of Heaven." And he continues, "This would be the . . . regular tendency of the will in all its determinations, were it determined by that, which is consider'd . . . the greater good; *but that it is not so is visible in Experience*" (*Essay* 2:21:38; emphasis mine). This strongly suggests that appeal to God does not "have what it takes" to determine behavior, and that eliminates the advantage that Waldron sees in theological over secular arguments. Another philosopher who reads Locke's theory in secular terms is A. John Simmons. See Simmons, *The Lockean Theory of Rights* (Princeton: Princeton University Press, 1992), 10.

have thought about his project. However, to follow Locke on this is a fool's errand because, in the current secular era, claims about what God wants or commands are taken to be both unprovable and highly speculative, and likely to convince only religious believers – and not all of them, since many believers will count such claims presumptuous. For them, God exists but His intentions are a mystery beyond our ken.

Consequently, I propose a secular interpretation in the hope of reaching and persuading a larger audience. I shall attempt to draw together various elements in Locke's argument for the natural right to liberty that I believe form the basis for a compelling secular argument. I shall proceed as follows. In Section 3.1, "A Lockean Argument for the Right to Liberty," I present an argument for the natural right to liberty based on the argument that Locke puts forth in the *Second Treatise of Civil Government*, strengthened by views that Locke expresses in his *Essay Concerning Human Understanding* and in his *Letter Concerning Tolerance*. I shall show that Locke holds that rational competence to make correct moral inferences is the ground of the entitlement to the right to liberty, the ground of moral responsibility, and the ground of the moral obligation to respect the natural right to liberty. I shall then point out that, if we have such a rational competence, we have a compelling secular basis for believing that we do in fact have a natural right to liberty. In Section 3.2, "Our Rational Moral Competence," I shall defend the claim that we have a rational competence to make correct moral inferences by showing that it is assumed in Anglo-American law and by moral philosophers in their practice, and that it is widely believed in by human beings in all cultures. Together with Section 3.1, this establishes the existence of the natural right to liberty as an article of knowledge. In Section 3.3, "From Liberty to Lockean Contractarianism," I argue that the existence of a natural right to liberty makes it morally necessary that requirements of justice, beyond recognition of the right to liberty, be the object of a social contract. One implication of this is that, though I shall eventually make use of Rawls's original position, the contractarianism that underlies Marxian Liberalism is Lockean rather than Rawlsian in nature. In this section, I will explain how in some conditions theoretical consent is morally equivalent to actual consent.

3.1   A Lockean Argument for the Right to Liberty

I start from a plain reading of two of Locke's statements. Asking "what estate men are naturally in," that is, what condition humans are in prior to, or in the absence of, political institutions that give some people special authority over others, Locke answers:

> A state . . . of equality, wherein all power and jurisdiction is recipro-
> cal, no one having more than another, there being nothing more
> evident than that creatures of the same species and rank . . . should
> also be equal one amongst another. (*ST*, ii:4)

And, then, a few paragraphs later:

> The state of Nature has a law of Nature to govern it, which obliges
> every one, and *reason*, which is that law, *teaches all mankind who will
> but consult it*, that being all equal and independent, no one ought to
> harm another in his life, health, liberty or possessions. (*ST*, ii:6;
> emphasis added)

Since we are reading Locke in secular terms, we can take him to mean by "a law of Nature" an objectively true moral law or require-ment or principle or rule.

Note that the two quotations make different claims. Only the second asserts that people have a right not to be harmed by others in their liberty, the right that I shall call the *natural right to liberty*. The first asserts only that people are equal, and only negatively. It denies that there is inequality of natural "power and jurisdiction." That is, it denies the existence of any special *natural authority* of one person over anyone else (that is, *of one sane adult person over any other sane adult person* – I won't always repeat this qualification; it should be assumed unless the context indicates otherwise). *Natural authority* is the kind of authority that parents are thought to have over their children. It is natural because it flows from the nature of parents (as rational adults) and of children (as not yet capable of guiding their lives rationally) and the nature of their relationship (a guardianship necessitated by the weakness and vulnerability of the children), not from any state's law or from any agreement between the parents and the children.

That human adults have no special natural authority over other human adults does not imply that people have a right not to be harmed or coerced by others. (For example, lions have no special natural authority over gazelles, but that does not mean that gazelles have a natural right not to be eaten by lions.) Thus this claim does not assert that people have a right not to be pushed around by other people. It does not assert a right to liberty. It rules out pushing other adults around *on the basis of a claim to authority over them*; but it says nothing about someone who would push others around without claiming authority. Only the second quotation asserts a right not to be harmed or coerced or bossed around by others, and thus a right to liberty. Put otherwise, the first quotation asserts that adults have no special natural authority over other adults; only the second quotation asserts that adults have special natural authority over themselves.

Before considering further the significance of these two claims, look at the setting about which Locke makes them. The setting is what Locke calls a "state of Nature," that is, a condition in which no social or political authority exists. Since we have no records of such a state and, in fact, since it is doubtful that it ever existed, appeals to the state of nature are often viewed with skepticism. But the state of nature is not meant to be a real condition. It is, like Rawls's original position (of which it is a not-so-distant ancestor), a mental experiment.

To undertake the "state of nature" mental experiment, we imagine away differences in social and political rank and authority in order to think of (sane, adult) humans in a "natural" condition. I put "natural" in quotation marks because what remains when we make this imaginary subtraction is still noticeably a product of human activity; it includes human social relations, such as families, and, of course, language. Having performed this mental subtraction, what we see with our mind's eye, according to Locke, is people whose condition is broadly alike. Locke claims that, when we picture humans in this way, nothing is more evident than that they are morally equal in the negative sense that no one has more authority over others than others have over them.

Locke's second quoted statement affirms a moral right not to be harmed. He gives two reasons for this. One is the negative equality affirmed in the first quoted statement. The second reason is that people are independent. Thus the product of the two quoted statements is that, because humans are "all equal and independent, no one ought to harm another in his life, health, liberty or possessions."

There are statements elsewhere in Locke's writings that can be used to add more detail to the claim that humans are "all equal and independent" (*ST*, ii:6), and that therefore make clearer how Locke could think that such equality and independence was sufficient to ground a natural right not to be harmed. In addition to the negative equality that we have already seen, there is further the fact that humans are equal in that what they believe and how they live their lives are of *intense interest* to them, to use an apt phrase of Waldron's.[2] Though Waldron takes this to be because they are interested in their divine salvation, it applies equally if they are not. Indeed, Locke asserts that, without the hope of salvation, how one lives this earthly life becomes the ultimate question. In his *Essay Concerning Human Understanding*, he wrote: "if there be no Prospect beyond the Grave, the inference is certainly right, *Let us eat and drink*, let us enjoy what we delight in, *for to morrow we shall die*" (*Essay*, 2:21:55). So, one either hopes for salvation or one doesn't and, either way,

---

[2]Waldron, *God, Locke, and Equality*, 79.

what one believes and how one lives is of intense interest.[3] This is given added support by the fact that we are *embodied*. Locke writes that "when we say that *Man is subject to Law*: We mean nothing by *Man*, but a corporeal rational Creature" (*Essay*, 3:11:16). That we are embodied means that human beings are equal in the further sense that, though the content of their needs and desires differ, they all have needs and desires and, in general, care deeply about having (at least the most important of) them satisfied. This, too, is of intense interest.

Moreover, in addition to humans being independent in the sense of physically separate, there is a further independence that we have as rational beings. In his *Letter Concerning Toleration*, Locke contends that power to compel anyone to a certain religious faith cannot be thought to "be vested in the Magistrate by the *consent of the People*, because no man can so far abandon the care of his own Salvation, as blindly to leave it to the choice of any other." The immediate reason he gives for this is that

> no Man can, if he would, conform his Faith to the Dictates of another. All the Life and Power of true Religion consists in inward and full perswasion of the mind; and Faith is not Faith without believing. (*Letter*, 26)

[3]Consider, for example, that, in both *Political Liberalism* and *A Theory of Justice*, John Rawls appeals to the importance that religious beliefs have for religious people as part of a secular argument for freedom of conscience. He writes: "if but one of the alternative principles of justice available to the parties [in the original position] guarantees equal liberty of conscience, this principle is to be adopted. . . . For the veil of ignorance implies that the parties do not know whether the beliefs espoused by the persons they represent is a majority or a minority view. They cannot take chances by permitting a lesser liberty of conscience to minority religions, say, on the possibility that those they represent espouse a majority or dominant religion and will therefore have an even greater liberty. For it may also happen that these persons belong to a minority faith and may suffer accordingly. If the parties [in the original position] were to gamble in this way, they would show that they did not take the religious, philosophical, or moral convictions of persons seriously, and, in effect, did not know what a religious, philosophical, or moral conviction was" (*PL*, 311; see similar remarks at *TJ*, 181).

Rational beings can only believe something if they are "fully satisfied in [their] own mind that [it] is true," and, thus, "such is the nature of Understanding, that it cannot be compell'd to the belief of anything by outward force" (*Letter*, 26, 27).

This is an argument that was very common among Enlightenment writers. For example, Voltaire wrote: "Our soul acts internally. Internal acts are thought, volition, inclinations, acquiescence in certain truths. All these acts are above coercion."[4] And Thomas Jefferson said, "Almighty God hath created the mind free, and manifested his Supreme will that free it shall remain by making it altogether insusceptible of restraint."[5] I suspect that this belief played a greater role in grounding Enlightenment liberalism than is normally recognized.[6] It is, in any event, clearly part of Locke's thought, and it provides additional reasons for viewing human beings as independent. Rational belief must in this way be independently arrived at. And for embodied rational creatures, this naturally spreads to create an inclination to live freely, that is, according to one's own independently formed beliefs about how to live.

Understanding our "being all equal and independent" as encompassing these three claims – human beings' natural negative equality, their equally intense interest in what they believe and how they live and in having their desires satisfied, the natural independence of their reason and their resulting desire to live according to their own independently formed beliefs – we can understand how Locke could hold that nothing is more evident than "that being all equal and independent, no one ought to harm another in his life, health, liberty, or possessions."

I think that the most that Locke is actually able to claim here is that, because humans are equal and independent, nothing is more evident than that each human has *a right not to be harmed in*

---

[4]François-Marie Arouet de Voltaire, "The Ecclesiastical Ministry," quoted in I. Kramnick, ed., *The Portable Enlightenment Reader* (New York: Penguin, 1995), 116.
[5]Thomas Jefferson, "A Bill for Establishing Religious Freedom," in *Papers of Thomas Jefferson*, ed. Julien Boyd (Princeton: Princeton University Press, 1950), vol. 2, 545.
[6]On the implications of this idea, see Jeffrey Reiman, *Critical Moral Liberalism: Theory and Practice* (Lanham, MD: Rowman and Littlefield, 1997), 5–11.

his or her life, health or liberty. We must omit the term "possessions" from Locke's famous phrase, because it is ambiguous between "what we physically possess" and "what we rightfully possess." If it is taken as the former, then it is doubtful in the extreme. We do not normally think, for example, that criminals have a right not to be harmed in their possession of stolen goods. If "possessions" is taken as "what people rightfully hold," then it requires a showing of rightfulness, which is to say, it requires that a right to private property be justified, which – as Locke recognized – requires a separate argument (which we will consider in Section 4.1). The conclusion that all have an equal right not to be harmed is made about us simply as corporeal rational beings. Property is a separate matter.

What then is *a right not to be harmed in one's life, health or liberty*? It is easy to understand what it means to harm someone in her life or health, but what does it mean to harm someone in her liberty? Most obviously, unwanted coercion harms a person in her liberty. But, harming people in their life or health is also coercion, and normally unwanted. Thus the right not to be harmed in one's life, health, or liberty is a general right not to be subjected to unwanted coercion. Since it amounts to a right to be able to live as one sees fit, I call it the *natural right to liberty*.

Humans have the right not to be harmed in their liberty, not because coercion or even harm are taken as bad in themselves. It's because rational adult human beings are equal and independent. That they are naturally alike in rank, coupled with the fact that they naturally want to satisfy their own desires and to live according to their own beliefs about how to live, *supports* the belief that they ought to have a right to do so. (Note that I say "supports" here, not "logically entails." The rational ability to go from such factual support to such a normative belief is an example of the competence to make normative inferences that I will argue presently grounds Locke's theory of rights.) Thus, we are entitled to believe that humans have a *natural right to liberty*, meaning a right to live according to their choices about how to live. That amounts to a natural right to bodily liberty, a right of humans to do with their bodies what they want as long as they do not interfere with the like right of others – and that, in turn, means that humans have a natural right to be free of unwanted coercion.

As we saw, Locke holds that this right is part of the natural law, which, as indicated above, we take as meaning objectively true moral rules. Locke holds that we are subject to such rules because our rationality enables us to understand them, and apply them to ourselves. In his *Essay*, Locke wrote that "were there a Monkey, or any other Creature to be found, that had the use of Reason, to such a degree, as to be able to understand general Signs, and to deduce Consequences about general *Ideas*, he would no doubt be subject to Law, and, in that Sense, be a Man, how much soever he differ'd in Shape from Others of that name" (*Essay*, 3:2:16). Possession of reason includes the competence to understand the true moral law, which is equally the competence to apply those true rules to ourselves. And that in turn is the condition of being morally responsible, that is being "subject to Law."

In the *Second Treatise*, Locke makes this clear in a different context. Locke accepts the commonsense belief that children do not yet have a natural right to liberty, and must be subject to their parents' supervision. When we come to have the right to liberty, he contends, is when we are of "the age of discretion," that is, when we possess the rational competence to understand the moral rules to which we are subject. But such a competence is an ability to make and apply correct moral judgments to ourselves. It is this competence that, for Locke, makes us morally responsible.

Discussing the grounds and limits of paternal authority over children, Locke argues that whatever gave the father the right to freedom will eventually give the same to the son. He writes:

> Is a man under the law of Nature? What made him free of that law? What gave him a free disposing of his property, according to his own will, within the compass of that law? I answer, an estate wherein he might be supposed capable to know that law, that so he might keep his actions within the bounds of it. When he has acquired that state, he is presumed to know how far that law is to be his guide, and how

far he may make use of his freedom, and so comes to have it; till then somebody must guide him, who is presumed to know how far the law allows a liberty. If such a state of reason, such an age of discretion made him free, the same shall make his son free too. (*ST*, vi:59)

Here, Locke holds that the level of maturity that entitles an adult to exercise the right to liberty is characterized by the rational competence to make valid moral judgments, and that competence is the ground of moral responsibility. Those who lack this competence must be guided by others who possess it. This means, incidentally, that the right to liberty is possessed by actual humans who are judged rational enough to be morally responsible by commonsense standards. It is not based on an ideal of perfect rationality or perfect freedom. It is (as we saw in Chapter 1) a right to the ordinary freedom of ordinary people.

This same rational competence that accounts for moral responsibility, and for when people gain the right to liberty, also helps us to make sense of Locke's account of the moral obligation to respect that right. That all rational people can be expected to make the correct moral judgment that people have a natural right to liberty means that all people know that all other rational people recognize that right, and thus that all can expect all others to respect it. Then, any sane adult who does not respect it is consciously flouting the reasonable expectations of his fellows. Such a person is reasonably judged a threat by the others, and reasonably dealt with defensively. Thus, writes Locke,

In transgressing the law of Nature, the offender declares himself to live by another rule than that of reason and common equity . . . , and so he becomes dangerous to mankind;... which being a trespass against the whole species, and the peace and safety of it, provided by the law of Nature, every man upon this score, by the right he hath to preserve mankind in general, may restrain, or where it is necessary, destroy things noxious to them, and so may bring such evil on any one who hath transgressed that law, as may make him repent the doing of it, and thereby deter him, and by his example, others from doing the like mischief. (*ST*, ii:8)

In short, the natural right of liberty obligates us because it is a reasonable judgment in response to our shared human condition – acting contrary to it is unreasonable – and because defensive action against those who are not willing to respect the right to liberty is the reasonable response to them. As some scholars have suggested, a Lockean theory of obligation is grounded both in reason and in the threat of sanction.[7]

We have seen that Locke takes it to be a rational inference from our equality and independence that we have a natural right to liberty. He also holds that we have a natural rational competence to make correct moral judgments, which is the basis of our moral responsibility, our right to exercise our liberty, and the ground of everyone's obligation to respect the right to liberty. With this, Locke's argument comes full circle. Locke's original argument for the natural right to liberty was that "reason . . . teaches all mankind who will but consult it, that being all equal and independent, no one ought to harm another in his . . . liberty" (*ST*, ii:6). Reason here refers to the same rational competence that Locke counts as making humans subject to moral law and entitled to act freely. *The natural rational competence that accounts for moral responsibility and moral obligation is the same competence that accounts for our knowledge of the truth of the original claim that we have a natural right to liberty.* It is worth turning now to a closer look at this competence.

3.2 Our Rational Moral Competence

Reflect on the kind of knowledge that Locke seems to be assuming we have when he asserts that the two statements quoted at the outset of Section 3.1 are true. In both of these statements, Locke writes as if ordinary human reason itself is capable of yielding some correct and very basic moral judgments in response to our shared human condition. Those judgments are that humans are negatively

---

[7]On Locke's views about the ground of moral obligation, see the discussion in Simmons, *Lockean Theory of Rights*, 26–28.

equal and independent, and that, because of that equality and independence, "no one ought to harm another in his life, health, [or]
liberty." (I continue to omit "possessions" for the reasons already
given.) These judgments are not stipulations or axioms, not self-
evident truths or logical entailments. They are what reasonable
people will rightly judge to be the proper treatment of their fellows
– the reasonable response to their fellows' similar conditions. They
are, as Locke says, "intelligible and plain to a rational creature" (*ST*,
ii:12).

I contend that we can make the best (secular) sense out of what
Locke is saying here by taking him to assume that the rational competence that he takes to be the ground of moral responsibility is the
same competence with which we know that, because humans are
equal and independent, they have a natural right to liberty. The
competence that makes us morally responsible is an ability to make
certain true moral judgments. If we have the competence to make
certain true moral judgments, that means we have generally the
competence to make correctly some normative inferences from
facts. *Then, this rational competence accounts for how Locke can claim to
know that we have the natural right to liberty.* In this section, I want to
support Locke's argument for the right to liberty, by showing that
we, too, assume that people have such a rational competence; we,
too, assume that that competence includes recognition of a right to
liberty; and we, too, assume that possession of that competence is
the condition for moral responsibility.

The claim that rational human beings have a competence to arrive
at correct moral judgments will be controversial. Since David Hume
at least, it has been denied that there is a rational way to cross the
divide between facts and values, between *what is* and *what ought to
be*. Hume wrote:

> In every system of morality, which I have hitherto met with, I have
> always remark'd, that the author proceeds for some time in the
> ordinary way of reasoning, and establishes the being of a God,
> or makes observations concerning human affairs; when of a sudden
> I am surpriz'd to find, that instead of the usual copulations of

propositions, is, and is not, I meet with no proposition that is not connected with an ought, or an ought not. This change is impercep-tible; but is, however, of the last consequence. For as this ought, or ought not, expresses some new relation or affirmation, 'tis necessary that it shou'd be observ'd and explain'd; and at the same time that a reason should be given, for what seems altogether inconceivable, how this new relation can be a deduction from others which are entirely different from it. But as authors do not commonly use this precaution, I shall presume to recommend it to the readers.[8]

Hume here claims that no belief about what ought to be done can be deduced from beliefs about what is. Put otherwise, no set of facts about what *is* the case logically entails a judgment of what *ought* to be the case. This is the famous *is-ought* or *fact-value* problem that has dogged moral philosophers for centuries.[9]

Hume is clearly right that what ought to be the case goes beyond, adds something to, the facts of the case. Thus, there can be no logical deduction from what is the case to what ought to be. No amount of facts about what is *entails* a statement about what ought to be. But entailment is a very strict logical relationship. When A entails B, then to affirm A and deny B is to commit a logical contradiction. And that, as philosophers say, is absurd.

The assumption that I am attributing to Locke, that we have a rational competence to make correct moral inferences from certain facts, is not in conflict with Hume's claim that facts do not entail normative conclusions. Though an entailment is a kind of inference, it's not the only possible kind of inference that rationally competent people can make. An inference can signify a looser relationship than entailment. It can be the judgment that some set of facts gives enough support to some belief as to justify holding that belief to be

---

[8]David Hume, *A Treatise of Human Nature*, 2nd edition (Oxford: Oxford University Press, 1978), Book III, part i, section 1, 469.
[9]On this, see W. D. Hudson, ed., *The Is/Ought Question* (London: Macmillan, 1969).

true – even if not true beyond any possible doubt. When I see the streets wet, I infer that it has rained. But I do not claim that to say that "the streets are wet" and "it did not rain" is to commit a logical contradiction. The streets might be wet for some other reason, say, that the street washers passed by recently. That it has rained is something that goes beyond the fact of the streets being wet. Nonetheless, my inference that it has rained from the wetness of the streets is often correct. And if I eliminate other possibilities, such as the street washers and so on, I reach a point at which I am entitled to treat my inference that it did rain from the fact of the wetness, plus the elimination of alternative explanations, as knowledge – even though those facts do not logically entail that it rained.

Likewise, in a correct moral inference, one goes beyond the facts of the case. I do not take Locke to claim that our being equal and independent *entails* that we have a right to liberty. There is no contradiction in claiming that we are equal and independent and denying that we have a right to liberty. My view is that Locke is claiming that we competently and correctly infer from the fact of our equality and independence to the existence of our natural right to liberty. We correctly judge that these facts give enough support to the belief in our natural right to liberty to justify calling that belief true. "True" here means, not true beyond any possible doubt, not true in the sense that its denial is absurd. It means, rather, true enough to act on, even true enough to be required to act on – a matter of *moral certainty*, not absolute certainty.

The competence that I take Locke to assume is different from our ability to discern entailments, but is also normally able to yield correct conclusions. And I contend that we do in fact generally believe that we have such a competence. Didn't Hume himself believe that certain *facts* about descriptive and evaluative statements entitled him to judge that he, and to recommend that we, *ought* to believe that factual premises cannot entail a moral conclusion? Perhaps the solution to the fact-value problem has eluded us because it is right under our eyes as it was right under Hume's: Our competence as rational beings includes the ability to make correct inferences that cross the gap between *is* and *ought*.

81

We do normally suppose that rational people have the competence to make correct moral judgments. First of all, note that some
normative inferences are so nearly universally made that they
become part of the rationality that we require for people to be
held morally responsible for their actions. Such rationality is *substantive*; it is not limited to logical consistency. Seriously deranged
people can be (maddeningly!) logically consistent in their beliefs
(think: Hannibal Lecter). Such people are held to be insane, and thus
not legally responsible, because they fail to make certain substantive inferences, including normative ones (in Hannibal Lecter's
case: that it is wrong to kill, cook, and feast upon one's fellow
humans).

The belief that insanity is an inability to make certain correct
substantive moral judgments is built into Anglo-American criminal
law. The defense of insanity against a criminal charge is the claim
that a person lacks the necessary conditions to be held legally
responsible for his actions. The traditional requirements of the
defense of insanity, as spelled out in the M'Naghten Rule, are that
the accused either lacks understanding of right and wrong, or lacks
the ability to act on this understanding. The first of these conditions
defines the rationality necessary to be held legally responsible in
substantive terms. One is not rational enough to be legally responsible simply because one's reasoning is logically consistent. One
must understand right and wrong. That means one must be able to
make the appropriate substantive moral inferences.

A person unable to make such substantive inferences is not legally
responsible for his acts. A person who thinks that he is the only one
who exists, or the only one who feels pain, may hold a consistent
view (much to the embarrassment of philosophers), but he lacks the
rationality necessary to be held legally responsible for his actions.
So too someone who fails to grasp that it is wrong to harm innocent
others. People who fail to grasp such things are thought to be, like
young children, appropriately subject to guardianship by those who
have the requisite level of rationality. When such people are dangerous, they must be restrained. Punishing them makes neither legal
nor moral sense.

That the requirements of legal responsibility are substantive means that they assume that rational beings all possess the competence to make certain theoretical (that is, factual) judgments (other people exist and feel pain) and certain practical (that is, moral) judgments (it is wrong to cause pain wantonly). A society that insists on possession of this competence as the condition of responsibility does not do so because it holds its own judgments of right and wrong to be self-evident or logically necessary. It does so because it trusts its own competence to make such judgments correctly.

Since our assumptions about the conditions of legal responsibility follow closely our assumptions about the conditions of moral responsibility, we can take the fact that legal responsibility assumes competence to make valid normative legal judgments of right and wrong as evidence that moral responsibility assumes competence to make valid moral judgments of right and wrong. (It should not be thought, by the way, that legal judgments of right and wrong are just factual judgments about what the law says. People are held responsible for making these judgments even if they do not know the law. That's why *ignorance of the law is no excuse*.) The substantive rationality that is the condition of legal responsibility is equally the condition of moral responsibility. Put otherwise, the competence to make valid moral judgments and the competence to count as morally responsible are the same competence. Those who do not recognize that it is wrong to harm innocent nonthreatening humans are not sufficiently rational to be legally, or morally, responsible.

In addition to being present in our law, belief in this natural rational competence to make correct moral inferences is also presupposed by contemporary moral philosophers. Modern moral philosophers always try to support their moral philosophical claims by showing that they yield beliefs about what is right and wrong or good and bad that match widely held moral intuitions. Such intuitions would be of no probative value if they didn't represent inferences (from situational facts to normative judgments) that humans are thought normally competent to make correctly. That such inferences are called "intuitions" has the effect of making the source of common moral beliefs mysterious, and suggests that the whole enterprise of moral reasoning and philosophizing is fundamentally nonrational. But these so-called intuitions are in fact inferences. From the facts about human life and its dearness, people commonly infer that killing innocent people to promote one's own ends is wrong; from the facts about suffering and its awfulness, people commonly infer that it is wrong willfully to cause people needless pain. And so on. If we replace the notion of intuitions with that of exercises of a rational competence to make valid moral judgments, the process of moral reasoning as well as the enterprise of moral philosophizing look more like rational endeavors.[10]

Once talk of intuitions is replaced by that of rational inferences or rational judgments, then our moral claims can be thought of as objects of knowledge with truth values – even if, of course, they cannot be shown to be truer than equally widely held contrary judgments, if such there be. When judgments conflict, there is no way, outside of yet other judgments, to determine which one is correct. The only evidence for the validity of a given normative judgment is that other reasonable people make it also. Since we judge as the exercise of a competence to judge, the fact that someone makes a given judgment is itself a reason to believe that that judgment is correct. Thus, appeal to what is widely judged to be the case, factually or morally, is part of showing that a given judgment is superior to its competitors. When judgments conflict, claims about which judgments are correct are essentially theories that aim best to explain the actual inferences that people make about both general principles and individual cases. Such theories, developed and defended, are moral philosophies.

---

[10]That I would replace the current language of "intuitions" with that of "reasonable judgments" should suffice to indicate that I in no way endorse the view, associated with G. E. Moore and W. D. Ross, that we have intuitions – in the sense of direct knowledge – of values or principles of right. These are claims of self-evidence that Locke would rightly reject (see *Essay*, 1:3:4), and I reject them too. Our competence to make correct moral inferences is not an ability to see or intuit self-evident facts, anymore than our competence to judge relative height is.

Rawls has been most explicit about this in characterizing his method of moral philosophizing as "reflective equilibrium." That method amounts to attempting to bring one's general moral principles in line with one's considered moral judgments about particular cases (that is, one's substantive moral inferences), and vice versa. Rawls points out that it is not only the appropriate method for justifying moral beliefs; a similar method applies as well to the justification of theoretical beliefs (*TJ*, 18–19, and 18 n. 7). But reflective equilibrium is not simply Rawls's method of moral philosophizing; it is essential to all modern moral philosophizing. No matter how a moral philosophy is arrived at, it will not be found plausible unless its conclusions generally match widely held judgments about particular cases. And since this assumes that we have the competence to make valid moral inferences – otherwise there would be no point in trying to get our principles in line with our considered judgments – we can say that modern moral philosophers assume the existence of this competence.

Finally, we all do normally judge that all people are equal, and that all have a basic right not to be harmed in their life, health, and liberty. When social and political authority are not in play, virtually everyone recognizes that it is wrong to harm innocent nonthreatening human beings in their life, health, or liberty. Even terrorists feel the need to justify their killing of innocents as necessary responses to great injustice; they do not claim that such killing is simply okay. And murderers are held to be guilty because they knowingly do wrong, that is, their legal guilt presupposes that they know that it is wrong to kill innocents but do so anyway. Since ignorance of the law is no excuse, this means that even if murderers don't know that there is a law against murder, they are expected to know that it is wrong to murder, that is to say, morally wrong.

Here's another way to see the prevalence of the belief that all people have a basic right not to be harmed in their life, health, and liberty: The Golden Rule is as near to a universally recognized moral standard as there is. Versions of the Golden Rule exist in virtually every tradition of moral teaching: in Hinduism ("Do naught to others which, if done to thee, would cause thee pain: this is the sum of duty"), Buddhism ("In five ways should a clansman minister to his friends and familiars, . . . by treating them as he treats himself"), Confucianism ("What you do not want done to yourself, do not do unto others"), Zoroastrianism ("Whatever thou dost not approve for thyself, do not approve for anyone else"), Judaism ("Whatsoever thou wouldest that men should not do unto thee, do not do that to them"), and Christianity ("As ye would that men should do to you, do ye also to them likewise" [Luke 6:31]). Among the ancient Greeks, Isocrates is quoted as saying "Do not do to others what you would not wish to suffer yourself," and Diogenes Laertius reports Aristotle saying "Treat your friends as you want them to treat you."[11] Though there appears to be no equivalent to the Golden Rule in the Koran, it does turn up in the Hadiths (reports of the sayings of Mohammed). There one finds: *"None of you truly believes until he wishes for his brother what he wishes for himself,"*[12] and: *"Whoever wishes to be delivered from the fire . . . should treat the people as he wishes to be treated by them."*[13]

It is hard to imagine that all of these traditions would have hit on the Golden Rule if it did not reflect a widely held belief. And, since no one wants to be harmed by another in his life, health, and liberty, the Golden Rule implies that no one should harm another in his life, health, and liberty. Accordingly, that must be a widely held belief. What is less frequently noticed is that the Golden Rule also presupposes the very equality of rank upon which Locke bases his inference to the right not to be harmed. This is because it assumes that imposing a harm on one person is as bad as imposing a like harm on another. Otherwise, it would not be appropriate to measure what one person may do to another by what that first person wants done to him.[14] In feudal law, for example, where

---

[11] Robert Ernest Hume, *The World's Living Religions* (New York: Charles Scribner's Sons, 1959), 276–278.
[12] Number 13 of Al-Nawawi's 40 Hadith Qudsi.
[13] Sahih Muslim Book 020, number 4546.
[14] This shows, by the way, that the Golden Rule is more than a principle of logical consistency. It only holds if one also believes that people are equal.

people were clearly not treated equally, the punishment for harming a noble was different from the punishment for harming a non-noble.[15] Such inegalitarian systems assume that imposing a harm on a person of high rank is worse than imposing the same harm on another person of lesser rank. Consequently, the Golden Rule is testimony that it is widely believed that people are naturally equal in rank and that, for that reason among others, it is wrong to harm them in their life, health, and liberty. And, that so many different cultures share the Golden Rule is testimony that these beliefs transcend Western culture and, thus, this argument for the natural right to liberty ought to satisfy those who suspect that such rights are Anglo- or Eurocentric.

Note in closing here that the model of moral knowledge embodied in the notion of a basic rational competence to make simple moral inferences is at odds with G. A. Cohen's argument that ultimate moral principles are fact-insensitive. Cohen claims that whenever a fact supports a moral principle, there must be a more fundamental principle that accounts for that supporting function. This claim, says Cohen, "rests upon the more general claim that there is always an explanation why any ground grounds. I have no argument for that more general claim – it strikes me as self-evidently true" (*RJE*, 236). But, if we have a basic competence to make some correct moral inferences from facts, that implies that some facts support some moral judgments though there is no explanation of that supporting relationship *in the form of a more fundamental moral principle*. We know that the facts support the judgments because we judge that they do, and we are competent (though not infallible) at making such judgments correctly. Moreover, the supposedly self-evident claim that there is always a principle that explains why any ground grounds is itself a normative judgment (epistemologically normative, not morally) that Cohen can only put forth because he believes he has a competence

---

[15] Hendrik Spruyt, *The Sovereign State and Its Competitors* (Princeton: Princeton University Press, 1994), 41.

to make some normative judgments from the facts of the human condition.

3.3   From Liberty to Lockean Contractarianism

Locke famously argues that people in a state of nature, that is, in a condition in which there are no political institutions – no legislators, no judges, no police – would find it rational to agree to a social contract that establishes a state that respects and protects individuals' natural rights. These rights are not produced by the agreement. Rather, it is because there are natural rights, especially the right to liberty, that the establishment of a state – with its potential to violate liberty – is legitimate only if agreed to. The individual's natural right to liberty requires that the state – and any other arrangement that might violate liberty – be the outcome of a social contract. The result is a form of contractarian philosophy that is morally driven, required by the preexistence of a moral right. I call it *Lockean contractarianism* in order to distinguish it from the Rawlsian variety, which starts from a position without moral rights and aims to establish all moral rights, so to speak, from scratch. In spite of the fact that Marxian Liberalism uses a contracting situation modeled on Rawls's original position, its contractarian approach is Lockean. Recourse to the social contract is required by the natural moral right to liberty that I have defended in this chapter.

The natural moral right to liberty is a negative right. It is a right to noninterference, not a right to others' assistance. It affirms positively that each sane adult has natural authority over him or herself, but it does not give any sane adult authority to require service from any other. Accordingly, it may be thought that the natural right to liberty is a sparse moral principle and, in a way, indeed it is. However, it has the important implication that no other requirement can rightly be forced on sane adults against their wills. That in turn implies (a) that the justification of requirements backed up by force must be found in people's consent to them, and (b) that all moral demands that are not consented to must be promoted by persuasion alone.

These implications immediately run into the problem that liberty itself appears to require the existence of institutions – a state with laws, judges, police – to protect it, which institutions must already exist if people are safely to reach an age at which they could consent to them. As Hobbes and Locke have argued, the liberty we would have without such institutions would be drastically limited by fear of violence from others, the need to protect oneself against such violence, and the irremediable uncertainty that one will be able successfully to exercise one's liberty. Since, not only current human beings, but future human beings will be subject to coercion by the state, it cannot be thought that consent to the state must be *actual* consent. At least in cases where the arrangements are necessary to provide for and protect a full and dependable liberty, and where provision is made to limit the incursions on liberty that such arrangements might themselves entail, we must be able to appeal to *theoretical* consent, namely to what *it would be reasonable for people to consent to* rather than to what they in fact consent to.

Locke's theory is about such theoretical consent. It does not require us to believe that there really was a social contract agreed to in a state of nature. Such a belief is, in any event, highly implausible. For all citizens to agree, the social contract would have to be renegotiated with each newly born person. And a one-time original agreement in a state of nature assumes that individuals lived without authority structures and yet had enough peace and sufficient understanding (not to mention linguistic ability) to formulate, consider, and agree to a contract. David Hume's classic critique of the notion that states were really based on a social contract is still very powerful. Hume contended that history shows that states are founded in violence rather than agreement; that the existence of any contract of allegiance to the state is unknown to citizens, and thus cannot be thought to involve their consent; and that the costs and risks of emigrating are too great to count residing in a country or availing oneself of its benefits as voluntary, and thus as an act of consent.[16] Hume seems quite right on these points, and his critique is devastating to any historical theory of the social contract.

But the Lockean theory that the state is based on a social contract agreed to in a state of nature is not a historical theory. It is a normative theory. It amounts to claiming that a state with a certain constitution would be consented to by rational people who are not in a state. This is a matter of theoretical consent, not actual consent.

It may fairly be asked how theoretical consent – consent that it would be rational for people to give, but that they do not actually give – can justify anything. In response, consider first that, for critical decisions that must be made when actual consent is impossible and actual preferences unknown (say, the decision whether to treat an unconscious person who will die without treatment), it is common to accept *consent that it would be rational for people to give* as equivalent to actual consent. Further, the difference between theoretical and actual consent is less than it seems. For its audience, even "actual" consent is theoretical. The uttering of "yes" is not consent, since it might be uttered by someone not competent to consent, a child or a crazy person. We infer consent from the uttering of "yes" coupled with evidence that the individual is competent. Part of that evidence is that *it would be rational to consent* in this case.[17]

Combining these ideas, we can treat theoretical consent to the state as equivalent to actual consent because it concerns a critical decision that must be made when actual consent is impossible, actual preferences unknown, and the only evidence we possess that people do consent is that it would be rational for them to consent. Indeed, there is no other way that a state can be consented to but

---

[16]David Hume, "Of the Original Contract," in David Hume, *Essays: Moral, Political, and Literary*, ed. E. Miller (Indianapolis: Liberty Fund, 1985), 465–487; see esp. pp. 470, 471, 475.

[17] "*The very* fact that a choice clearly is extremely detrimental to [individuals] may itself be grounds for concluding that it was made in a moment of incompetence; at that point it becomes reasonable to respect the choices they *would* have made had they been competent rather than the choices they actually made." Steven Luper, *The Philosophy of Death* (Cambridge: Cambridge University Press, 2009), 161.

theoretically, since a state that must wait on the actual consent of every newly appearing human being is no state at all. Given the existence of the right to liberty which requires that states are only justified if consented to, this means that the only way in which the state can be justified is by theoretical consent.

I am not here saying that whatever it would be reasonable for people to agree to can rightly be imposed on human beings independently of their actual consent. I am making the more limited claim that what can be shown to be necessary for the provision and protection of a robust and secure liberty, and thus that would be reasonable for people cognizant of their possession of a natural right to liberty to consent to, can be rightly imposed on human beings without waiting for their actual consent. In this case, their theoretical consent is morally equivalent to actual consent.

I take it as evident that, at least for the foreseeable future, a state is necessary for the existence of a secure right to a robust liberty. By a *secure* right to liberty, I mean a right to liberty one can confidently exercise and confidently plan on exercising in the future. A secure right to liberty cannot exist unless there are known laws defining its reach and punishing its violation, independent courts and judges to apply those laws to cases, and an executive apparatus to enforce those laws. For this reason, Kant holds that our right to liberty (as well as our right to property) is a right to a state, and thus that we have a duty to form a state, since otherwise we fail to respect others' rights (*MM*, 45, 86). Moreover, the state increases enormously the power of human beings to realize their goals and, in this way, extends the liberty of human beings by placing within their reach projects that require the concertation of large numbers of people. This makes for a *robust* liberty.

These facts show that it is rational for people to consent to the state theoretically. But they show more: *They show that it is rational for actual people to count that theoretical consent as morally equivalent to actual consent.* Suffice it to say that anyone who thinks that the state is morally justifiable (anyone not an anarchist, that is) must believe that the benefits of the state justify imposing state institutions on people without their having first consented in fact. And, among these nonanarchists, anyone who believes that it is wrong to impose things on people without their consent will have to accept a theoretical version of consent, that is, taking people to consent actually to what it would be reasonable for them to consent to.

Later, I shall argue that the right to private property must and can also be justified by appeal to theoretical consent. Unlike libertarians, I do not view property rights as natural rights on a par with the natural right to liberty. Indeed, I shall argue in the next chapter that, because property rights may actually limit the liberty of nonowners, such rights are a threat to the natural right to liberty. (This is why I omitted "possessions" from the statement of the natural right to liberty, early in this chapter. The moral compatibility of property and liberty must be shown; it is not automatic.) In some form however, that is, with protections for nonowners built in, property rights are necessary supports to a secure and robust liberty. And, since they cannot be based on actual consent, it is rational for actual persons to accept their theoretical consent to property rights as equivalent to actual consent.

With this we get a moral justification for the social contract strategy of arguing for the moral acceptability of certain collective arrangements by showing that they would be agreed to by people in a suitably defined imaginary condition. This is a *moral* justification of the strategy because it starts from the fact that people who have a natural right to liberty may not have arrangements forced upon them against their wills that they do not consent to. Thus the social contractarianism that grounds Marxian Liberalism is of a Lockean rather than a Rawlsian variety.

Rawls's theory has often been attacked for presupposing moral rights when it aims to ground moral rights. Locke's contract is not vulnerable to this objection. Precisely because the Lockean contract is morally required, it is openly based on appeal to an already existing moral right. And, if, as I have argued, the Lockean argument for that right is sound, then the morally required social contract is stronger than the Rawlsian one that is justified by its conformity with our intuitions (in early Rawls), or by its conformity to our liberal democratic culture (in late Rawls). The Lockean social contract is grounded in each person's natural right to liberty. And since that right is the object of a correct rational inference that human beings are competent to make, the right is knowable to all reasonable people, and the ground on which Lockean contractarianism sits is firm.

4

The Ambivalence of Property
Expression of Liberty and Threat
to Liberty

In this chapter, I will develop Marxian Liberalism's understanding of the relationship between private property and liberty. Here, what is important is to see that while ownership of private property promotes the liberty of the owner, it also threatens the liberty of the nonowner. I call this two-sided nature of property's relationship to liberty the *ambivalence of property*. The first side of the right to private property has been overlooked by Marxists, but it is recognized and accepted by Marxian Liberals. The second, darker side of the right to private property has normally been overlooked by liberals and libertarians. Once the second side is recognized, it follows that the right to private property is not a simple implication of the natural right to liberty. It is one of those arrangements that requires the consent of the people affected by it.

Analyzing the arguments for the right to property of Locke and Kant and Nozick and Narveson, we will see that the right to private property promotes the liberty of owners *and* limits the liberty of

As Free and as Just as Possible: The Theory of Marxian Liberalism, First Edition. Jeffrey Reiman.
© 2014 Jeffrey Reiman. Published 2014 by John Wiley & Sons, Ltd.

nonowners. However, talk of this "limit" understates the nature of the threat to liberty in large and unequal property holdings. Under the condition of *universal ownership* (in which virtually everything is owned by someone or, like the oceans, treated as unownable by anyone) – a condition reached long ago virtually everywhere in the world – the right to property is more than a limit on liberty. It is an arrangement in which nonowners will have to provide some service to owners if they are to get some property of their own, including a wage of their own to live on. With the recognition that large property holdings pose the unique threat to liberty of forcing servitude on nonowners, we reach the Marxian claim that private ownership of means of production is more than a limit on liberty; it is a powerful form of coercion. And we come upon a central discovery of Marxism, namely, that coercion can be built into the structure of society and, thus, can occur without overt violence. I call this social form of coercion *structural coercion*.

In this chapter, I proceed as follows. In the first two sections, I take up, respectively, Locke's argument from liberty to property and Kant's argument from liberty to property, as well as, in each case, a modern libertarian's version of the argument. I take it that all are broadly successful in showing that private property promotes its owner's liberty. However, in Section 4.1, "Locke, Nozick, and the Ambivalence of Property," where I take up Locke's discussion of the right of property in the state of nature, I show that he implicitly recognizes the threat of property to the natural right to liberty. There I take up as well libertarian philosopher Robert Nozick's Lockean view of the right to property, and show that it does not respond adequately to this threat. And, in Section 4.2, "Kant, Narveson, and the Ambivalence of Property," where I take up Kant's argument, I show that it too leads to the conclusion that property is a threat to the natural right to liberty, and that libertarian philosopher Jan Narveson's recent version of Kant's argument does not adequately respond to this threat. In Section 4.3, "Marx and the Structural Coerciveness of Property," I show that Marx went beyond Locke and Kant in seeing that property was not just a threat to liberty, but a form of social coercion.

4.1   Locke, Nozick, and the Ambivalence of Property

In the *Second Treatise of Civil Government*, Locke arrives at the full right to property in stages. First, we get the argument for the individual's natural right to liberty that we considered in Section 3.1. Remember that Locke's inclusion of possessions, in stating the natural right to liberty, had to be set aside to wait for an additional argument. Locke surely didn't mean *all* possessions, say, even stolen goods, but only *rightful* possessions – and a separate argument is needed to determine when possessions are rightful, as Locke clearly recognized. Leaving possessions until that separate argument is made, we characterized the right to liberty that Locke has argued for as a natural right to dispose of one's body as one sees fit as long as one does not interfere with the like right of others. This right may be extended to one's possessions in some appropriate way, if and when they are determined to be rightfully held.

To get from the right to natural liberty considered strictly as a right over one's own body to rightful possessions requires, for Locke, *two* arguments: (1) Locke starts by arguing for the right to own what one takes from nature for the purpose of personal consumption. This argument starts with the claim that people own their persons: Locke writes that "every man has a 'property' in his own 'person.' This nobody has any right to but himself" (*ST*, v:27). This last phrase shows that people's ownership of their persons is based on their natural right to liberty, since that right is an exclusive right to control one's person. Then: (2) From everyone's property in his person, Locke infers that "the 'labour' of his body and the 'work' of his hands . . . are properly his." And Locke takes that to imply that "Whatsoever . . . he removes out of the state that Nature hath provided and left it in, he hath mixed his labour with it, and joined to it something that is his own, and thereby makes it his property" (*ST*, v:27).

Locke makes three important points about this property right. First, it is limited to things to be used before they spoil; it is not a right simply to accumulate as much as one can: "As much as any one can make use of to any advantage of life before it spoils, so much he may by his labour fix a property in" (*ST*, v:31). Second, removing something from its natural state creates a right to own it only "where there is enough, and as good left in common for others" (*ST*, v:27). And third, this right does not depend on the consent of anybody else: "If such a consent as that was necessary, man had starved, notwithstanding the plenty God had given him" (*ST*, v:28).

The first point, that the right is only to things to be used before spoiling, makes the right only *a right to property for consumption*. The second point, that enough and as good be left in common for others, requires that to have a genuine right to property in what one has acquired in the unowned state, an acquisition must leave other people the real possibility of making similar acquisitions of unowned stuff. (Nozick dubs this the *Lockean proviso*, though he interprets it as the requirement that no one ought to be made worse off by another's acquisition, which, I shall argue presently, is a significant weakening of Locke's requirement [*ASU*, 175].) And the third point, that the right does not depend on consent of others, tells us that the right to property for consumption is a natural right that arises in the same way as does the natural right to liberty.

From here, Locke proceeds to argue for a larger right to property, the right to own as much as one can accumulate including what property one can store in the form of money. Since this is also a right to own considerably larger property than others own, I will call it *a right to large and unequal property*. It is, for all intents and purposes, the right to property one finds in modern Western nations, such as the United States. That Locke argues for this larger right to property in the state of nature, prior to the formation of the polity, seems to make him the odd man out among the classical social contractarian philosophers. Hobbes, Rousseau, and Kant all held that there is something like the right to liberty in the state of nature. They also held that there is, at some point, a right to large and unequal property. Unlike Locke, however, all three held that the larger right to property emerges only *after people have left the state of nature* by consenting to form a state. Thus Hobbes, Rousseau, and Kant took the right to property to be, not a natural right, but one that is created by the agreement of those affected by it.

Locke's difference from these other social contractarians is less than it first appears to be. Though it arises in the state of nature, Locke argues that the larger right to property is based on people's consent. He finds evidence of this consent in the conventional value of money, which, because it stores value in the form of gold or silver, allows holdings beyond what one can consume before it spoils. Locke writes:

> since gold and silver, being little useful to the life of man, in propor-
> tion to food, raiment, and carriage, has its value only from the consent
> of men – . . . it is plain that the consent of men have agreed to a
> disproportionate and unequal possession of the earth. (*ST*, v:50)

In short, Locke contends that since the value of money is conventional, it has been consented to. And since money makes possible large and unequal property holdings, they too have been consented to. Thus, Locke gives us, in the state of nature, a pre-contract contractarian argument for the right to large and unequal property.

It is not a very persuasive argument. That something is conventional doesn't mean that it is consented to (for something to count as consented to, it must be possible to dissent: try dissenting from the conventional meanings of "yes" and "no"); and, furthermore, were it consented to, people would have had the chance to tie conditions to their consent, but no such opportunity was afforded. Moreover, that something is consented to doesn't mean that whatever it makes possible is thereby consented to (even if we did consent to the conventional meanings of language, that wouldn't imply that we consented to all that they made possible, such as lying).

More important than the quality of the argument, however, is the fact that Locke thought he had to make it. I think that he thought he had to make it because the right to large and unequal property is a substantial restriction of the natural right to liberty. Go back in the state of nature to the point at which the natural right to liberty exists, and other rights do not yet exist. At that point, all of us have the right to go wherever we wish, as long as we do not trespass upon others' bodies. When we add the right to property for consumption, it brings only minor limits: Now we also cannot trespass on whatever little pile of things others have accumulated and are about to consume. These limits are naturally small and – given Locke's requirement "that enough and as good be left in common for others" – without significant effect. Moreover, since our bodies and our capacities for consumption are broadly similar, the limits are virtually the same for all. Thus, the rights to liberty and to property for consumption keep relations between humans symmetric: we each have as much freedom as others, and we each have as much authority over others as they have over us.

If, however, we now add a right to large and unequal property, *things change dramatically.* When this large piece of land is now my rightful property, you may no longer walk on it without my permission. Since there is little if any limit to how much land I may own, this can be a very substantial limitation on where you were previously free to walk. And, since there is no assurance that you own an equally large tract of land or any land at all, this is a limitation on you that is not necessarily balanced by an equal limitation on me – indeed, you and I may now stand in an asymmetrical relation in which I have significantly more freedom to go where I wish than you do. Moreover, with a right to large and unequal property, it won't be long before just about everything is owned by someone. Once this condition of *universal ownership* arrives, then, outside of publicly owned spaces, there will be nowhere that non-owners may freely roam without the permission of others. Eric Freyfogle writes:

> Consider what happens when a person becomes the first owner of a tract of land and puts up no-trespassing signs around the perimeter. Before then, any person could wander onto the land and use it; the landscape was a commons for all to enjoy, collecting wood and berries, bringing their livestock, and looking for game. Now, with no-trespassing signs up, these people can no longer make use of this

> particular land. Only the owner can do so, and those who have
> gained permission to enter. . . . The landowner, to be sure, has gained
> greater freedom over this exclusive piece of land. The owner's liberty
> has gone up. At the same time, everyone else's liberty has gone
> down.[1]

Bear in mind that this loss of liberty for everyone else is the immediate effect of private ownership. I shall argue that ultimately a system of private property increases everyone's liberty. This is what will make it reasonable for everyone to consent to private property. Nonetheless, it must be noted that, whatever else it does, private property starts by limiting the liberty of nonowners. That is what makes it necessary for private property to be consented to in order to be moral.

On Locke's theory, the state must be consented to precisely because people have a natural right to liberty that a state may significantly restrict. The right to liberty itself entails that such a restriction on liberty may not legitimately be imposed on anyone without her (exercising her right to liberty by) authorizing that restriction. Since the right to large and unequal property also significantly restricts liberty, that larger right to property needs to be consented to for the same reason that the authority of the state over its subjects needs to be consented to. Indeed, the right to large and unequal property is a kind of authority over others. You cannot walk on or use my property unless I give you permission to do so. In that sense, the larger right to property is exactly on a par with the authority of the state, albeit parceled out to some individuals. If the authority of the state is imposed without consent, it violates the natural right to liberty – and the same is true if the right to large and unequal property is imposed without consent.

Now consider a modern version of Locke's theory. Robert Nozick's theory of the right to property consists of three principles: a *principle of just acquisition* which applies to the original acquisition of

[1] Eric T. Freyfogle, *On Private Property: Finding Common Ground on the Ownership of Land* (Boston: Beacon Press, 2007), 7.

property from the unowned state, a *principle of just transfer* which applies to the ways in which property once owned passes from one owner to another, and a *principle of rectification* to correct property holdings that have resulted from violations of either of the first two principles. The principle of just acquisition is modeled broadly on Locke's theory that unowned things become private property when labor is mixed with them.

Nozick acknowledges Locke's claim that such a right only arises if nonowners are left with enough and as good in common. Nozick calls this the *Lockean proviso* (*ASU*, 175, 178–182). He accepts that this proviso limits all original acquisition, and thus affects all property ownership derived from such acquisition – which is to say all property other than one's body and labor. Precisely because he thinks this attaches to all property ownership, and thus such ownership as occurs even once everything is owned and nothing left "in common," Nozick omits the phrase "in common" from his statement of the Lockean proviso. That is, he drops from the proviso the requirement that there be unowned property left for others to appropriate. Instead, it becomes the requirement that no one be made worse off because of someone else's acquisition. This is weaker than Locke's requirement. Conveniently, Nozick's version leaves room, not only for the justice of private ownership after everything is owned, but for capitalism. That is, capitalism can easily satisfy the watered-down version of Locke's condition because capitalism makes a lot more goods available to people. Thus, presumably, everyone is richer in a capitalist society than in one without private property. And then no one is made worse off by another's acquisition.

Note, however, what Nozick's Lockean proviso does not do. It does not guarantee that others will have the same opportunity to acquire property as those who have already acquired some. Moreover, it does not guarantee that others will have the same freedom of movement as those who already own some property. Once the condition of universal ownership is reached and just about everything is owned, others may roam on owned property only with the permission of its owner. And they may obtain a share in capitalism's bounty of goods, but only if they provide services for those who own property. Thus, what Nozick's proviso does not do is repair the loss in liberty that the original acquisition of property set in motion, and that universal ownership seals. I do not argue that a system of private property cannot solve the problem of property's limitations on liberty. I do contend, however, that the virtually unlimited right to property that Locke and Nozick defend is part of the problem, not the solution. And the same is true of the virtually unlimited right to property defended by Kant and Narveson, to which I now turn.

4.2   Kant, Narveson, and the Ambivalence of Property

Immanuel Kant makes an argument for property that does not follow Locke in deriving property from ownership of the person and the mixing of one's own labor with unowned things. Kant argues to the right of property directly from the right to liberty itself. Narveson does so too. Here, I shall consider Kant's argument for the right to property and show that it leads to the same conclusion that Locke's did: though the right promotes the liberty of the owner, it is a threat to the liberty of the nonowner. I shall then show that Narveson's version of the argument does not avoid this outcome.

Kant's argument for the right to property occurs in that part of *The Metaphysics of Morals* (*MM*) titled "The Doctrine of Right." The doctrine of right is, for Kant, that aspect of morality that addresses justice and just laws, and thus applies uniquely to those things which can be subject to coercion. For Kant that means external behavior, not internal motives. The requirements that apply to our internal motives are discussed by Kant in that part of *The Metaphysics of Morals* that is called "The Doctrine of Virtue."

As is well known, Kant held that we are subject morally to a *categorical imperative* that commands us to act only on maxims (that is, subjective intentions) that we can wholeheartedly will to be universal laws. If I am considering acting on the maxim that I may kill a non-threatening person when I can get away with it, I must test that maxim by asking if I could wholeheartedly will that there be a universal law permitting people to kill others who pose no threat to them, when they could get away with doing so. Since such a law would render everyone's life insecure, including my own, I cannot will it. Thus, I know that acting on my maxim is immoral or, as Kant would say, contrary to moral duty. And, this tells me that it is my moral duty not to murder.[2]

Since the doctrine of right applies only to external actions, it is concerned only with the conformity of an action with the categorical imperative, not with its maxim: "The conformity of an action to [this] law of duty is its *legality* (*legalitas*); the conformity of the maxim of an action with the law is the *morality* (*moralitas*) of the action" (*MM*, 17). Accordingly, Kant formulates a "Universal Principle of Right" which holds that "Any action is right if it can coexist with everyone's freedom in accordance with a universal law" (*MM*, 24). This is, in effect, the application of the categorical imperative to external action alone. That is, if I may only intentionally perform an external action that could be permitted to all by a universal law, then I can only intentionally perform those actions which are compatible with everyone else's freedom to perform those same actions. What is distinctive about the Universal Principle of Right is that the principle does not require that I take it as my maxim. All that it requires is that I act in conformity with the principle no matter what my motivation. Thus it allows for the use of coercion to assure that people's behavior complies with the principle, and that freedom is protected.

Kant takes the freedom protected by Universal Principle of Right to be our only innate right (*MM*, 30). Thus, like Locke, Kant takes liberty to be a natural right, one that we have in the state of nature

---

[2]For the argument for this way of determining our duty, see generally, Immanuel Kant, *Groundwork of the Metaphysics of Morals* (Cambridge: Cambridge University Press, 1998), 7–33.

and that, accordingly, precedes any other right, such as the right to property. Also like Locke, Kant derives the right to property from the innate right to liberty – but he does so by establishing a closer link between liberty and property than Locke does. Where Locke goes from liberty to ownership of one's person, and from there to the right to property, Kant skips the middle step and goes directly from liberty to the right to property. In fact, Kant rejects the idea of people owning themselves, holding that only things, not persons, can be owned (*MM*, 41, 56).

Kant distinguishes physical or empirical possession of something from owning it. I only have a property right in something "if I may assume that I could be wronged by another's use of the thing even *though I am not in* [physical] *possession of it*" (*MM*, 37). If I am in physical possession of something unowned, and another tries to take it from me, he violates my right to liberty, not any right of property (*MM*, 38). To distinguish the right to property from physical possession, Kant sometimes calls ownership intelligible possession or *possessio noumenon* (*MM*, 39–40). The problem is to defend a right to intelligible possession.

Kant's strategy in proving the existence of a right of property, of the right to intelligible possession of something external to the individual, is to disprove the contradictory, that is, to show that it cannot be true that nothing can be rightly owned. He writes:

> . . . an object of my choice is something that I have the *physical* power to use. If it were nevertheless absolutely not within my *rightful* power to make use of it, that is, if the use of it could not coexist with the freedom of everyone in accordance with a universal law ([and thus] would be wrong), then freedom would be depriving itself of the use of its choice with regard to an object of choice, by putting *usable* objects beyond any possibility of being *used*; in other words, it would annihilate them in the practical [that is, moral] respect and make them into *res nullius* [things with no owner], even though in the use of things choice was formally consistent with everyone's outer freedom in accordance with universal laws. . . . [T]his would be a contradiction of outer freedom with itself. . . . It is therefore an *a priori* presupposition of practical reason to regard and treat any object

of my choice as something which could objectively be mine or yours. (*MM*, 41)

Kant's point is that freedom requires use of external things. And Kant must be thinking of such use as including that one be able to leave the thing one is using aside for a while (say, while one is sleeping, or out buying groceries or tools) and still have the right to use it upon return. Accordingly, the freedom of everyone requires that everyone be able to have rights to things *when they are not in physical possession of them*. Then, the claim that we cannot have such a right would contradict external freedom because it would deny us the rightful use of the external world that freedom requires, "even though in the use of things choice was formally consistent with everyone's outer freedom in accordance with universal laws." Accordingly, we can have rights to property.

Kant recognizes that the right to property is a right to exclude others from the use of some external thing, and such a right puts others under a moral obligation not to trespass. Thus, Kant recognizes that the right to property is a restriction on the natural right to liberty – the innate freedom – of everyone else. Accordingly, the right to property requires the consent of the others: "By my unilateral choice I cannot bind another to refrain from using a thing, an obligation that he would not otherwise have; hence I can do this only through the united choice of all who possess it in common" (*MM*, 49). For everyone to consent to individuals' exclusive use of some thing, all people must be thought of as originally possessing (in some way) all things – otherwise they would not be able to grant anyone the right to exclude them from using some of those things. This last claim makes sense if we take the original common possession to reflect everyone's natural right to liberty, which includes the right to physically possess whatever is not owned. It is because people have this right that they can consent to grant individuals rights to own specific parts of the earth.

Kant claims that the argument thus far creates only a *provisional* right to property. A conclusive right to property requires the formation of the state, or what Kant calls "the civil condition." This is because the right to property imposes obligations on everyone else, which are binding on them only if they can be assured that everyone will respect similar obligations toward them. Such assurance can only be given by "a collective general (*common*) and powerful will" able to impose a coercive law. And "the condition of being under a general external (i.e., public) lawgiving accompanied with power [to impose a coercive law] is the civil condition" (*MM*, 45), that is, a state. Kant takes this to entail that individuals have the right to force their fellows in the state of nature to form a state. But we need not follow Kant that far.

Kant saw that property is ambivalent *vis-à-vis* liberty; it both promotes and limits liberty. The right of property enables people to exercise their liberty by using things. Thus property promotes owners' liberty. But, Kant saw as well that one person's ownership of property puts others under obligations to which they would not otherwise be subject. Thus property limits nonowners' liberty. And Kant recognized that the limits might be severe. He saw that accumulation of property could lead to significant inequality such that "the welfare of one very much depends on the will of another (that of the poor on the rich), [and thus] one must obey . . . while the other commands, one must serve (as laborer) while the other pays."[3] It is for this reason that this right must be consented to by all. However, when he turns to what would be consented to by all, he considers no alternative to the virtually unlimited right to property that he saw around him. It did not occur to him that it might only be rational for all to consent to a right to property along with (at least) a guarantee that everyone will have enough property to exercise their liberty. In short, Kant saw the problem of the threat to liberty from private property, but he did not provide a solution to it.

Now consider a modern version of Kant's argument: Narveson makes an argument for the right to property that is similar to Kant's.

---

[3]Immanuel Kant, "On the Proverb: That May Be True in Theory, But Is of No Practical Use," in *Perpetual Peace and Other Essays* (Indianapolis: Hackett, 1983; "On the Proverb" originally published 1793), 73.

He contends that we all have a right to liberty because everyone consents to it in return for consent to their right to liberty. Liberty is the freedom to act. Like Kant, Narveson emphasizes that free actions require using things in the world. From this fact, Narveson concludes that our right to liberty *includes* our right to property, that is, our right to acquire unowned things in the world and then to do what we want with them as long as we don't violate other people's rights. Thus Narveson ties the right to property to the right to liberty even more tightly than does Kant. And this might protect Narveson from the conclusion we reached regarding Kant's argument. Narveson writes:

> Libertarianism proclaims that we all have a general right to liberty, and to have that right is, precisely, to have a right that others refrain from interfering with, negating, or undermining that liberty (i.e., interfering with, negating, or undermining the course of action, or inaction, that the right-holder has in mind to engage in).[4]

And then he asks:

> How then do we get to property? In brief, the answer is that many of our actions involve the use of various bits of the world outside of ourselves. We want to be able to engage in those actions successfully, and to do this requires, generally, that others not intervene to upset those trains of actions, given the plans governing them.[5]

And then:

> How do I induce you to refrain from such interferences? The proposed answer is that I make a very general deal, or arrangement, or agreement, with you: You refrain from interfering with me, in regard to certain bits of the world, and I refrain from interfering with you in your use of certain other bits of it. This is the proposed answer

[4]Jan Narveson, "Property and Rights," *Social Philosophy & Policy* 27, no.1 (Winter 2010), 114.
[5]Narveson, "Property and Rights," 114.

because, given that we are both capable of such interferences, mutual refraining is of mutual benefit for us.[6]

Since Narveson believes that our right to liberty includes our right to property, he takes this appeal for others' consent not to interfere with my exercise of my right to property, as part of the original consent of all to everyone's right to liberty.[7] Thus he writes that "When *A* allows *B* to acquire, and *B* allows *A* to acquire, they are trading liberties."[8] The deal that Narveson proposes above, then, is meant simply to spell out the logic of the inclusion of property in the right to liberty. But, look closely at the deal: "You refrain from interfering with me, in regard to certain bits of the world, *and I refrain from interfering with you in your use of certain other bits of it."* You respect my property and I will respect your property. That will certainly be reasonable for us both, *if we both have property to be respected.* It is rational for you to allow me to acquire because I allow you to acquire, if there is something for you to acquire. So, it seems that Narveson is granting the quite *un*libertarian claim that it is reasonable for everyone to agree not to interfere with others' exercises of their right to acquire property on the condition that everyone is guaranteed to be able to acquire some property of their own. But the fact is that Narveson is talking about acquisition of unowned things. And there is no guarantee that, because there are unowned things for me to acquire, there will be unowned things for you to acquire. So, Narveson is really talking about the freedom to acquire *if there is something to acquire* – he is not affirming the guarantee that you will be able to acquire something. But then the mutuality of benefits that made Narveson's deal seem reasonable for both parties evaporates.

Narveson's argument might seem to avoid the problems that arose for Kant's and Locke's argument for two reasons. First of all, Narveson expressly argues that original acquisition – that is,

[6]Narveson, "Property and Rights," 115.
[7]Narveson, personal correspondence, November 9, 2011.
[8]Narveson, "Property and Rights," 112.

acquisition of *unowned* things – does not harm others. Such acquisition cannot harm others since it does not take anything that belongs to them.[9] But this is not persuasive. Even if they don't own a thing, others can be harmed by being deprived of the use of something that they were previously free to use. This would only be blocked if Narveson thought, as Locke did, that the right to make unowned stuff one's property was conditioned on there being "enough, and as good left in common for others." But Narveson says nothing of the kind; nor is that surprising since this qualification (taken literally) amounts to a guarantee that others are able to get a decent share of property.

The second reason that Narveson's argument might avoid the problems that arose for Kant and Locke is more fundamental. Narveson does not argue that there is first a right to liberty *and then* a right to property; he takes the right to liberty as including the right to property. Accordingly, there is not liberty around first that then can be limited by another's claim to property. To have a right to liberty is to have a right to property.

The problem here is not that Narveson takes the right to liberty to include the right to property, but that he takes it to include *a virtually unlimited right to property*. That won't normally be a problem as long as the right is exercised while leaving "enough and as good" for others. But eventually it will mean that all of nature comes to be owned by someone (or, like the oceans, unownable). Then, future acquirers will be limited in their liberty to acquire property in a way that original acquirers were not. This will be the case even if, as Narveson contends, there are always new ideas to be had which, until someone has them, are unowned.[10] Since new (and bankable) ideas are had rarely, it still remains the case that future acquirers are limited in their liberty to acquire in ways that original acquirers were not. Consent to liberty including a virtually unlimited right to property is not mutually beneficial for all.

[9]Narveson, "Property and Rights," 109–110.
[10]Narveson, "Property and Rights," 119.

This means, as it did with Locke and Kant, that, contrary to what Narveson asserts, the "deal, or arrangement, or agreement" that people will accept is not simply "you refrain from interfering with my acquisition and I will refrain from interfering with yours." When just about everything ownable is owned, existing owners are already interfering with latecomers' acquisitions. And that means that the original situation of roughly equal rights to liberty no longer obtains. It means in effect that those who are born earlier will have greater rights to liberty than those who are born later, which is surely arbitrary from a moral point of view. As it is from Narveson's own point of view: He has written that "if we think that all men have certain rights, then it follows that we think that people living in the year 2469 have them, just as much as we do now, and that people living six millennia ago had them. . . . It short, time as such would seem to be quite irrelevant to the attribution of fundamental rights."[11]

This implies that the "deal, or arrangement, or agreement" that Narveson thinks justifies private property may be mutually reasonable to contemporaries, particularly when there remains unowned stuff to acquire. But ownership established now will continue to limit people's liberty in the future. Your grandchild will not be able to use freely what I bequeath to my grandchild. And where you and I may have lived while unowned stuff was available for appropriation, there's no guarantee that our grandchildren will. Why, then, should your grandchild accept my grandchild's claim to own what I have bequeathed him? What deal could be made with your grandchild comparable to the deal I might have made with you? It seems clear that the deal that all people (who may ever be limited by property) would find mutually reasonable to accept regarding property is one in which latecomers (including the innocent descendants of those who could have acquired property originally but did not) will have some protections against the risk of owning nothing – a genuine risk once universal ownership is reached. And that in

[11]Jan Narveson, "Moral Problems of Population," *Monist* 57, no. 1 (1973), 65–66.

turn means that what it will be rational for all to agree to is a right to property with at least a guarantee against ending up with no property at all.

4.3 Marx and the Structural Coerciveness of Property

Analyzing Locke's and Kant's (and Nozick's and Narveson's) arguments for the right to property has shown us that the right to large and unequal property holdings is a threat to the liberty of nonowners. But this understates the nature of the threat. Once the condition of universal ownership is reached – as, for all intents and purposes, has been the case now for some time – the right to property does more than restrict the liberty of nonowners to go where they wish. With everything owned, the right to property is the power to have nonowners work for one, since nonowners will have to work for some owner of property to get property at all, including the food and clothes and shelter that they need to live. They will have to serve others to earn a living, which means to live at all.

This condition reaches its height in capitalism, where a relatively small number of people own the means of production – things necessary for productive labor, such as machines and factories and land and raw materials – and the rest own virtually no means of production beyond the muscles in their backs. Thus, as we saw, Marx described the wage-worker in capitalism as a "man who is compelled to sell himself of his own free will," and characterized capitalism as a system of "forced labour – no matter how much it may seem to result from a free contractual agreement" (C, I, 766; III, 819). And not only Marx believed this. Rousseau, for example, wrote:

> When inheritances so increased in number and extent as to occupy the whole of the land, and to border on one another . . . , the super-numeraries . . . were obliged to receive their subsistence, or to steal

it, from the rich, and this soon bred, according to their different char-
acters, dominion and slavery, or violence and rapine.[12]

When Marx says that the wage-worker "is compelled to sell
himself of his own free-will," or that capitalism is a system of
"forced labour – no matter how much it may seem to result from
free contractual agreement," he points to the fact that, in capitalism,
the coercive aspect of property ownership tends to be invisible.
Marx held that capitalism, like serfdom and slavery before it, is "a
coercive relation" (*C*, I, 309). What distinguishes the capitalist coercive relation from that of serfdom and slavery is that the force upon
which the capitalist relation rests is not direct physical violence.
Rather it is an indirect force built into the very fact that the capitalists own the means of production and the laborers own nothing but
their labor-power. Lacking ownership of the means of production,
workers lack their own access to the means of producing a livelihood. They are therefore compelled to work for the capitalist on his
terms, since the alternative is pauperism or starvation. Thus, wrote
Marx: "The dull compulsion of economic relations completes the
subjection of the labourer to the capitalist. Direct force, outside
economic conditions, is of course still used, but only exceptionally"
(*C*, I, 737).

Marx discovered that coercion can work through the structure of
society itself (what Marx here calls "economic relations") without
needing direct force or overt violence in the normal course of events.
From the fact that society is organized so that some own the means
of production and the rest do not, nonowners are compelled to work
for owners. I call this mechanism of compulsion *structural
coercion*.

I contend that it was Marx's *dereified* view of social phenomena
that enabled him to see structural coercion for what it is. Marx saw
that social institutions were nothing but patterns of human behav-

---

[12] Jean-Jacques Rousseau, *A Discourse on the Origin of Inequality*, in *The Social Contract
and Discourses* (London: Dent and Sons, 1973; originally published 1755), 87.

ior. As, interestingly, does John Rawls, who wrote: "The social system is not an unchangeable order beyond human control but a pattern of human action" (*TJ*, 88). Marx wrote of capitalism, "capital is not a thing, but a social relation between persons" (*C*, I, 766). Marx may have been influenced by Kant here, since Kant recognized that property ownership was not a relation of a person to a thing, but "a relation of a person to persons" (*MM*, 55). But this dereifying vision had even earlier roots in modern political philosophy. Hobbes, for example, held that, in choosing to leave the state of nature by creating a polity, people consent to organize themselves into a single artificial person. Of this, he wrote:

> This is more than consent, or concord; it is a real unity of them all, in one and the same person, made by covenant of every man with every man. . . . This done the multitude so united in one person is called a COMMONWEALTH, in Latin CIVITAS. This is the generation of that great LEVIATHAN.[13]

The agreement to form a state is "more than consent" because it is creative. It is consent, to be sure, but an especially powerful instance of consent, namely, consent to do what is needed to transform a multitude of individuals acting on their several wills, into a people organized so that it can act with a single will. This is literally a distinctive physical structuring of the group in the sense that it requires that people act physically (as well as mentally) in the ways – as chief executive, minister, legislator, voter, bureaucrat, judge, prosecutor, lawyer, police officer, witness, jury member, prison guard, soldier, tax-paying and law-abiding citizen, and so on – that are necessary to organize themselves into a group able dependably to act with a single will. For this reason, the commonwealth is literally a large unified agent that is created – continually created – by its citizens. All the great modern political philosophers who followed Hobbes – Locke, Rousseau, Kant, even Hegel in his

[13]Thomas Hobbes, *Leviathan* (Indianapolis: Hackett, 1994; originally published 1651), pt. II, chap. xvii, p. 109.

113

way – agreed that the state was the whole people organized politically.

Marx extended this idea to economic realities. Because he saw both economic and political institutions as patterns of human behavior, he was able to go beyond the philosophers who saw that property was a limitation on liberty, and see that those limitations were imposed by people on people – indeed, imposed continually by people on people. Thus they constituted coercion, rather than mere limitations.

Structural coercion is structural both in its effects and in its origins. Take the effects first. Unlike the usual strong-arm stuff that singles out particular individuals as its targets, this coercion works on people by virtue of their location in the social structure (for example, as members of some class, say, nonowners of means of production), and it affects individuals more or less "statistically." By this I mean that such coercion affects individuals by imposing an array of fates on some group while leaving it open how particular individuals in that group get sorted, or sort themselves, into those fates. The term "structural" is appropriate for such coercion because it works the way that a physical structure such as a bottleneck (in the road) imposes fates on groups, forcing a majority of cars to slow down while leaving it to chance and other factors who makes up that majority and who gets into the minority that slips easily through. Structural coercion is structural in its origin also: Though the coercion works to make the class of nonowners serve the class of owners, it is not the owning class that forces the non-owning class – rather the structure of the ownership or class system itself forces this service. Since this structure or system is a pattern of human action, it is the whole society, or virtually the whole society, that does the forcing.

To get a handle on the notion of structural force, picture a large crowd of spectators who must pass through a human bottleneck as they leave a stadium. I mean "human bottleneck" quite literally. Imagine that people are standing shoulder to shoulder in the shape of a bottleneck and that the crowd must pass through this human funnel to get out of the stadium. The people making up the human bottleneck are there with varying degrees of intentionalness, some are there just minding their own business and some are there because they want the crowd to have to pass through just this sort of shape. But all are inclined to stay where they are because they want to, or believe they should or must, or because they are conditioned to, or some combination of these. If people in the crowd try to break through the human bottleneck, they will at least be resisted, and where they succeed in making an opening, people from other points on the bottleneck will move to seal it up and prevent their passing through. And other bottleneckers will at least support this and even offer to lend a hand. The crowd leaving the stadium, then, will find in this bottleneck varying degrees of resistance to their attempts to break through it, but enough so that they will have to adapt their flow to the shape.

It is natural to say here that the crowd is forced into a certain pattern by the structure of the human bottleneck. Note that this force works its effects "statistically." Some people – say, those who move quickly to the head of the crowd – will hardly be slowed or constrained at all, they may follow the same path they would have had there been no one else there. And some may manage to wriggle through holes in the bottleneck before they are sealed up. But most will have to follow the shape of the bottleneck. Moreover, this force originates structurally. To be sure, the bottleneck structure is manned by real individuals, but they play their roles more or less unthinkingly, and none of those who play their roles thinkingly could succeed in keeping the crowd in the bottleneck shape were it not for the rest of the people making up the bottleneck. The result of them all generally playing their roles is to force virtually the whole crowd to take on the shape of the bottleneck, while leaving undetermined which individual will end up in each particular spot inside that shape.

The institution of private property is like the human bottleneck. A large number of people play roles – as judges, lawyers, police officers, laborers, consumers, real estate agents, voters, and so on – in that institution, thinkingly and unthinkingly, more or less actively. And it is the overall shape of those roles that forces a certain pattern of options on the people subject to it, while leaving it open exactly which options are forced on which particular individuals.

There is no logical problem with people playing roles in the structures that limit their own freedom. A military command structure, for example, forces obedience on every soldier by the general likelihood that other soldiers will obey orders to punish disobedients, and these others are coerced (and thus likely) to obey because of yet others, and so on. Each individual soldier is among the "other soldiers" for everyone else. It follows that every soldier plays a role in the structure that limits every soldier's freedom. Thus, soldiers will play roles in the structures that limit their own freedom. Insofar as workers pay taxes, respect "No Trespassing" signs, and the like, they play roles in the structure of private ownership that in turn coerces them.

Nor is there any logical problem in calling a social structure a mechanism of coercion. The features of standard cases of force are here recognizable if somewhat altered in form. First, in the standard cases we take force to limit people's options by making all their alternatives but one either unacceptable or prohibitively costly (as in "your money or your life"). With structural coercion, people's options are limited by their social position to a range of things they can do, with options outside this range unacceptable or prohibitively costly. So, by virtue of occupying a social position defined, say, by lack of control over means of production, a person will be limited to a range of ways in which he can achieve a living, because alternatives outside this range (such as starvation or begging or crime) are unacceptable or prohibitively costly.

Second, in the standard cases of coercion, it is exercised intentionally by human beings. Structural coercion is a kind of leverage over people to which they are vulnerable by virtue of their location in the social structure. But the social structure – say, a caste or property system – is nothing but a pattern of human behavior. There is no doubt, then, that it is exerted by human beings. And at least some of the human beings playing roles in this structure – for example, the police – know that they are coercing people. If the actions of the rest of the people making up the structure are not intentional, they could be made intentional by making people aware of the effects of their actions. If enough people became aware, they could alter this coercion or rightly be held to intend it.

More controversial is the following. In the standard cases, the target of coercion has no real choice over his fate, either because all his alternatives save one are unacceptable, or because he has no alternatives at all (perhaps he has been bound or drugged). In structural coercion, by contrast, there is some play. Structural coercion works to constrain a group of individuals to some array of situations, leaving it to them or to other factors to determine how they are distributed among those situations. Therefore, between the coercing structure and its effects there can be room for the operation of free and rational choice on the part of individuals affected. That is, while people are constrained to the set of situations in the array (because alternatives outside the array are unacceptable or prohibitively costly), they may be able to exercise real choice among those in the array, selecting the one that they find most desirable. Nonetheless, I contend that, as long as the group is constrained such that its members must end up distributed among the situations in the array determined by the structure, all the individuals are "forced into" the particular situations in which they end up – even if they exercised some choice on the way there. In short, structural coercion can operate through free choice. And the reason for this is that coercion need not only take advantage of your fear (say, of dying) – it can also work, indeed often more effectively, by taking advantage of your rationality.

Suppose an outlaw is lying in wait for a stagecoach, in which he knows there will be six passengers each wearing a gold watch worth twenty dollars and each carrying about that amount in cash. Our outlaw wants to emerge with three watches and sixty dollars but is indifferent about who gives which. He resolves to give the passengers a chance to choose which they will give, although if their choices don't arrive at his desired outcome, he will rescind the privilege and just take three watches and sixty dollars. Stopping the coach, gun in hand, he orders the passengers to give him either their watch or their cash. The passengers regard their watches and their twenty dollars as comparably desirable, though each has a decided if small preference for one or the other. As luck would have it, their preferences result in the outlaw's desired outcome, and three give up their watches and three their cash. Now, take one passenger at random who, say, has given up his watch. Was he not forced to give up the watch? It certainly seems odd to say that he wasn't forced to give up his watch because he had an acceptable alternative (giving up his $20). To say that seems to focus excessively on what happens in the last moment just before the passenger handed over his watch, and to pay too little attention to the fact that the situation had been set up so that there was a good chance that by allowing him (and the others) to choose (rationally, in light of their preferences), the outlaw would succeed in subordinating their wills to his ends. Moreover, if you say that he wasn't forced to give up his watch, you would have to say that he was not robbed but gave away his watch freely – which is preposterous. I take it then that a person can be said to be forced to do something even if he has rationally chosen that thing from among other acceptable alternatives, provided that the whole array of alternatives can be said to be forced upon him.

This will be no news to con artists and spy-story authors. They well know that a free choice can be the last link in the chain that ties a person to a coerced fate. It is possible to get someone to do your bidding by setting up a situation in which doing your bidding is your victim's most rational choice, even if there are other choices which are acceptable though less rational for him. It is easy to overlook this, since when a person does what is most rational for her because it is most rational, and not just because it is the only thing acceptable, she seems to be acting freely. And, to an extent she is (much as the worker who is compelled to sell himself of his own free will does indeed exercise his own free will). But rather than showing that she (or the worker) is thus not coerced, what that shows is that *coercion can work through free choice*. An intelligent coercer can take advantage of the fact that, left free, people will normally do what is most rational for them. And this is an advantage because when people do another's bidding this way, they are less likely to see (or feel) that they are being coerced. Accordingly, coercion can be more effective because less visible if it can work through people's predictable free choices. When Marx wrote that the wage-worker "is compelled to sell himself of his own free will" (C, I, 766), he was not being arch or paradoxical. He was telling us both how coercion works in capitalism and why it is unseen.

The very existence of the social roles of capitalist and worker – defined by ownership and nonownership of means of production, respectively – and enacted by human beings doing what is most rational for them, within the constraints of those roles, is what coerces the worker to work for the capitalist. It coerces in the same way that a social structure that allotted to one group ownership and thus control of all the available oxygen would coerce. Beyond what was necessary to defend this group against challenges to its ownership of the oxygen, no additional force would be necessary for the coercion to operate. Indeed, it would operate quite effectively by means of bargains freely struck in which the non-oxygen-owners had to offer something to the owners to get the chance to breathe. They, too, would be compelled to sell themselves of their own free will. The same can be said of capitalism. Once its structure of social roles is in place, all that is necessary is that individuals choose, from among the alternatives available to them in their roles, the course of action that best serves their self-interest, and they will be coerced to work for capitalists without the need for overt violence.

As with the oxygen-owning society, so too with capitalism, overt force is used or threatened to defend owners against challenges to their ownership. That is just another way of saying that, in capitalism, the state uses overt force to protect private property. And this force is used to protect both the property of the capitalist (her factories and resources) and the property of the worker (his body, that is, his ability to labor). This differs crucially from the way in which overt force is exercised in social relations like slavery. In slavery, the use of overt force is part of the normal exercise of the master's power. In capitalism, overt force is used to defend all against forceful interference with their right to dispose of whatever property

119

they happen to own, be it means of production or labor-power. Accordingly, such force is not part of the capitalist's power but is left to a third party that, in this respect, can function neutrally toward all owners – the state.

With both capitalists and workers protected in their capacity to dispose of what they own, the process by which workers are coerced to work can proceed apace. This effect can be achieved with the state functioning neutrally. Although the state normally favors the interests of capitalists over workers,[14] it can serve the process of forced extraction of unpaid labor by protecting both capitalists and workers alike in their freedom to dispose of what they happen to own. It just turns out that what capitalists happen to own are machines and factories and raw materials, and what workers happen to own is their ability to labor. Capitalism, then, naturally appears as a system of free exchanges between people with equal rights (over unequal amounts of property). Thus, Marx writes that the sphere

> within whose boundaries the sale and purchase of labour-power goes on is in fact a very Eden of the innate rights of man. There alone rule[s] Freedom . . . because both buyer and seller of a commodity, say of labour-power, are constrained only by their free will. (C, I, 176)

Though capitalism is, for Marx, a coercive, indeed, enslaving system, it appears as a free arrangement, in which people confront one another as equals, each with the right to own property and dispose of it as he or she sees fit. That some own factories and others own nothing but their bodies appears as a natural difference, as morally insignificant as the difference in people's height. The coerciveness of the enormous power that the capitalist has over the worker dis-

[14]See, for example, G. William Domhoff, *Who Rules America?* (Englewood Cliffs, NJ: Prentice-Hall, 1967); M. Green, J. Fallows, and D. Zwick, The Ralph Nader Congress Project, *Who Runs Congress?* (New York: Grossman, 1972); Edward S. Greenberg, *Serving the Few: Corporate Capitalism and the Bias of Government Policy* (New York: Wiley, 1974); and Ralph Miliband, *The State in Capitalist Society* (London: Merlin Press, 2009; originally published 1969).

appears from view. For this reason, and because people come to take the institutions in which they grow up as natural, structural force tends to be invisible. This invisibility is the core of what Marx called *ideology* – and by which, as we saw, he meant false beliefs that hide the injustice of a society. Libertarians, like Nozick or Narveson, who defend capitalism as a purely free system fail to see the force built into the structure of property ownership. They fall for capitalist ideology. So too do liberals, who, though they effectively see the coerciveness in poverty and racism, rarely see it in private property itself. In this sense, Marxian Liberalism is liberalism without ideological blinders.

5

The Labor Theory of the Difference Principle

In this chapter, I present the moral version of the labor theory of value and show how Rawls's difference principle can be interpreted in its light. I argue that, so understood, the difference principle can be defended against the common objection that it is biased in favor of the less advantaged in society. I close by answering the objection to the use of incentives under the difference principle that has been made by Jan Narveson and G. A. Cohen. This discussion will set the stage for consideration (in Chapter 6) of what parties in the Marxian-Liberal original position will agree to regarding the right to property. Section 5.1 is entitled "The Moral Version of the Labor Theory of Value," Section 5.2 is "The Labor Theory of the Difference Principle," Section 5.3 is "Finding a Just Distribution," Section 5.4 is "Is the Difference Principle Biased?," and Section 5.5 is "Answering Narveson and Cohen on Incentives."

As Free and as Just as Possible: The Theory of Marxian Liberalism, First Edition. Jeffrey Reiman.
© 2014 Jeffrey Reiman. Published 2014 by John Wiley & Sons, Ltd.

5.1   The Moral Version of the Labor Theory of Value

Marx held that the market values of commodities tend to reflect (through various refractions) the relative amounts of time upon which they have been labored. This in turn is taken to imply that the prices of commodities could ultimately be transformed into the amounts of labor-time normally expended in their production. Such transformations are now widely thought to be impossible, thus rendering the labor theory of value generally vulnerable, and many Marxists willing to jettison it. I shall not try to defend the theory as a theory of price-formation. But I do think that a moral version of the theory, which makes no claim to account for prices, is defensible, and must be defended if we are to be able morally to assess different property systems and the distributions to which they give rise. This will be all the more necessary if such systems are characterized by structural coercion.

Suppose that we are surveying the various property systems that have existed in history so that we might assess them morally. We will need a neutral way of characterizing what it is that people give one another in the various systems (where "give" is understood very broadly to refer to any way in which some person undergoes a loss that ends up as a gain to another). By neutral, I mean a way of characterizing what is given that does not presuppose the validity of any particular system of property. Accordingly, we cannot say that what people give others is equivalent to "what they give of what they own in the legal sense." The reason is that it is precisely what people legally own that is being examined when we morally assess different property systems. If, say, a system of legal ownership is not morally justified, then in giving what I "own legally," I may really not be giving anything but only passing on what is actually given by someone else. It is precisely such matters that we would want to be able to identify for purposes of our moral assessment. Thus we need a way of characterizing what people give each other in a property system that is independent of what people legally own. Then, while remaining neutral on its morality, we will be able to say of any property system how it works to get some people to give things to others.

It is striking how frequently this feature of the problem of establishing fundamental principles of distributive justice is overlooked. For example, many people take the difference principle to be imposing sacrifices or losses on the better off. But this assumes that the better off are entitled to whatever is being taken from them, when the difference principle aims to determine what people are entitled to in the first place. So accustomed are we to the fact of individual ownership that it appears as a fact of nature. Once it is recognized as a human institution, evaluation of it must not presuppose its acceptance in any form.

When nothing that presupposes the validity of the property system can be used, all that remains that workers give in production is their time and energy, in a word, their labor, or as Marx had it, their "labor-time" (which he understood to include a standard measure of energy exerted).[1] And this labor-time is really given in the sense that it is *used up*. As finite human beings, workers have only finite time and energy, and thus they have less left over when they have given some up. Marx writes that "however varied the useful kinds of labour . . . may be, it is a physiological fact, that they are functions of the human organism, and that each such function, whatever may be its nature or form, is essentially the expenditure of human brain, nerves, muscles, &c. . . . In all states of society, the labour-time that it costs to produce the means of subsistence, must necessarily be an object of interest to mankind" (C, I, 71).

The same cannot be said, for example, of people's talents. Their talents are the result of their natural gifts plus the time and energy they devoted to developing those gifts. That time and energy count of course, and they must be factored into labor-time, so that the talented labor devoted to producing something now must include some measure of the earlier labor that went into producing that

---

[1] "The labour-time socially necessary is that required to produce an article under the normal conditions of production, and with the average degree of skill and intensity prevalent at the time" (C, I, 39).

level of talent. But the "natural gifts" themselves are, as the word suggests, *given to* people and thus merely passed on by them. What's more, talents are not used up in exercising them. If anything, they are augmented by use rather than depleted.

Outside of ownership, labor, and talent, all that is left in any part of the social product are the natural materials that went into it. And these (less the labor that went into extracting them or working them up into usable form) are not given by anyone to anyone else unless they are already owned. Thus we cannot use natural materials as our measure anymore than we can use talents.

Try the following thought experiment. Suppose that A and B are equal in their talents, and that C enslaves them both, forcing A to work two eight-hour days and B to work one eight-hour day at the same level of intensity (relative to their capacities). I expect that readers will agree that what happens to A here is worse than what happens to B and that it is roughly twice as bad (or, equivalently, that what C does to A is worse, roughly by a factor of two, than what he does to B). Suppose that A and B are each forced to work one eight-hour day, though A is forced to work at twice the level of intensity that B is (again relative to their capacities). Here too, I expect that readers will agree that what happens to (or what C does to) A is worse than what happens to (or what C does to) B, and that it is roughly twice as bad. Suppose now that X is twice as talented as Y, though both have devoted the same amount of time and energy to reaching their respective levels of talent, and that Z enslaves them both, forcing them each to work at their respective levels of talent for one eight-hour day at the same level of intensity. Is X's enslavement twice as bad as Y's? Is it worse at all? I think the reader will agree that their enslavements are equally bad. Doesn't it follow from this that (all other things being equal) taking more time and energy from one person than from another amounts to taking more from the first, while taking more talented labor from one than from another does not? This reflects the recognition that what people give in laboring is their time and energy and not their talents.

It might be objected that counting labor as given by workers presupposes that workers own it. But it only presupposes that labor is physically their own, in the way that their pains and their deaths are their own. This is a natural fact. People give themselves in laboring; they literally use themselves up. *Labor done, however willingly or even joyously, is life itself spent.* I suspect that it is this natural fact that accounts for the appeal of the labor theory of value to Marxists. Then, since moral philosophical considerations rule out thinking of individuals as already owning some goods, and talents and natural resources are not given by anyone to anyone, we are left with the recognition that what individuals give in producing the social product is their labor.

If we imagined that distributive principles were established at the beginning of human history, before any system of property was established, it would be obvious that the only cost to human beings of any batch of goods is the labor that goes into them. Depletion of finite natural resources might also be reckoned a cost, but not a cost to anyone in particular. Such depletion would impose a limit on the absolute size of any generation's shares under any distributive principle. It would not affect the issue of the relative size of individuals' shares, over which the difference principle and its competitors primarily contend. Consequently, we can ignore this cost for our purposes.

If the social product is being distributed among those who have produced it, then individuals are not simply receiving the goods that they themselves have produced. Rather, each receives goods that others have labored to produce. It follows that alternative principles of distribution establish, not merely different allocations of things, but *different proportions in which individuals work for one another*. Since their time and energy are finite, rational individuals will be concerned with how much of that time and energy will be spent serving their own purposes, and how much will be spent serving others. Consequently, it is appropriate to consider alternative distributions as representing different proportions in which individuals labor for one another.

Since "laboring for" is a social relation, I shall refer to the fact that economic distributions represent proportions in which individuals labor for one another as the *social dimension* of economic distributions. I contend that it is recognition of the crucial nature of this social dimension to creatures whose time and energy is finite that makes it appropriate to consider economic distributions as distributions of labor for the purpose of morally evaluating those distributions.

It might seem that little hinges on whether we think of economic distributions as distributions of goods, money, or labor, since each can be exchanged for – and thus be thought to represent – either of the other two. But, in fact, much hinges on this, since focus on money or goods *hides*, while focus on labor *reveals*, the social dimension of economic distributions. If we think of a distribution in terms of goods or money, then we shall see it as a matter of the relative size of each individual's share, how much money or goods each has. The relations between shares will be either quantitative (one has more, another has less) or psychological (those with less may feel envious of those with more, and those with more may feel superior to those with less). What we shall not see is that, where one person possesses a good produced by another, the labor of that other has been put at the possessor's disposal. And where the goods produced by some group of cooperating individuals are distributed among them unequally, some will have more of other people's labor at their disposal than those others have of theirs.

The same can be said of money. If one person earns one hundred thousand dollars a year and others earn ten thousand a year, this is more than a difference in the size of each individual's share. It means as well that, in return for one year of his labor, the first person can have ten of the others work for him (provide him with products or services) for a year. This is not to say that such unequal distributions cannot be justified – rather, it is to say clearly what it is that must be justified to justify such distributions. Following Marx, I call the fact that focus on money or goods hides the social dimension of economic distributions the *money illusion*, although it should be clear that this refers equally to goods or money.[2]

---

[2] "It is . . . this money-form of the world of commodities that actually conceals, instead of disclosing, the social character of private labour, and the social relations between the individual producers" (C, I, 76).

5.2   The Labor Theory of the Difference Principle

The difference principle holds that economic and social inequalities are just only insofar as they are to the greatest benefit of the least-advantaged group in the distribution (*TJ*, 266), and via the lexical version, to the groups above. As Rawls presents it, the difference principle applies to all social and economic goods (other than liberty, which is covered by his first principle of justice). In the present discussion, the difference principle is taken strictly as a principle of economic distribution. An economic distribution is not just, according to the difference principle, as long as it is still possible, either by transfers within the distributive scheme or by replacing that scheme with another, to reduce (or increase) the shares of the better-off groups in ways that improve the shares of worse-off groups over the long run (*TJ*, 68). So, for example, if, in two relevantly similar societies differing only in their distributive system, the worst-off share in one is smaller than in another system, then it is still possible to improve the worst-off share in the first system, and thus redesign of the first system along the lines of the second is required by the difference principle.

Rawls assumes that inequalities can work to maximize the share of the worst off by serving as incentives for people with above-average abilities to work in ways that increase productivity overall: "Their better prospects act as incentives so that the economic process is more efficient, innovation proceeds at a faster pace, and so on" (*TJ*, 68). (In Section 5.5 I address a recent criticism of this idea; until then, I assume that it is acceptable.) Rawls is clear that the difference principle is about people's shares *over the course of their lifetimes*. When he talks about how the principle operates, he speaks of "life prospects" or "expectations" (*TJ*, 67–68), and he makes clear that individuals' "expectation indicates their life prospects as viewed from their social station" (*TJ*, 56). This is important to bear in mind, since any unequal distribution can be altered in a way that immediately benefits those with smaller shares. If, however, the greater shares of the better off are functioning successfully as incentives to bring out higher productivity, then the reduction in inequality will have the long-term effect of decreasing the absolute size of the smaller shares and will be ruled out by the difference principle.

So understood, the difference principle requires redistribution from the better off to the worse off until that point after which the absolute size of the worse-off shares begins to diminish. Speaking of the conditions under which inequality in the life prospects of members of an entrepreneurial and a working class would be just, Rawls writes: "The inequality in expectation is permissible only if lowering it would make the working class even more worse off" (*TJ*, 68). This feature of the difference principle has led a number of commentators to suspect that it is lopsided in favor of those at the lower end of society. Thomas Nagel, for example, finds Rawls's theory resting on the presumption "that sacrifice at the bottom is always worse than sacrifice at the top," or "that sacrifices which lessen social inequality are acceptable while sacrifices which increase inequality are not."[3] And R. M. Hare writes that Rawls's strategy yields "principles of justice according to which it would always be just to impose any loss, however great, upon a better-off group in order to bring a gain, however small, to the least-advantaged group, however affluent the latter's starting point. If intuitions are to be used, this is surely counterintuitive."[4]

Against this, Rawls maintains that the difference principle is "a principle of mutual benefit," one under which individuals "do not gain at one another's expense since only reciprocal advantages are allowed." Since "we do not deserve our place in the distribution of native endowments," the better-off individual is not entitled to claim that he deserves a greater share simply because he is more

[3]Thomas Nagel, "Rawls on Justice," in *Reading Rawls*, ed. Norman Daniels (New York: Basic Books, 1975), 13.
[4]R. M. Hare, "Rawls' Theory of Justice," in Daniels, ed., *Reading Rawls*, 107; see also Robert Paul Wolff, *Understanding Rawls* (Princeton: Princeton University Press, 1977), 173–174.

talented. Thus "it is incorrect that individuals with greater natural endowments . . . have a right to a cooperative scheme that enables them to acquire even further benefits in ways that do not contribute to the advantages of others. . . . From a suitably general standpoint, the difference principle appears acceptable to both the more advantaged and the less advantaged individual" (*TJ*, 88–89).

Rawls's argument here is not very satisfactory. Even if the better-off or more talented individual is not entitled "to acquire . . . benefits in ways that do not contribute to the advantages of others," it does not follow that he is entitled to acquire benefits only in ways that maximize the welfare of others. For example, leaving distributions to the workings of the free market also forbids anyone to benefit in ways that do not contribute to the welfare of others, since if the market is free then only mutually beneficial exchanges will be agreed to, that is, only exchanges that all parties perceive as improving their welfare. As such, Rawls's argument does not establish the superiority of subjecting distributions to the difference principle over letting the free market run its course, producing whatever inequalities it may.

Moreover, that the more talented do not deserve their greater talent does not in itself imply that they are entitled to benefit from those talents only in ways that benefit others. No doubt, the fact that people do not deserve their greater talents supports the notion that they are not entitled to benefit from those talents in ways that make others worse off. But why aren't they entitled to benefit from their talents in ways that have no net effect, positive or negative, on others? On the face of it, it seems that Rawls is confusing justice with benevolence and insisting that the more talented have a positive duty to benefit others (regardless of what those others do for or to them) as a condition of the just enjoyment of the benefits of their own greater talents.

What is more, even if we grant Rawls that people are not entitled to benefit from their talents in ways that do not improve the welfare of others, then this is surely true for both the more and the less talented. Yet the difference principle, in requiring reduction in the shares of the better off in order to maximize those of the worse off,

130

seems to permit the latter to benefit in ways that do not improve the welfare of others. This suggests that the principle that no one should benefit from his abilities in ways that do not benefit others is being applied only to those with greater abilities, and this supports the charge that the difference principle is biased in favor of the least advantaged.[5] Indeed, we seem drawn to the conclusion that, if the principle that no one should benefit from his abilities in ways that do not benefit others is either applied evenhandedly to all groups in society, or replaced with the less questionable principle that no one should benefit in ways that worsen the conditions of others, the difference principle is undermined.

The difference principle can be defended against these charges, once we interpret the difference principle in light of the moral version of the labor theory of value. The implications of this reinterpretation of the difference principle are quite far reaching. For example, if we take economic distributions as distributions of goods or money, redistributing from the better-off group to the worse off according to the difference principle appears to be imposing a sacrifice on the former group for the benefit of the latter. Faced with this, we shall naturally be prone to ask for a justification for taking from the pockets of the rich to give to the poor. If, however, we understand an economic distribution as a distribution of titles to the labor of others, the greater shares of the better off will be seen to be made up, not of *their* goods or money, but of *other people's* labor. Then we shall be prone to ask for a justification for allotting the better off even as great a share of other people's labor as the difference principle allows them.

---

[5]Robert Nozick, for example, imagines the more talented members of society responding to the less talented members' proposal that they cooperate according to the difference principle. "How generous these proposed terms are might be seen by imagining that the better endowed make the almost symmetrical proposal: 'Look, worse endowed: you gain by cooperating with *us*. If you want our cooperation you'll have to accept reasonable terms. We propose these terms: We'll cooperate with you so long as *we* get as much as possible. . . .' If these terms seem outrageous, as they are, why don't the terms proposed by those worse endowed seem the same?" (*ASU*, 195).

Viewing economic distributions as distributions of labor enables us to see the superiority of the difference principle to the free market and, I believe, to all alternative principles. Further, it shows that either insisting that the principle that no one benefit from his talents in ways that do not improve the welfare of others be applied even-handedly to the more and the less talented, or replacing this with the principle that no one benefit in ways that worsen the condition of others, supports the difference principle, rather than undermining it. It shows that, either way, the difference principle is truly a principle of mutual benefit or reciprocity, the only principle according to which each benefit conferred by one person on another is matched by a reciprocating benefit. This should dispose of the notion that the difference principle is biased in favor of the least advantaged.

That we should evaluate different distributive principles in terms of the distributions of labor to which they give rise does not mean that it is never appropriate to consider the size of the shares of goods that individuals end up with as a result of different distributive principles. Rather, this consideration is appropriate at a different and later point in the moral evaluation of such principles. Obviously, if economic distributions were only a matter of labor, that labor would be pointless. What makes it rational for individuals to contribute their labor to the social product is that they receive goods in return. Consequently, the size of the shares in goods that result from alternative distributions is an appropriate consideration in determining which among the alternatives it would be rational for all to choose.

Thus the appropriate way to evaluate alternative distributive principles is to view them as different systems of the proportions in which individuals labor for one another, and then to consider the shares of goods that each such system yields in order to determine which it would be most rational for all to accept. This will be all the more appropriate when it is recognized that the economic system is structurally coercive. Then the proportions in which people work for each other will be the proportions in which they are forced to work. This (as we shall see in Chapter 6) makes the economic system a terrain on which the battle to protect liberty must be fought.

5.3 Finding a Just Distribution

Consider how the problem of arriving at a just economic distribution appears in light of the conclusions just reached. First of all, it is clear that we cannot approach this problem assuming that people with greater talents automatically deserve greater rewards. Rawls maintains that "we do not deserve our place in the distribution of native endowments," and thus that it is incorrect to think that those with greater gifts are more worthy and for that reason deserve greater rewards (*TJ*, 89). This is, to be sure, one of my considered judgments, but I am not as confident as Rawls is that this view is widely shared. The point, however, can be made much more directly and without dubious appeal to such wide agreement. Once we recognize that the substance of economic rewards is other people's labor, then it is obvious that the simple fact that A has greater talent than B is no reason to assert that A deserves some portion of B's labor.

Nor can we assume, in the fashion of the defenders of the free market, that any exchange reached voluntarily by A and B is just. This puts the cart before the horse. It assumes in advance that the free market is the standard of justice, when what is needed is a determination of the standard of justice against which we could determine whether the free market did or did not yield just results. Moreover, since those with greater talent will probably be able to hold out for better terms than those with less talent, taking free market exchanges as our standard has the effect of smuggling the notion that greater talents deserve greater rewards back into our conception of a just distribution. Furthermore, we know that exchanges that broadly count as voluntary are affected by the relative power, wealth, or need of the exchangers, all of which factors may be arbitrary from the point of view of justice and thus may lead to unjust distributions if allowed to function. Thus neither greater rewards to greater talents nor free market exchanges will assuredly result in a just economic distribution. Nor, of course, am I claiming that either assuredly results in the reverse. Rather, the question of what constitutes a just distribution must be asked from a position of neutrality on these matters. From such a position, we can ask whether greater rewards to greater talents and free market exchanges are just.

If an economic distribution is a system of proportions in which individuals work for one another, we can find a just distribution by asking for reasonable terms for the exchange of labor (in one form or another) between persons. For this, we must first find some measure of labor that is independent of the laborer's level of talent. If we build the laborer's level of talent into the measure of his labor, then we will build into our reasonable terms for the exchange of labor the assumption that more talented labor automatically deserves greater reward. This not only violates our neutrality on this issue, but it again puts the cart before the horse, since what we want is a measure we can use to determine if and when more talented labor does deserve a greater reward, that is, a claim on a greater share of the labor of less-talented others. Nor does such a measure bias us against greater rewards for greater talents. The point is that we cannot determine whether it is reasonable for some quantity of skilled labor to exchange for (earn title to) a greater quantity of unskilled labor, unless we have a quantitative measure of labor that is indifferent to whether it is skilled or not.

Two quantitative measures of labor that are indifferent to level of talent are time labored and intensity of effort. It is useful to think of the latter as energy expended. These give us not only an objective measure of labor independent of talent, but also a measure of the worth of labor to the laborer that is independent of his or her talent. That is, though individuals may differ in their natural gifts, they are alike in that their labor is a definite quantity of their total lifetime spent and a definite quantity of their total life energy expended – neither of which can be replaced. Moreover, while both these measures are independent of talent or natural gifts, neither is independent of the training that goes into developing talents or gifts. Such training is also measurable in time or energy and can be thought of as factored into the time labored or energy expended in any given exchange. Following Marx, I select time labored as the standard since it is more easily measured than effort or energy, and, as Marx does, I shall assume that labor is done at the average level of expenditure of energy. Labor-time spent at non-average levels will be measurable in terms of the standard unit of labor-time.

Measuring labor in terms of time labored, we can evaluate distributions by comparing distributions in which the goods or money each person receives represents an amount of labor-time by others that is unequal to the amount of labor-time that she has contributed herself, to a distribution in which labor-time is exchanged equally. Assume (for simplicity's sake) that everyone works the same amount of time. Then, we can say that, in an equal distribution, everyone contributes and receives the products of the same amount of labor-time, say t hours. We can represent this distribution as a series of exchanges between everyone and everyone else in which each gives and receives t hours of labor-time, in the form of services or products. If an equal distribution can be represented as such a series of exchanges, it can be represented even more simply as an exchange between any two members of society selected at random. Assume that we select A and B, who are exchanging t for t and thus ending up with equal shares of labor-time. Suppose, then, that A asserts that she is more talented than B and thus entitled to something better than an equal share. A claims that her t hours of labor-time given to B should bring $t + n$ hours of labor-time from B to her in return.

We must remember that A and B are to be thought of, not as traders bringing goods from distant zones, but as members of a single economic system, a cooperative scheme in which what each gives and gets affects the total amount produced and thus the absolute value of everyone's share. In this light, it will be reasonable for B to contribute $t + n$ hours of labor-time to A in return for A's t hours of labor-time, if the result is to increase output in a way that makes B better off than he was when he was giving and receiving t hours. And, of course, it must make B better off in an amount greater than the output of n alone, since he could conceivably have worked the additional n hours for himself and added the resultant output to what he received when all were giving and receiving t.

Thus it will be rational for B to contribute $t + n$ hours of her labor-time to A where the result is to increase B's share by m (*a quantity of goods, not labor-time*, as A's labor-time for B is still t), where m is the surplus over B's share when he and A contributed t, plus what B could produce for himself with n. Presumably, this could happen where giving B's $t + n$ to A worked as an incentive to bring out A's greater talents in a way that raised overall output and increased B's share by m. We can say that it would be rational for A and B to exchange t hours of A's labor-time for $t + n$ hours of B's, whenever the increment of n hours to A is sufficient to encourage her to devote her talents to the cooperative venture in a way that results in an increment to B of m goods.

A numerical example will help here. Imagine that a society has only two groups, those with greater-than-average talents, the As, and those with average abilities, the Bs. We can then think of the economic distribution in this society as an exchange of labor-time between an A and a B as representatives of their groups. Assume that As produce loaves of bread and Bs produce cups of sugar and that the average level of output in the society is one loaf or one cup per hour labored. Assuming that without a special incentive As produce at the average level, an equal distribution (for a day's labor of eight hours) looks like Table 5.1:

Table 5.1 Equal distribution

	A	B
Labor time given to the other	8 hours	8 hours
Goods produced for the other	8 loaves	8 cups

In this case, A and B each contribute eight hours of their labor-time to each other, in the form of an exchange of eight loaves for eight cups. A receives one cup for an hour of her labor, and B receives one loaf for an hour of his.

Assume now that with some incentive A can double her output, and that the minimum increment that will function as an incentive to bring out this heightened productivity voluntarily is a 50 percent increase in what she earns per hour. Nothing less makes enough of a difference to A. Since B always works at the average level of productivity, this will require B to work proportionately 50 percent longer. Since this is the minimum incentive that A will accept and the lowest increase in productivity she gives in return, we can refer to this case as that of the lowest minimum incentive.[6] Under it, the resulting distribution would be as in Table 5.2:

Table 5.2   Lowest minimum incentive

	A	B
Labor time given to the other	8 hours	12 hours
Goods produced for the other	16 loaves	12 cups

In this case, A trades eight hours of her labor-time for twelve hours of B's (the t for $t + n$ in our previous discussion), in the form of an exchange of sixteen loaves for twelve cups. The range of inequality here is that A earns 150 percent of what B earns, that is, A receives, for a day of her labor (based on an eight-hour workday), money sufficient to purchase a day and a half of B's labor. Here A receives

[6]Needless to say, it will not be easy to determine what these minimum incentives and lowest increases will be. They cannot be assumed to be simply equivalent to what people say they will take and give in return. Presumably they could be identified by collecting data on different arrangements within societies as well as on other societies with different levels of incentives and of productivity. In the examples here, I assume that they have been so identified. I say more about this issue in Section 5.5.

one and one-half cups for an hour of her labor and B receives one and one-third loaves for an hour of his. The exchange, for A, is reasonable *ex hypothesi*, that is, we set it at the minimum incentive that A would find reasonable to bring forth her more productive efforts voluntarily. The exchange is reasonable for B because he receives an additional one-third loaf for every hour of his work over and above what he had in the equal distribution (the *m* in our previous discussion).

Let us assume further that A can produce even more than sixteen loaves in a day. Her maximum productivity is twenty-four loaves. For this, the minimum incentive that she will accept is a 100 percent increase in what she earns per hour (compared to equal distribution). Since B always works at the average level of productivity, this incentive will require B to work proportionately 100 percent longer (compared to equal distribution). Since this incentive is the minimum that A will accept for her new level of productivity, and since this is her highest level of productivity, we can refer to this case as that of the highest minimum incentive. Under it, the resulting distribution would be as in Table 5.3:

Table 5.3 Highest minimum incentive

	A	B
Labor-time given to the other	8 hours	16 hours
Goods produced for the other	24 loaves	16 cups

In this case, A trades eight hours of her labor-time for sixteen hours of B's, in the form of an exchange of twenty-four loaves for sixteen cups. The range of inequality is that A earns twice what B earns, that is, A receives, for a day's labor-time, money sufficient to purchase two days of B's labor. Here, A receives two cups for an hour of her labor and B receives one and one-half loaves for an hour of his. Once again, for A, the exchange is reasonable *ex hypothesi*. It is reasonable for B because he receives an additional one-half loaf for every hour of his work over and above what he had in the equal distribution (a higher m than in Table 5.2).

Though sixteen cups is the minimum that A will take for the twenty-four loaves she produces in a day, there is a range above sixteen that she could ask for which would still leave B better off than he was under equal distribution. So, for example, if A were to demand twenty-three cups in return for her twenty-four loaves, B would have to work twenty-three hours to get the twenty-four loaves, and thus he would end up earning $1\,^{1}/_{23}$ loaves for each hour labored, which is still better than the one loaf per hour he received under equal distribution. Thus, assuming that sixteen cups is A's bottom line, were A to offer her twenty-four loaves to B on the free market, B would find it rational to pay anywhere from sixteen to twenty-three cups in return. Thus we can say that were these exchanges left to the market, the resultant distribution would be indeterminate in this range since any trade of twenty-four loaves for anything between sixteen and twenty-three cups would be beneficial to A and B.

Note that I am assuming here that, wherever the trade is set within this indeterminate range, all the effects of market forces – competition, supply and demand, and so on – have already done their work, and no further reduction in prices can be expected. Defenders of the free market (at least in the textbook version) are likely to balk at this assumption, holding that, under conditions of perfect competition, the selling price will always be the lowest the seller will accept, since otherwise someone will undersell her. This assumes that perfect competition is occurring in the actual world, and that accumulated wealth on one side and need and restricted opportunity on the other – factors that are arbitrary or dubious from the standpoint of economic justice – are not functioning to permit sellers to sell above what they would be satisfied with, when that is precisely what has to be determined. Put otherwise, those who question whether the free market yields just outcomes are likely to suspect that the level playing field that is portrayed in economics textbooks does not exist in the real world. And thus we must evaluate market exchanges without assuming that it does.

Accordingly, I take it that under the free market, the resulting distribution would be as in Table 5.4:

Table 5.4 Free market range

	A	B
Labor-time given to the other	8 hours	16–23 hours
Goods produced for the other	24 loaves	16–23 cups

In this case, A trades eight hours of her labor-time for anywhere from sixteen to twenty-three hours of B's in the form of an exchange of twenty-four loaves for anything from sixteen to twenty-three cups. The maximum range of inequality that could result from these exchanges would have A earning $2\,7/8$ as much as B: A would receive, for a day's labor, money sufficient to purchase $2\,7/8$ days (twenty-three hours) of B's labor. For A, any of these exchanges are reasonable *ex hypothesi*: they start at her minimal acceptable incentive and improve from there. Any of these exchanges are reasonable for B because he receives at least $1\,1/23$ loaves per hour, which is still more than the one loaf an hour he receives under equal distribution. (I am momentarily ignoring Table 5.2 to keep matters simple. If it were included, that would only change the range of possible mutually beneficial market exchanges, not the point being made.)

Of the four cases discussed, the difference principle requires the third, where A and B exchange twenty-four loaves for sixteen cups. This is the case in which the inequality between the best-off and the worst-off representative persons, A and B, is reduced to the minimum (sixteen hours of B's labor in return for eight hours of A's) compatible with maximizing the worst-off's share (B gets twenty-four loaves, or one and one-half per hour). Were the inequality reduced further, A would not produce twenty-four loaves a day, and thus B's share would decline. Were the inequality to be increased, B would be giving more than sixteen hours to A. Thus B's share (per hour) would decline and, in any event, the inequality would be more than is necessary to maximize B's share. Using the notation introduced earlier, we can say that the difference principle permits inequalities, exchanges of t for $t + n$ hours of labor-time, where n is the smallest increment that will produce the largest m for the worst-off person in the distribution. In the third case, n is eight hours of B's labor-time and m is the surplus of half a loaf per hour that B gets over what he would have in an equal distribution.

5.4 Is the Difference Principle Biased?

Consider now how the objection that the difference principle is biased in favor of the worse off and against the better off arises, and how it is cast in new light by viewing economic distributions as distributions of labor. If A could have gotten twenty-three cups for her twenty-four loaves on the market and the difference principle allows her only sixteen cups, then this does seem a lopsided affair, since no limitation is placed on B's share, and the exchange of twenty-three cups for twenty-four loaves would also have improved B's position. Moreover, if our distributive system operates on a free market basis with taxation and transfer payments used to bring distributions in line with the difference principle, A will first have gotten her twenty-three cups and then the government will come along, forcibly confiscate seven of these, and transfer them back to B. This looks, at best, like Robin Hood stealing from the rich to give to the poor and, at worst, like forcing A to labor for B on terms not of her choosing.[7]

This is how the redistribution ordered by the difference principle looks if we think of an economic distribution as a matter of individuals' shares in money or goods. If, instead, we view the

---

[7] "Taxation on earnings from labor is on a par with forced labor" (*ASU*, 169, see also 172).

distribution as a matter of individuals' shares in other people's labor, things take on an entirely different cast. In this light, the seven cups that A might get on the market (above the sixteen allowed by the difference principle) represent *seven additional hours of B's labor-time for A*. What gives A the right to have B labor these additional seven hours for her? We cannot simply say that she has this right because B would agree to it on the free market, because that assumes in advance that free market exchanges are just, which is what we are trying to determine. Such exchanges may simply reflect A's greater power to hold her products off the market, and this may be a power that is unjust or that produces unjust outcomes. To stay neutral on the question of the justice of market exchanges, we must ask what benefits B derives from working these additional seven hours for A. The answer is *none*. This additional labor-time produces no benefits for B that he could not already have working sixteen hours to produce the sixteen cups that (*ex hypothesi*) A would have accepted for her twenty-four loaves.

Considering economic distributions as distributions of labor, it becomes clear that in limiting A to sixteen cups from B, the difference principle is not confiscating seven cups from A. *It is prohibiting A from obtaining additional labor-time from B without benefiting B in return*. B's labor beyond the sixteen hours necessary to produce sixteen cups results in no additional benefit for B. If, on the market, A can get more than sixteen hours of labor from B without conferring additional benefits on B, then this must reflect A's favorable market position, due to B's need or A's mere possession of greater talent (that is, as distinct from her using it to benefit others), facts that are arbitrary from the standpoint of justice. This is what the difference principle prohibits.

This shows how the difference principle is truly a principle of reciprocity or mutual benefit. In setting the distribution at twenty-four loaves for sixteen cups, it assures that A and B are benefited for all of the labor that each contributes to the other. A is benefited; *ex hypothesi*, sixteen is the minimum she would find reasonable compensation for producing her twenty-four loaves. B, on the other hand, in producing the sixteen cups, does only that much additional labor (compared to the equal exchange of labor in Table 5.1) for which he receives benefits in return. *For A to ask for more is to ask B to work for her additionally for no additional compensation.* This is (or could have been) Rawls's answer to the charge that the difference principle is biased in favor of the less advantaged and biased against the more advantaged. The only limit on the latter's greater share is that every increment of greater-than-equal labor that others contribute to her must make those others better off as well. This is why the difference principle is "acceptable to both the more advantaged and the less advantaged individual" (*TJ*, 89).

This also enables us to see clearly the difference between the difference principle and free market exchanges. We can represent the ranges of inequality in our example by the fraction $(t + n)/t$, since A's income is $(t + n)/t$ times B's (that is, A is paid for t hours of her labor-time enough money to purchase the products of $t + n$ hours of B's labor-time). Such inequalities are reasonable if they produce a surplus m for B over what B could have gotten for his $t + n$ hours under conditions of equality. We can think of an unequal distribution, then, as an exchange in which B contributes n to A in return for A's m to B. The free market allows any exchange of n for m that leaves both parties better off than before the exchange. (In our examples, this means that n can vary between eight and fifteen hours of B's labor-time, above the eight hours represented by t.) The difference principle, by contrast, allows only the smallest n that will encourage A to produce m in return (this n is eight hours in our examples). If a larger n will produce a larger m, then the difference principle requires this larger n. (This is why the difference principle requires the third rather than the second of the cases in our example.)

The difference between free market exchanges and the difference principle, then, is this: The market requires only that the total n yield a surplus of m to B. The difference principle requires that every unit of n from B to A yield a unit of m for B. Thus the market would allow n to go to fifteen hours because this total still leaves B with a surplus (an additional $1/23$ loaf per hour). But the difference principle limits n to eight hours because the units of n beyond this yield no

143

additional unit of *m* to B. Here lies the superiority of the difference principle – as a principle of reciprocal benefit (*TJ*, 88) – to free market exchanges.

The *money illusion* obscures the nature of this limit on A's share. The money illusion leads to the error of thinking that the difference principle simply imposes sacrifices on the better off for the benefit of the worse off. It makes the difference principle appear as confiscating A's money (or goods) and giving them to B, *when in fact the principle is limiting B's labor for A*. Once the money illusion is dispelled, the share of the best off is seen to be constituted by the labor of others. Limiting this share is not imposing a sacrifice on the best off; it is making sure that those whose labor constitutes this share receive compensation in return and give no extra labor that does not receive such compensation. On the other hand, the best-off's share is allowed to rise to that point necessary to make it reasonable for her to work voluntarily in the ways that benefit those whose labor constitutes that share. This shows, I believe, more clearly than Rawls has been able to, that the difference principle is a principle of reciprocal advantage.

Earlier, I maintained that viewing the difference principle as distributing labor rather than money or goods would show that the defense of the difference principle is compatible, first, with insisting that both more talented and less talented persons benefit from their talents only in ways that benefit others and, second, with the less controversial notion that persons should not benefit from their talents in ways that worsen the condition of others. Now we can see that it is only when the difference principle is thought of as taking the more talented person's money and giving it to the less talented that the difference principle seems to require only of the more talented that they benefit in ways that improve others.

Viewing the difference principle as distributing labor-time, however, we see that when it "takes" the more talented person's money it is in reality limiting her share of the less talented person's labor-time, and it is limiting it at the point at which each person benefits from their talents only on terms that benefit the other: The more talented gets her greater-than-equal share ($t + n$)

only insofar as she gives a compensating benefit (*m*) to the less talented. And the less talented receives this benefit only insofar as he gives his greater-than-equal labor time in return. All that the difference principle does when it "takes" money from the more talented is limit the *n* hours of labor-time by the less talented for the more talented *to that point after which no further benefit is contributed by the more talented to the less*. This only prevents the more talented from earning additional increments of *n* without conferring additional benefits on those whose labor constitutes *n*. On the other hand, by allowing *n* to rise as high as is necessary to maximize *m*, the difference principle insists that the less talented receive benefits *only in return for exercising their lesser talents in ways that benefit the more talented as much as is necessary to make it reasonable for the more talented to produce and contribute* m *in return*. Thus both groups benefit from their talents only insofar as they benefit others.

As for the second precept referred to above – that no one should benefit from their talents in ways that worsen the condition of others – it is again only the money illusion that makes it appear that the difference principle confuses benevolence with justice and imposes a positive duty on the more talented to benefit others as a condition of the more talented ones reaping the benefits of their own greater talents. If the difference principle distributes labor-time rather than money, then it is not insisting that the more talented give some of their money away to the less – it is insisting that the more talented take no more labor-time from the less talented than they give benefits for in return. Inasmuch as the difference principle prevents the more talented from benefiting in ways that cost the less talented more labor-time without benefiting them in return, the difference principle is preventing the more talented from benefiting in ways that worsen the condition of the less talented.

These challenges to the difference principle can be met because viewing economic distributions as distributions of labor brings to light the *social dimension* of economic distributions, the way in which the benefits of one person are the burdens of another. Focus on money or goods, by contrast, makes economic distributions appear as relations between separate individuals each of whom starts with

145

some quantity of benefits unrelated to the burdens of others. Viewing economic distributions as distributions of money is seeing them occurring among the separate islands of an archipelago. Requiring a rich islander to give his money or goods to a poor islander across the sea then appears as forcing charity in the guise of justice. Viewing economic distributions as distributions of labor, by contrast, has the effect of draining the water from the archipelago and revealing how the islands are connected as peaks of an unbroken landmass. From this view, the wealth of rich "islanders" is seen connected to, indeed, constituted by, the labor of poor ones. Requiring the rich person to give his money to the poor then appears only as limiting the rich person's control over the poor one's labor – and this brings the issue clearly out of the realm of charity and into that of justice. Is it any wonder that, in arguing against the difference principle, Nozick imagines Robinson Crusoes working on separate islands (*ASU*, 185)?

Note that reference to greater talent in this discussion implies here no belief in the greater inherent worth of some than others. Greater talent is defined internally to any ongoing economic system. It represents any above-average capacity to produce more of the things that people desire in that system. Now, once a system with the rationale I have outlined got going, there would be no particular limit on the size of $t + n$ relative to t, as long as a suitably large m were returned to the worse off. If $t + n$ became so large that an individual could not himself spend it in his lifetime or did not wish to, he could give or bequeath some of it to others, who might not have to work at all. As long as this magnitude of $t + n$ were necessary[8] to evoke the m, this distribution would still be justified according to the difference principle. Moreover, as long as it were reasonable for the worse off to contribute their $t + n$ to those with greater talents in return for m, it would be reasonable for them as well to contribute their $t + n$ to a scheme that yielded them m even if this meant that the $t + n$ did not end up in the hands of those

[8] I say more about the meaning of this "necessity" in Section 5.5. See also note 6, above.

146

whose talents went into m.[9] That is, once economic distributions are seen as distributions of labor, any distribution that satisfies the difference principle, by minimizing inequality between the best- and the worst-off groups and maximizing the share of the worst-off group (and, *à la* the *lexical difference principle* [see Section 2.2, above], the shares of all groups in between), *is a distribution in which no one labors more for others than is necessary to yield him benefits in return.* Thus any such society is truly one in which people labor for one another on mutually beneficial terms.

These last remarks show the conditions under which a capitalist economy would be one in which people labor for one another on terms that are fair to better and worse off alike. Since the free market is open-ended in its outcomes, it might spontaneously yield the distribution required by the difference principle. If not, this would have to be achieved by government intervention in the form of redistributive taxation or other policies, aimed at reducing inequalities and improving the share of the worse off until the point of diminishing returns. The result would still be essentially a capitalist economy. (Rawls spends considerable time in *A Theory of Justice* describing the institutions of such a capitalist economy [*TJ*, 228–251]; and I discuss this in Section 7.3, below.)

5.5   Answering Narveson and Cohen on Incentives

Jan Narveson, on the right, and G. A. Cohen, on the left, have criticized Rawls's contention that unequal incentives are just according to the difference principle. Since Marxian Liberalism's use of the

---

[9]Cf. *ASU*, 189. Nozick takes Rawls's difference principle to imply that individual contributions to the social product can be isolated, so that incentives can be given to the correct persons. But Rawls never insists on this. He speaks only of "economic inequalities [being] arranged so that they are . . . to the greatest benefit of the least advantaged" (*TJ*, 266). Nothing in that requires directly rewarding the more talented or productive in proportion to their contributions. It requires only that the overall scheme functions to maximize the share of the worst-off group.

difference principle in capitalism also relies on incentives, it is important to show that this criticism can be rebutted. I start by considering Narveson's version.

Narveson notes that in Rawls's original position, parties are initially drawn to an equal distribution (we shall see this as well in the Marxian-Liberal original position). Subsequently, they find it more in their interest to give this up for an unequal distribution where inequalities are necessary to maximize everyone's share from that of the worst off on up. Narveson takes this to mean that "equal distribution is *prima facie* just, and inequalities require special justification of the kind stated."[10] Then, noting that the inequalities that are said to be necessary are incentives for more productive labor, Narveson writes:

> Incentives are psychological matters, which concern one's principles of action. If I hold out for, or accept, a greater payment for my services than someone else is getting for his, I am voluntarily consenting to an inequality. I cannot argue that this higher payment is "necessary," that I am *forced* to have more than you. Obviously, I could, if I wanted to, accept the same wage as everyone else. Alternatively, I can accept more, but then turn around and give the excess to those who have less. The question we are discussing is whether, in justice, I *ought* to do this. And to say that incentives are "necessary" for this purpose is to engage in confusion, or possibly even in self-deception.[11]

Given that an equal distribution is *prima facie* just, and inequalities can only be justified if they are *necessary* to maximize the worst-off's share, Narveson contends that incentives are not justified because not truly necessary. They amount to more talented people simply insisting on getting more. Likewise, Cohen says that incentives are only "necessary" because, if they are not given, the

---

[10]Jan Narveson, *Respecting Persons in Theory and Practice* (Lanham, MD: Rowman and Littlefield, 2002), 19.

[11]Narveson, *Respecting Persons*, 21.

more talented will go on strike to the detriment of the rest of society (*RJE*, 33).

In response, note first of all that it is a mistake to count the initial appeal of equal distribution in the original position as amounting to the claim that equal distribution is *prima facie* just. Rawls's theory aims at establishing moral principles by showing that they would be agreed to in the original position. Accordingly, there are no moral principles *inside* Rawls's original position, that is, prior to being agreed to. Until then there are only different candidates for what is in everyone's interest. Moreover, the parties are mutually disinterested, and thus they cannot judge a distribution in any terms other than how it serves their individual interest. Equality as a moral value is a standard that compares one person's reward to another's, thus it is a standard that cannot be used by mutually disinterested people. The appeal of equality to the parties in the original position, then, is strictly a matter of what seems to be in everyone's interest until it is pointed out that inequality might make everyone better off than equality. When the parties realize this, they agree to the difference principle, and then and only then is there a moral principle.

It is a bit more complicated to state the analogous point in terms of Marxian Liberalism, since Marxian Liberalism's contractarianism is of the Lockean rather than Rawlsian variety. Parties enter the Marxian-Liberal original position with one moral principle, namely, that everyone has a natural right to liberty. Nonetheless, that principle logically precedes the Marxian-Liberal original position, and there are no other moral principles until they are agreed to therein.[12]

[12]One might say a similar thing about Rawls's original position. Rawls has designed the original position to embody the principle of the inviolability of persons; and this principle functions prior to agreement (see, for example, *TJ*, 3). Or, if one accepts the suggestion made above (Section 2.2), that Rawls appeals to a more fundamental principle of justice according to which justice is the set of requirements that are mutually reasonable to all people, then this principle also functions prior to agreement. Nonetheless, neither of these principles emerges *inside the original position*. In any event, it is clear that neither Rawls nor Marxian Liberalism builds a moral principle of equal distribution into the design of the original position.

Thus the initial appeal of equality in the Marxian-Liberal original position is no more a moral principle, not even a *prima facie* one, than it is in Rawls's original position.

We shall see that this helps in answering Narveson, but only as the first step. We still must respond to his objection that incentives are not *necessary* for maximizing the share of the worst off because more talented people have it in their power to do their more-productive-than-average labor without insisting on an incentive. It should be no surprise that this will depend on what one means by "necessary."

Suppose that when, in the Marxian-Liberal original position, someone proposes allowing incentives to function as inequalities if they maximize the share of the worst off, someone else objects by saying that more talented people should simply do their more productive work for the same reward that everyone else gets who does their share of society's needed labor. After all, people do not deserve their greater talents. They are, as we say, *gifts*.

In response to this, we can imagine another party pointing out that history shows that, no matter how desirable such an egalitarian system might appear, it does not work. Systems that expect all to work for the same reward, no matter how productive their labor is, do not in fact increase productivity so that the share of the worst off can be maximized. What history shows is that capitalism, with its inequality-producing incentives, does do this. So, in fact, while it is not *strictly necessary* (in the sense of impossible to avoid) that more productive workers get incentives, it is *practically necessary* for maximizing the share of the worst off, that a system be adopted that provides such incentives.

Since the parties in the original position have no moral commitment to equality, and since they are concerned strictly with what is in their interest, they will opt for a system that is actually likely to work to maximize the share of the worst off. This means that the parties will determine what is *necessary* based on realistic expectations about human behavior, not simply on what people might do because they could do it. There are numerous reasons why this is appropriate. One is that the parties in the original position do not know which particular individuals they will be. Thus, they cannot know if they will be altruistic or selfish. They must consider what people will *typically* do. Moreover, the parties' interest is in what others in society actually do, not in their benevolent motives. Thus, the parties can, indeed *must* (since it is in their interest to do so), evaluate principles of justice in light of reasonable expectations about typical human behavior.

At this point, we can bring Cohen into the discussion, since he recognizes that it may well be *sensible* to offer incentives to draw out more-talented people's productive labor voluntarily (*RJE*, xv, 83–84). Incentives may even "be part of a package that is, all things considered, more just than any other," but they cannot be thought to be "through-and-through just" (*RJE*, 7). For Cohen, only equal distribution is through-and-through just. To an extent, Marxian Liberalism can accept this notion, given its historical conception of justice. Recall that that conception is that justice calls for the maximum provision for the interests of others that can reasonably be required of people given their human nature (see Section 2.5). Unequal incentives are not part of the perfect justice of the future, if, as Marxists think, people will be much more altruistic than they are today. Unequal incentives result from the leverage that the more talented have because of their natural gifts (which they do not deserve), plus their self-interestedness in exercising that leverage (which enables the more talented to capture gains that could in principle be used to make the worst off even better off). But this self-interestedness is (at least for Marxism) a product of capitalism itself and, thus, within capitalism, it is an aspect of people's actual human nature that limits what can be reasonably required of them. For Marxian Liberalism, this makes incentives historically just, that is, truly just in the current historical era. But Cohen insists that the incentives are unjust, even if they constitute "the best injustice we can get" (*RJE*, 85).

Before answering Cohen's argument, note that, when we consider the inequalities that the difference principle will allow, we should not assume that those inequalities are equivalent to the inequalities in current-day capitalist societies. There is considerable reason to believe that the worst-off people in, say, modern-day England or America, could be made significantly better off than they are – say, by redistributive taxation – without lowering overall productivity. Cohen acknowledges this fact: "a society that implements John Rawls's two principles of justice will not display the degree of inequality that characterizes contemporary Britain" (*RJE*, 62). Nonetheless, I think that much of the intuitive appeal of Cohen's argument comes from his characterization of how hard life is for people at the bottom of current British society, cold in the winter due to high fuel prices, "wretched," and so on (*RJE*, 31, 34, 59–62).

Also important is that Cohen allows that there is "a legitimate personal prerogative" (*RJE*, 10; see also 68 n. 37, 70 n. 39), some range in which morality allows people to pursue their self-interest. Cohen makes no effort to identify this range. He gives us no principle or argument for determining the scope of rightful self-interestedness. Nonetheless, Cohen contends that "a modest right of self-interest *seems insufficient* to justify the range of inequalities . . . under discussion" (*RJE*, 61; emphasis added). I share Cohen's intuition that existing inequalities in America or Britain are not justified by the moral right of self-interest. But this tells us nothing about a society governed by the difference principle where inequalities are likely to be considerably smaller, and life at the bottom considerably better, than in existing capitalist societies. We shall return to the legitimate personal prerogative shortly.

Like Narveson, Cohen appeals to Rawls's claim that real people in a society governed by the two principles of justice will endorse those principles (*RJE*, 68, 74–76). I agree with Cohen that limiting the principles of justice to the basic structure of society is not defensible (*RJE*, 116–140; see also Section 2.2, note 9, above; and Section 7.1, note 1, below). Accordingly, Cohen (like Narveson)[13] imagines the better off having to justify their demand for greater incentives in a conversation with the less advantaged once they are in the

---

[13]Cohen opens his discussion quoting such a conversation from Narveson's "Rawls on Equal Distribution of Wealth," *Philosophia* 7 (1978), 281–292 (cited in *RJE*, 27).

society designed on the principles agreed to in the original position. Since the better off *could* do their more talented work without incentives, Cohen, like Narveson, contends that they cannot justify those incentives as *necessary* to maximize the shares of the less advantaged.

What Cohen and Narveson are missing here is that the better off have at hand an easy way to justify their incentives, one that the members of a society governed by principles agreed to in the original position *must agree to*. The better off can appeal to the difference principle *because that principle is equally a principle determining the scope of legitimate pursuit of self-interest*. Cohen recognizes the complementary relation between the difference principle and the right of self-interest, one begins where the other ends: "the individual who affirms the difference principle must have some regard to it in his economic choices, whatever regard, that is, which starts where his personal prerogative stops" (*RJE*, 10). But he does not consider the implications of this complementarity.

In acknowledging a legitimate personal prerogative, Cohen has identified an interest that everyone in the original position has, namely, the interest in not having a degree of altruism imposed on them that will be experienced as oppressively demanding, given their actual human nature. This is implied in the fact that the parties stand in the circumstances of justice, such that they have "confin'd generosity" and only limited altruism (*TJ*, 109, 248). Thus, we can imagine the parties in the original position, who do not know whether they will be more or less talented, as having two conflicting interests: an interest in an ample right of self-interest, and an interest in not doing poorly because the more talented ones are pursuing their self-interest at the less talented ones' expense. The difference principle resolves this conflict by setting the maximum limit of rightful pursuit of self-interest at the point at which that pursuit actually works to maximize the share of the worst off. It sets it, not at the point at which the more talented are capable of foregoing incentives, but at the point at which an actual social system, executed by humans as we know them, will work to maximize the share of the worst off.

No doubt it will be difficult to determine this point in an actual economy. Societies will have to engage in experimentation with more and less inequality to see how much inequality really maximizes the worst-off share; and they will have to look seriously at the results of different experiments in different nations, and so on. But the principle is clear: That degree of inequality that actually works to maximize the share of the worst off is the maximum limit of the legitimate personal prerogative, the rightful range in which people may pursue their self-interest. It should be clear that this does not justify every grasping conduct, such as price-gouging or other practices, widely agreed even by capitalists to be unethical, and not necessary to the functioning of the system. It justifies the normal self-interested pursuit of incentives that makes capitalism work to raise the standard of living of society.

Thus, if, as both Cohen and Narveson imagine, the less advantaged ask the more advantaged to justify their better shares, the more advantaged can say that they are acting according to the difference principle, which everyone would agree to in the original position – which is to say under conditions designed to make agreements just because, for example, behind the veil of ignorance, no one can tailor agreements to her own needs or abilities. Thus, the better off can say to the worse off:

> Look, I understand that you would like more, but I am only asking for an incentive that it would be reasonable for you to agree to if you did not know whether you would be more or less talented, well or poorly off. As the difference principle requires, the incentive I am insisting on is one that actually works to make you the best off that you can be without violating the interest that we all have in not having a degree of altruism imposed on us that we would experience as oppressive. This interest reflects the fact that we "stand in the circumstances of justice" and thus we "have no grounds for complaining of one another's motives."[14]

---

[14]The quoted phrases are from *TJ*, 131.

And, precisely because, as Rawls holds, members of a society based on principles agreed to in the original position will endorse those principles, it follows that the worst off will endorse them as well and accept this justification offered by the better off.

For this reason, incentives justified by the difference principle are compatible with community between the better and the worse off. Cohen thinks that such incentives are incompatible with community between the better and the worse off because he believes that the better off cannot justify them to the worse off; thus the better off must act as if they are "not accountable to their interrogators," which means "they are foreswearing community" with the rest of society (*RJE*, 44). Cohen takes as distinctive of liberalism that it allows the choices of private economic actors to be "self-seeking" and "show no respect for . . . justice" (*RJE*, 2). He claims that when the more talented demand incentives for the talent they happen to be born with, they do not show such respect for others (*RJE*, 76). But this is mistaken. Once the difference principle is seen as determining the just size of the right to pursue self-interest, then one can agree with Cohen that the difference principle does not apply only to the basic structure and individuals must apply it to their own behavior. The better off can do this because the difference principle entails that their pursuit of incentives is just. Thus Rawls is right in saying that, in a society governed by his two principles of justice, "persons express their respect for one another in the very constitution of their society" (*TJ*, 156).[15] And since the worse off also must apply the difference principle to their behavior, they must accept the justification offered by the better off.

This argument works because justice is a standard that is fitted to actual human nature (as argued in Chapter 1), and the difference

---

[15]For this reason, I do not consider "the social bases of self-respect" a separate primary good that might then be distributed by the principles of justice, as Rawls suggests in his last work (*JF*, 60). I take it that a just society will convey respect to people in the structure of society, which is constituted by their fellows' behavior. Members of such a society will then have all the social bases for self-respect that can be given – the rest will be up to them.

principle is understood in light of what will actually maximize the share of the worst off. Cohen admits that his position is utopian (*RJE*, 1). He goes to great lengths to prove that "infeasibility of application does not defeat the claim of a [moral] principle" (*RJE*, 20, see 229–273), that is, to defend his right to hold impracticable moral standards. Accordingly, he concedes that a criticism he credits to Samuel Scheffler calls his egalitarianism into question as a practical proposal, but not as a moral value. He writes:

> It needs to be shown that a society of people who believe in equality and act accordingly is reproducible, that it is not fated to collapse under disintegrative strains. Such societies seem to be possible on a small scale, and we need to explore what constraints of human nature and organization make them difficult – as they undoubtedly are – on a larger scale, and whether those difficulties approach impossibility. As a practical proposal, normative egalitarianism requires a corresponding psychology. If the research program to which the Sheffler objection points were to deliver negative results, equality might still be a tenable value [since infeasibility does not defeat the claim of a moral principle], but it could not, unmodified, represent a policy goal. (*RJE*, 52)

For Marxian Liberalism, this absence of an egalitarian psychology along with the recognition that large-scale egalitarian societies are undoubtedly difficult to sustain is quite damning. Until the research program that Cohen proposes shows otherwise, indeed, until history itself shows otherwise, what we know is that capitalism with unequal incentives works to raise material productivity, and egalitarian socialism does not (at least not after agrarian society has been brought into the industrial era). This effectively rules out Cohen's egalitarianism in the present historical era, and puts it off to a later one. If Marxists' optimistic predictions about human nature are true, then eventually social conditions will produce a human nature to which generosity and cooperation are natural. History will produce the egalitarian psychology whose need Cohen acknowledges, and whose absence he laments.

But, as Marx recognized and Marxian Liberalism agrees, this requires the completion of capitalism's historical mission. Abundance itself will lead to less conflictual social relations and thus to the very change in human nature that egalitarian society needs for it to be a realistic policy goal. Then Cohen's egalitarian ideal will lose its utopian halo and be a realistic policy goal. Indeed, then it will not even have to be a policy goal, just a description of how people spontaneously treat their fellows. Until then, for the present and the foreseeable future, capitalism – constrained by the difference principle to allow the smallest unequal incentives practically necessary to maximize the standard of living of the worst off – is just. Historically just, but truly just nonetheless, because it calls for the maximum provision for the interests of others that it is reasonable to demand of currently existing people.

6

The Marxian-Liberal Original Position

In this chapter, I formulate a Marxian-Liberal version of Rawls's original position and use it to determine what it would be rational for all to consent to regarding the right to private property and the nature of the state. This original position functions as a thought experiment just like Rawls's version except that, here, we assume that we have reached a point in time when the factual beliefs making up the *Marxian theory of the conditions of liberty*, as well as some factual beliefs characteristically held by liberals, are recognized as common knowledge along with widely accepted facts of history and conclusions of natural and social science. All of these beliefs are part of the general knowledge possessed by the parties in the Marxian-Liberal original position. I shall argue that it will be rational for these parties to agree to a right to property subject to Rawls's difference principle understood in light of the moral version of the labor theory of value – and to a limited state empowered to protect liberty and to implement the difference principle.

As Free and as Just as Possible: The Theory of Marxian Liberalism, First Edition. Jeffrey Reiman.
© 2014 Jeffrey Reiman. Published 2014 by John Wiley & Sons, Ltd.

My argument in this chapter will unfold as follows. In Section 6.1, "Property and Subjugation," I indicate how recognition of the structural coerciveness of private property shapes the problem of protecting and promoting liberty. In particular, I contend that, where traditional liberal theories make a crucial distinction between the problem of justifying liberty against coercion in the political realm and the problem of justifying economic distributions, recognition of structural coercion collapses these problems into one. Economic distribution is a measure of the proportions in which people are forced to labor for one another, and thus the problem of justifying economic distribution is part of the problem of protecting liberty against coercion. In Section 6.2, "The Limits of Property," I argue, on historical and conceptual grounds, that the problem of justifying a right to private property is necessarily a matter of justifying a right of a certain shape, characteristically determined by some set of limits. Thus, in the Marxian-Liberal original position, we will not ask whether people will or will not agree to a right to private property, we will ask whether there is a right to private property *of a certain shape* (with perhaps certain limits built into it) to which it will be rational for the parties to agree. In Section 6.3, "The Marxian Theory of the Conditions of Liberty," I spell out the Marxian beliefs that are part of the general knowledge of the parties in the Marxian-Liberal original position. In Section 6.4, "Inside the Marxian-Liberal Original Position," I argue that it will be rational for the parties to agree to a principle guaranteeing equal basic liberties for all, to a right to private property limited by the difference principle, to a principle establishing a general right not to be subject to unwanted coercion, and to a state limited to enforcing these principles. Here, I contend that Marxian Liberalism provides the deduction of the difference principle that Rawls hoped for but did not achieve in *A Theory of Justice* (see *TJ*, 104–105). In Section 6.5, "The Difference Principle as a Historical Principle of Justice," I show that the difference principle allows for movement from the capitalist principle of just distribution to the socialist principle, and then to the communist, as historical conditions change.

6.1 Property and Subjugation

In Rawls's theory of justice, there are two basic principles, a principle that guarantees equal individual liberty for all, and the difference principle (plus requirements of fair opportunity and reasonable intergenerational savings) that governs social and economic inequalities (see Section 2.2). Formulation of these principles, writes Rawls,

> presupposes that, for the purposes of a theory of justice, the social structure may be viewed as having two more or less distinct parts, the first principle applying to the one, the second principle to the other. Thus we distinguish between the aspects of the social system that define and secure the equal basic liberties and the aspects that specify and establish social and economic inequalities. (*TJ*, 53)

This distinction harks back to Hegel's distinction between the *state* and *civil society*, the former a realm of political coercion in which people are to have equal rights, and the latter a realm of social freedom in which people end up with unequal wealth and status. The distinction is at least implicit in the writings of the liberal philosophers who preceded Hegel, such as Locke, who, as we saw, defended an equal right to liberty and a right to large and unequal property, and Kant who did the same. Kant affirmed the *equality of subjects* in a just state, and added: "This complete equality of men as subjects in a nation is completely consistent with the greatest inequality in the quantity and degree of possessions that they have."[1]

In his essay "On the Jewish Question," Marx attacked the distinction between the state and civil society. He wrote:

> The perfected political state is, by its nature, the *species-life* of man [his social life as an equal member of the human species] as opposed

---

[1]Kant, "On the Proverb: That May Be True in Theory, But Is of No Practical Use," in Immanuel Kant, *Perpetual Peace and Other Essays* (Indianapolis: Hackett, 1983; "On the Proverb" originally published 1793), 73.

to his material life. All the presuppositions of this egoistic [material] life continue to exist in *civil society outside* the political sphere, as the qualities of civil society. . . . He lives in the *political community* where he regards himself as a *communal being*, and in *civil society* where he acts simply as a *private individual*, treats other men as means . . . , and becomes the plaything of alien powers. (*MER*, 34)

Thus, Marx takes the distinction between the political state and civil society (meaning, chiefly, the economy) as distinguishing between a realm of society in which people act subject to rules aimed at the common good, and a realm in which they pursue their private advantage. In the political realm people are to treat one another morally and humanely as equal citizens. In the economic realm, people treat one another as means, and live as playthings of powers beyond their control. For Marx, then, the distinction between the political state and civil society effectively puts the economic beyond the reach of the shared moral rules that govern the political realm.

Behind this critique is Marx's view of capitalist private property as coercive. The political realm must treat people morally and as equals because it is a realm of coercive power which needs special justification. The economic realm is, putatively, a realm of freedom, so it need not be governed by moral rules or treat people equally, beyond affirming their equal freedom to use whatever they happen to own on the market. Thus, the distinction between the political state and civil society is of a piece with the ideological invisibility of the structural coercion of private property. By separating the political realm, whose coerciveness is overt and recognized, from the economic realm, where coercion is structural and unseen, the latter is taken as a realm of freedom. Differences in property are taken as only differences in goods, and the enormous power over workers that ownership of means of production gives is hidden from view. People are led to believe that the coercion occurs only in the political realm, where it represents the interests and protects the freedom of all, while the coerciveness of private property that makes people "the plaything of alien powers" is allowed to operate unimpeded in the economic realm.

By recognizing the structurally coercive nature of private property, Marxian Liberalism strips away this ideological mask. Accordingly, Marxian Liberalism does not recognize the political and the economic realms as *morally* distinct. They remain *functionally* distinct, of course, so that we can still speak of political considerations (concerning the nature of the state and the laws) and economic conditions (concerning the organization of work and the distribution of its product). Marx, himself, recognized their functional distinction when he affirmed, in "On the Jewish Question," that "political emancipation certainly represents a great progress" (*MER*, 35). But, morally, both are arenas in which coercion occurs, and thus in which liberty must be protected.

The need to protect liberty in the economic realm is difficult to see because of the invisibility of structural coercion. However, we can use the moral version of the labor theory of value to see through the invisibility of structural coercion. Viewing economic distributions as distributions of people's labor embodied in the goods they end up with, we see the proportions in which people are forced to work for others. Where people are required to work for each other in equal amounts, such forced labor is, in the absence of indications of wrongdoing, morally benign. This is because the exchange of equal amounts of labor means that the same amount of time and energy workers give up comes back to them in a different form, leaving them in effect as if they had labored for themselves. However, where they are required to work for others in unequal amounts, then, some are structurally coerced to work more for others than those others work for them. I call such structurally coerced unequal labor *social subjugation*.

When the parties in the Marxian-Liberal original position take up the issue of the right to private property, their right to and interest in liberty will lead them to want a right to private property with limits built into it aimed at eliminating social subjugation – though, as we shall see, other considerations will lead them to tolerate some social subjugation. Some may object that property is property, and that building limits into a right to property violates the nature of that right. I take up this objection in the following section.

6.2   The Limits of Property

The objection just stated ("that property is property . . .") assumes that there is a "natural" or "essential" meaning of the right of property, namely, that a property owner may do whatever she wants with her property as long as she doesn't violate the rights of others to liberty or to use their own property. But, in fact, property rights have taken a large variety of forms in history, most commonly as rights encumbered with various limits and responsibilities. Thus, any argument for a right to property must specify the *shape* of the right – the particular set of powers and limits included in the right – and justify the right with that shape. "It is idle," wrote R. H. Tawney, "to present a case for or against private property without specifying the particular forms of property to which reference is made."[2]

One implication of the variability of the right to property is that it cannot be assumed that justice is determined by some right of property with a predetermined shape. The relationship is the opposite: *Justice must determine the shape of the right to property*. A theory of economic justice is a theory of the shape of the right of property. If it is unjust that some get at birth unearned advantages that others lack, then, the shape of the right to property must be tailored to enable just rectification of that inequality in advantages. The right to property must fit the requirements of justice, not vice versa.

Against this, it might be countered that one can, in principle, go in either direction: from justice to rights, or from rights to justice. Thus, this rejoinder runs, we could develop a theory of natural rights including a right to property, and then define justice as whatever conforms to those rights. The problem with this, however, is that, to develop a theory of the natural right to property, one must defend, not merely a right to property, but a right in one shape rather than another. That particular shape of the right will have to be argued for. To be convincing, that argument will have to show

---

[2]R. H. Tawney, *The Acquisitive Society* (New York: Harcourt, Brace, 1921), 54.

that the right so shaped does not lead to evident injustice. The upshot is that the right to property will necessarily have to be shaped to fit the requirements of justice.

In the remainder of this section, I give both historical and conceptual reasons for my claim that there is no natural or essential shape to the right of property.

Legal history shows that ownership comes in many forms. It is "a bundle of rights, privileges, and obligations. . . . Ownership does not always mean absolute ownership."[3] Ownership in *fee simple* is the least restricted form of legal control over property in common law countries, but it is not without limits. It is subject to taxation, easements, and the government's power of eminent domain, that is, the power of states to take private property for public use (normally in return for fair compensation).[4] Of the power of eminent domain, Freyfogel writes: "the settlement of the United States was greatly assisted because governments held and willingly exercised this power."[5] It was used, for example, to grant private railroads land on which to construct their rail lines.

In the Middle Ages, ownership of property was subject to extensive built-in limits. V. G. Kiernan writes that "Medieval-feudal concepts of landownership" made "land the object not of a single undivided right but of a network of rights, and entitling all from prince to ploughman, if very unequally, to a share."[6] In medieval Europe and continuing into the Renaissance, the practice of *primogeniture*, requiring that property be passed on from father to eldest son, was a common limit on the right of property. Slightly less restrictive was *entail*, limiting an estate to a line of descendants. Of

[3]*Corpus Juris Secundum: Property* 73, sec. 43 (Eagan, MN: Thomson West, 2004), 48.
[4]W. L. Burdick, *Handbook of the Law of Real Property* (St. Paul, MN: West Publishing, 1914), 61–67.
[5]Eric T. Freyfogle, *On Private Property: Finding Common Ground on the Ownership of Land* (Boston: Beacon Press, 2007), xx.
[6]V. G. Kiernan, "Private Property in History," in Jack Goody, Joan Thirsk, and E. P. Thompson, eds., *Family and Inheritance: Rural Society in Western Europe, 1200–1800* (Cambridge: Cambridge University Press, 1976), 376.

this, writes Viernan, "Clearly . . . there could be no untrammeled possession for the heir himself, who was only the occupant, one of a long line each following the other in turn."[7] In addition, there were moral limits to the right of property. For example, St. Thomas Aquinas held that it was permissible for a man in desperate straits to steal. Kiernan notes that ownership among the ancient Hebrews, among the Arabs, and in traditional Hindu and Muslim and Chinese societies, was similarly subject to complex limits.[8]

Roman law had a notion of private property that was much less limited than the feudal notion. It was the return to Roman law in the Renaissance that provided intellectual support for the modern, largely unlimited, conception of the right to property. Nonetheless, Roman law knew many limits on the right, such as *servitudes*. A servitude was a "burden on property obliging the owner to allow someone else to use it for some purpose – or preventing the owner from using it in a way that inconveniences another."[9] Peter Garnsey writes that "a servitude cuts into *dominium*; it takes something away from the owner's absolute control of his property."[10] *Praedial servitudes* were burdens related to neighboring property. Among those recognized in Roman law were *iter* (the right to cross the neighbor's land), *actus* (the right to drive cattle across a neighbor's land), *via* (the right to have a road across a neighbor's land), and *aquaeductus* (the right to have an aqueduct across a neighbor's land).[11]

Modern-day property rights can be limited by *easements*, which normally grant rights to owners of adjacent property. Among these are *access easement* ("an easement allowing one or more persons to travel across another's land to get to a nearby location, such as a

---

[7]Kiernan, "Private Property in History," 376–377.
[8]Kiernan, "Private Property in History," 387–391.
[9]Peter Garnsey, *Thinking about Property: From Antiquity to the Age of Revolution* (New York: Cambridge University Press, 2007), 186.
[10]Garnsey, *Thinking about Property*, 188.
[11]Alan Watson, *Roman Law and Comparative Law* (Athens, GA: University of Georgia Press, 1991), 49.

road"), *light-and-air easement* ("preventing an adjoining owner from constructing a building that would prevent light or air from reaching the dominant estate," that is, the land benefiting from the easement), *public easement* ("for the benefit of an entire community, such as the right to travel down a street or a sidewalk").[12]

In addition to this historical evidence of the variety of shapes taken by the right to property, the fact is that the concept of the right of property is inherently unspecified, and thus necessarily subject to variation in the shapes it may take. For example, nothing in the concept of a right to property spells out how far that right reaches. Of Locke's theory of property acquisition by mixing one's labor with unowned things, Nozick wonders: "If a private astronaut clears a place on Mars, has he mixed his labor with (so he comes to own) the whole planet, the whole uninhabited universe, or just a particular plot?" (*ASU*, 174). This doesn't even get to the question of air rights and mineral rights, that is, how high above and deep below one's cleared patch of land one's right to property reaches. Narveson recognizes that ownership of land doesn't necessarily include unlimited ownership of the air above or the ground below. About the latter, he writes: "I don't see that [the owner of the surface] has any obvious 'natural' claim to rights, as it were, all the way down. One might note that for such [cases], there is the problem that all places on the surface of the Earth are such that if you go straight down, they will all meet at the center. Then what? Clearly, we cannot simply extrapolate from the situation on the surface."[13] One might hold that ownership of the surface of the earth is ownership of the infinite imaginary cone that goes from the edges of the property down, ever narrowing, to the exact centerpoint of the earth and up, endlessly widening, into outer space. But no one would think that this is essential to the concept of the right to property.

---

[12]Bryan A. Garner, ed., *Black's Law Dictionary*, 7th ed. (St. Paul, MN: West Group, 1999), 527–528.

[13]Jan Narveson, "Property and Rights," *Social Philosophy & Policy* 27, no.1 (Winter 2010), 122.

A. M. Honoré identified eleven elements of the notion of property ownership.[14] Lawrence Becker divided one of Honoré's elements into three, and contends that ownership contains the following thirteen elements:

1   The right to exclusive control of a thing.
2   The right to enjoyment of the benefits of a thing.
3   The right to manage the use of a thing.
4   The right to income from letting others use a thing.
5   The right to consume or destroy a thing.
6   The right to effect changes in a thing less extensive than annihilation.
7   The right to transfer a thing during one's life by exchange or gift.
8   The right to bequeath a thing.
9   The right to security, that is, to immunity from expropriation of one's ownership rights.
10 The absence of term, that is, the absence of a time limit to one's ownership rights.
11 The prohibition on harmful use of a thing.
12 Liability to having the thing taken away as payment for a debt.
13 Residuary rules governing transfer of a thing to another where ownership rights have expired or been abandoned.[15]

Of these thirteen elements, Becker writes: "Each of the elements is capable of a variety of definitions. . . . Full ownership – that is, the concatenation of all these elements – therefore has as many different varieties as there are different definitions of the elements."[16] As for the minimum content of a right to property, Becker holds that "if anyone holds even one of [the first] eight elements [possession, use, management, income, consumption or destruction, modification,

---

[14] A. M. Honoré, "Ownership," in A. G. Guest, ed., *Oxford Essays in Jurisprudence*, First Series (Oxford: Clarendon Press, 1961), 107–147.
[15] Lawrence C. Becker, "The Moral Basis of Property Rights," in J. R. Pennock and J. W. Chapman, eds., *NOMOS XXII: Property* (New York: New York University Press, 1980), 190–191.
[16] Becker, "The Moral Basis of Property Rights," 191.

alienation, or transmission] plus security [the ninth] . . . then it makes sense to say that that person has a property right." And further: "The varieties of property rights, then, consist of any set of the thirteen elements that includes at least one of the first eight plus security. There are 4,080 such combinations[!]."[17] This number does not include variations in the definition of the elements. Thus, in fact, there are many more than 4,080 possible shapes to the right to property. From this it follows that there is no natural or essential content to the right of private property. Any argument for a right to private property will necessarily be an argument for a right with a particular shape. Accordingly, a right to private property can have numerous limits built into it without thereby stopping being a right to private property.

This indeterminacy in the concept of property is why I said at the outset – in the context of distinguishing Marxian Liberalism from Left-Libertarianism – that a right to property ownership must be derivative in a theory of justice, rather than foundational. A theory of justice is needed to determine the shape of a morally acceptable right to property.

6.3   The Marxian Theory of the Conditions of Liberty

The specific Marxian beliefs that together make up the Marxian theory of the conditions of liberty are that coercion can function structurally, and does so in the institution of private ownership, especially, private ownership of means of production; that structural coercion tends to be invisible and therefore that *a moral version of the labor theory of value* is needed to evaluate property systems morally; and, finally, what I call *the fungibility of material and social subjugation*. All of these beliefs will be part of the general knowledge possessed by parties in the Marxian-Liberal original position. These

[17]Becker, "The Moral Basis of Property Rights," 192.

beliefs are not chosen at random. They are those aspects of Marxism that liberals, concerned to protect and promote freedom, would naturally consider of crucial importance. All of these beliefs except *the fungibility of material and social subjugation* have already been discussed. I turn to it now.

Though Marx thought capitalism was a coercive system that unjustly forced unpaid surplus labor out of workers, he held it nonetheless to be progressive. He wrote:

> It is one of the civilizing aspects of capital that it enforces [the extraction of] surplus-labour in a manner and under conditions which are more advantageous to the development of the productive forces, social relations, and the creation of the elements for a new and higher form than under the preceding forms of slavery and serfdom. (*C*, III, 819)

Note that Marx includes the *manner* and *conditions* in and under which capitalism extracts surplus labor as among its progressive features. This I take to refer to the ways in which social and political conditions of life and labor in capitalism are superior to those in slavery or serfdom. Chief among these conditions are the liberal freedoms that have normally accompanied capitalist development, especially in its mature phases. Thus, we have seen Marx commend the liberal rights embodied in the French Declaration of the Rights of Man and the Citizen and in the American Revolutionary-era state constitutions as "a great progress," even if it "is not the final form of human emancipation" (*MER*, 35).

Here, however, I am primarily concerned with capitalism's progressivity with regard to "the development of the productive forces." This is because, for Marx, the development of material productivity promises to provide the conditions for genuine freedom. Marx wrote:

> Just as the savage must wrestle with Nature to satisfy his wants, to maintain and reproduce life, so must civilized man, and he must

do so in all social formations and under all possible modes of production. With his development this realm of physical necessity expands as a result of his wants; but, at the same time, *the forces of production which satisfy these wants also increase. Freedom in this field* can only consist in socialized man, the associated producers, rationally regulating their interchange with Nature, bringing it under common control, instead of being ruled by it as by the blind forces of Nature; and *achieving this with the least expenditure of energy* and under conditions most favourable to, and worthy of, their human nature. But it nonetheless still remains a realm of necessity. *Beyond it begins that development of human energy which is an end in itself, the true realm of freedom, which, however, can blossom forth only with this realm of necessity as its basis.* (C, III, 820; emphasis added)

As the emphasized passages suggest, Marx thought that heightened material productivity brought freedom in two ways. First, it enabled human beings to satisfy their expanding wants. Second, it enabled human beings to satisfy those wants with less and less labor, leading finally to "the true realm of freedom" beyond the realm of necessary labor, though with that necessary labor as its basis. (I leave aside here the increase in freedom that comes from greater worker control in the workplace, since that is not a result of increased material productivity. I return to this consideration later, in Section 7.3.) For the present, note that increased material productivity increases freedom in the form of greater material means to satisfy human desires, and in the form of reduced necessary labor. I call these the *material conditions of freedom*. Since the lack of these conditions limits freedom, I call that lack *material subjugation*.

Material subjugation refers to the limits on freedom that come from the fact that human beings' freedom is subject to the constraints of the material world, such that (a) people need material objects to have genuine freedom in the sense of the real possibility of acting on their choices (this includes obvious things that enhance people's ability to act on their choices, such as food and phones and cars, but also cures to diseases and other protections against life's perils),[18] and (b) people must work on nature to wring from it the objects covered under (a). The belief that an ample supply of material goods is a necessary condition of genuine freedom is behind the Marxian critique of liberal rights as merely formal: rights without material means to act on them give no real freedom. (For Rawls's recognition of this fact, see *JF*, 177; and Section 2.2, above.)

Since Marx's theory of the conditions of liberty holds that freedom is limited both by the structural coercion of private property and by deprivation of the material conditions of freedom, I take the theory to affirm the fungibility of material subjugation and social subjugation. This is the belief that, though being constrained by material deprivation is not a form of coercion, its effect on freedom is equivalent to that of being constrained by human coercion.

The belief is implicit in Marx's view that history is progressive. "In broad outlines," writes Marx, "the Asiatic, ancient, feudal and modern bourgeois modes of production can be designated as progressive epochs in the economic formation of society" (*MER*, 5). Since, for Marx, history – up to and including capitalism – is a story of social subjugation accompanied by increasing power over nature, the progressivity of history implies that such social subjugation is a price worth paying for the reduction in material subjugation that increasing power over material nature brings, and thus that social and material subjugation are comparable, and fungible: one can rationally be traded for the other. This is all the more evident if Marx is taken as subscribing to the view voiced by Engels, that the earliest societies were characterized by a so-called primitive communism. Since those societies were more egalitarian than the ones that followed, history could count as progressive only if those subsequent

---

[18]This general idea is accepted by Philippe van Parijs in *Real Freedom for All: What (if Anything) Can Justify Capitalism?* (Oxford: Oxford University Press, 1995), and by Amartya Sen in *The Idea of Justice* (Cambridge, MA: Harvard University Press, 2009).

societies with greater social subjugation were seen as trade-offs necessary for reducing material subjugation.[19]

I turn now to consideration of how these various beliefs will work in the Marxian-Liberal original position.

6.4   Inside the Marxian-Liberal Original Position

We are now prepared to consider what would be consented to in the Marxian-Liberal original position. In Section 3.3, I argued that consent to the state must be theoretical, and that, given that the state is both necessary for the protection of liberty and that the state cannot perform that function if it must await the actual consent of every newly arriving person, theoretical consent to the state is morally equivalent to actual consent. The same goes for the right to property. We see in Locke's and Kant's arguments, as well as from history, that some right to private ownership of parts of the world is necessary for effective freedom; and we recognize as well that a right to property cannot serve this function if it must wait on the actual consent of every newly arriving person. Accordingly, here too, theoretical consent is morally equivalent to actual consent.

To determine what will be the object of theoretical consent, Marxian Liberalism deploys a version of the imaginary choice situation that Rawls calls the *original position*. In Section 2.2, I described Rawls's notion of the original position with its veil of ignorance, and the parties therein characterized as rational and mutually disinterested, with an interest in acting on their own purposes whatever these turn out to be, and possessing general factual knowledge. What's more, the parties cannot gamble on what position they will be in in the society on whose principles they agree. In the Marxian-Liberal original position, all of these features obtain with the addition that the parties' factual knowledge includes key beliefs from liberalism and from Marxism.

---

[19]See Frederick Engels, *The Origin of the Family, Private Property and the State* (New York: International Publishers, 1970; originally published 1884), 103, 112–114.

The liberal beliefs that the parties hold are that people already have a natural right to liberty in the form of a right not to be subjected to unwanted coercion, that people have an interest in being able to exercise this liberty, that private property is a necessary condition of individual liberty, and that a state is needed to define and protect the rights to both liberty and property. The specific Marxian beliefs are that coercion can function structurally and that it does in the case of private property, that *a moral version of the labor theory of value* is needed to evaluate property systems, and what I have called *the fungibility of material and social subjugation*. One belief that follows from combining these liberal and Marxian beliefs (and that is backed up by the parties' general knowledge of history)[20] is that a democratic state is needed to protect citizens against the coerciveness of private property and its consequences.

Note that, apart from the natural right to liberty, none of these liberal or Marxian beliefs is a moral principle. They are factual beliefs that could in principle become part of generally accepted knowledge and thus part of the general factual knowledge possessed by parties in Rawls's own version of the original position. The beliefs get what moral force they have by being coupled with the natural right to liberty.

In light of this knowledge and, in particular, in light of their interest in being able to exercise their liberty, the parties will agree to a principle protecting equal basic liberties for all, modeled on Rawls's first principle of justice. This principle will protect the familiar rights of liberal polities, such as those enshrined in the U.S. Bill of Rights. As we shall see later in this section, the parties will give this principle lexical priority over the principle governing the right to property, for reasons related to those which Rawls gives for the lexical priority of his first principle of justice over the second. Moreover, they will insist that their state serve their liberty

---

[20]In the nineteenth and twentieth centuries, capitalist countries saw the growth of popular suffrage leading to increased use of the state's power to regulate capitalism for the common good and, in particular, to protect workers from the vagaries of the market.

by being a democratic state truly controlled by citizens with roughly equal influence on political decisions. Thus, they will agree to the requirement that the political liberties – the rights necessary for political participation – be maintained at fair value so as to be effective.

In addition, the parties recognize that the protection of basic liberties and the principle governing the right to property do not eliminate all the ways in which people might be subjected to unwanted coercion. For example, protection of the basic liberties does not guarantee that there will not be laws against victimless crimes, such as recreational drug use, or commercial sex. However, the natural right to liberty prohibits the use of coercion to prohibit such activities by sane adults. Thus, to make sure that the natural right to liberty is fully protected, the parties will agree to a third principle prohibiting unwanted coercion not necessary for protecting the basic liberties and for implementing the principle they select for governing the right to private property. On the basis of this third principle, liberty will be protected against the common (nonstructural) forms of coercion not already prohibited by the first principle, such as physical assaults and fraud as well, since fraud functions like coercion to subvert choice (a victim of fraud thinks he is acting on his choice, but is really doing his swindler's bidding).

That private property is necessary for liberty is something that the parties have learned from Locke and Kant, but also from history and (surprisingly) as an implication of their Marxian beliefs. That ownership of means of production is coercive is a Marxian reason for doubting that individual freedom can exist if such ownership is taken out of individuals' hands and placed under state (or other collective) control. The oppressive nature of twentieth-century communist states is powerful evidence for such doubt. Moreover, private, and thus relatively decentralized, ownership of property is the material basis for the freedoms that generally characterize capitalist societies and that have been generally absent from communist ones. For this reason, we cannot assume that placing ownership of the means of production in the hands of a modern liberal democratic state will protect against the abuse of the enormous coercive power that that would represent. On Marxian grounds, liberal democratic states are as free as they are because of capitalism's relatively decentralized ownership of property.[21]

What's more, the parties know that freedom has material conditions, so that their interest in liberty gives them an interest in a rapidly rising material standard of living. They know as well from history that capitalist societies tend rapidly to increase material productivity and thus the general standard of living.[22] As we saw in Chapter 1, they know this also from reading the *Communist Manifesto*, where Marx and Engels asked rhetorically of capitalism, "what earlier century had even a presentiment that such productive forces slumbered in the lap of social labour?" (*MER*, 477). The parties know from history that socialist and communist societies tend to be economically stagnant.

The parties will therefore agree to some right to private property including ownership of means of production because they know that capitalism with its private ownership of means of production will both support liberal democratic institutions and rapidly raise their standard of living, and thus increase their access to the material conditions of freedom. The parties know from history that the right to property comes in numerous forms with numerous built-in limits, and thus that the question they must answer is what form of the right to property with what, if any, limits it would be rational for them to consent to.

---

[21] The belief that the state in capitalist societies is shaped by the material conditions of capitalism is not in conflict with the parties' belief, mentioned above, that they need a state to protect them against the coerciveness of private property. Numerous Marxist authors have recognized that, while the state in capitalist societies works generally to protect the long-term interests of the capitalist class, it has a certain autonomy vis-à-vis that class that is necessary for it to serve that class's long-term interests (for example, it enables the state to rise above the conflicting interests of competing capitalists). This autonomy also enables the state to protect the workers against the vagaries of the free market, and thus more generally to protect them against the coerciveness of private property. See, for example, Ralph Miliband, *The State in Capitalist Society* (London: Merlin Press, 2009; originally published 1969); and Nicos Poulantzas, *State, Power, and Socialism* (London: Verso, 2001).

[22] See Chapter 1, notes 15–19, and accompanying text.

Defenders of the relatively unlimited right to large and unequal property tend to offer capitalism's great productivity as a reason people would consent to capitalism's right to virtually unlimited property. Locke does it (see, for example, *ST*, v:43); and Nozick does too (*ASU*, 117). But this move is a bit too quick. It would not be rational for people to consent to what leads to greater productivity as an end in itself, that is, without assurance that they will benefit from it – especially knowing that they are agreeing to potentially large limits on their natural right to liberty. Thus, the right to property that can be justified by consent of those affected by it will be a right with, at a minimum, limits built into it that guarantee that everyone will end up with a decent share. But this is just a minimum, and a vague minimum at that. The parties will go further.

Because of the *moral version of the labor theory of value*, parties in the Marxian-Liberal original position understand that the money or goods that a person gets in an economic system are not simply "his" money or goods, but "other people's labor." Thus, inequalities in people's economic shares are not merely distributive differences. Indeed, since a property regime is a system of structural coercion, inequalities represent the fact that some people are being forced to work more for others than those others work for them. Because of the complexity of a modern economy, this is spread through the system, not limited only to relations between capitalists and workers. If the average worker's salary is $20,000 a year, then someone who earns $100,000 a year has the labor-time of five workers at his disposal in return for his own labor-time (and not even for that much, if his earnings are from stocks or other investments). And given that the property system coerces this arrangement, the result is a relationship of unequal forced labor mediated by the economic system. I have called this unequal forced labor *social subjugation*.

We need distributive measures for this because the invisibility of structural coercion hides the fact of social subjugation. In *Capital*, Marx took distributive measures as indications of exploitation: "The rate of surplus-value [the ratio between the value received by the capitalist in the form of profit, and the value that the capitalist gives to the worker in the form of his wage] is . . . an exact expression of the degree of exploitation . . . of the labourer by the capitalist" (C, I, 218). Accordingly, parties in the Marxian-Liberal original position will not simply consider the right to private property in terms of the benefits it may bring them, they will look at it as a system of social subjugation and consider whether, or what, benefits might make that system worth accepting.

We can, as Rawls does, suppose that the parties in the original position will first be drawn to accept a property system with a built-in limit guaranteeing that everyone will labor for everyone else in equal amounts. They would be drawn to this, not by its moral appeal, since there are no moral principles in the Marxian-Liberal original position other than the preexisting natural right to liberty. Aside from this right, the parties in the original position, in both Rawls's and Marxian-Liberalism's version, know that they have an interest in liberty itself, that is, in being able to act on their choices. Since the parties know that exchanging an equal amount of labor is equivalent to doing that much labor for oneself, and since they cannot gamble on being the recipient of a greater-than-equal exchange, it would appear to be in their interest to insist on equality in the exchange of labor-time.

However, since the parties in the Marxian-Liberal original position believe in the fungibility of material subjugation and social subjugation, the parties would find it rational to agree to some inequalities in exchanges of labor-time, that is, to some social subjugation, if there were counterbalancing reductions in material subjugation. The parties know from history that socialist societies that insist broadly on equality of labor-time tend to be stagnant economies, and they know from history (and from Marxism) that capitalist economies that allow inequalities of labor-time primarily in the form of incentives for more productive labor tend to have extremely productive economies. Thus, it would be reasonable for them to agree to an unequal capitalist economy rather than an equal socialist economy, if they can be guaranteed that they will get the compensating increase in freedom that comes from reducing material subjugation, that is, from increasing their material standard of living. In short, the parties' interest in exercising their liberty, combined with the Marxian belief that increasing possession of material goods is a condition of increasing freedom, give the parties a strong interest in a system that increases their material standard of living. And this is all the more so, if the basic liberties are guaranteed.

Social subjugation could be accepted if it were compensated for by a reduction in material subjugation, either in the form of more material goods or less required labor. For simplicity's sake, I shall assume that workers who gain increases in material goods (as pay for their labor) can trade these for reductions in labor-time that are compatible with efficient production. Then, we can say that parties in the Marxian-Liberal original position can accept inequalities (measured in labor-time) that amount to social subjugation, if they are counterbalanced by the reductions in material subjugation that come from increases in the workers' material standard of living (measured in goods).

Since the parties want both to maximize their material standard of living and to minimize social subjugation understood as being on the wrong end of an unequal labor exchange, they need a principle that spells out the proper trade-off between these two goals. From Marxism, they understand that social subjugation is a price worth paying for raising the material standard of living. Moreover, they believe this on independent grounds as well. They understand from history that increases in the material standard of living tend to be cumulative. Each generation normally starts at the material standard of living attained by their parents over the course of their lifetimes. Thus any rise in the material standard of living will normally raise the floor for all subsequent generations. This means that everyone living and yet to live will benefit from raising the material standard of living at any point in time.[23] Moreover, compared to reductions in social subjugation whose gains are limited to achieving equal labor exchanges, increases in material standard of living

[23]Since the natural environment is everyone's home, I take it that the parties understand their interest in raising their material standard of living as subject to due respect for the natural environment, which is in everyone's interest.

have no inherent limit. For the foreseeable future at least, they promise indefinitely increasing power over nature and thus indefinitely increasing freedom to act on one's choices. Finally, also for the foreseeable future, even if equal labor exchanges are achieved, workers will still be required to work. Their lives would still be largely shaped by material subjugation, with little appreciable gain.

Thus the most significant growth in freedom will come from the increase in their material standard of living which promises not only more goods with which to act on one's choices, but also the reduction in required work that raising material productivity makes possible. These points gain even more force in light of the first principle guaranteeing equal basic liberties to all, since it eliminates the worst features of serfdom and slavery. Consequently, because the parties want both to maximize their standard of living and to minimize social subjugation, while giving priority to the former, it will be rational for them to agree to the idea that they should maximize their material standard of living and accept the least amount of social subjugation necessary for that.

Note the crucial difference between the thinking in the Marxian-Liberal original position and what goes on in Rawls's original position. In Rawls's version, parties must maximize the share of income or goods for each person, not knowing which one they will be. In the Marxian-Liberal original position, parties aim at *two interrelated but distinct goals*: They must maximize each person's share of material goods *and* minimize social subjugation. The parties must achieve these two goals for everyone because agreement in the original position must be unanimous among individuals who cannot gamble on where they will end up under the principles agreed to.

The two goals are interrelated because the size of a person's share in material goods reflects the labor he gets from others. Assuming everyone works the same length of time, the larger a person's share in material goods, the more of other people's labor he gets in return for a unit of his own labor. Likewise, the smaller a person's share in material goods is, the less that person receives in labor from others in return for a unit of his own. That means that the smaller a person's share, the more he must work for others to get his share – or, equivalently, the more he is subjected to social subjugation. Consequently, if, in designing a distributive scheme, you increase one person's share by reducing the size of a smaller share, you increase the amount of labor the one with the reduced share must do in exchange for the labor of others that produces her share – which is to say you increase social subjugation for that person.

It follows that the only way to design a distribution in which the shares of material goods are maximized, while reducing social subjugation to the least necessary for that maximization, *for all people,* it is necessary *to maximize the absolute share of material goods for each person while not reducing the absolute share of material goods of anyone who has a smaller share than that person.* You can maximize *some* people's shares of material goods, and minimize social subjugation for them, by lowering the shares of people with less than them. However, the only way to do it for *all* people is by maximizing their shares without reducing the shares of those with less than them. But, then, each share can only be maximized subject to the condition that all the shares smaller than it are maximized.

Consequently, the only way to reduce social subjugation to the minimum necessary to maximize people's material standard of living *for all people* is to maximize the absolute material standard of living for the worst off people and then, without reducing that, maximize the standard of living of the next worst off group, and so on, moving up through the other positions above it. *Bear in mind that this is a characterization of the shares in a just distribution, not a proposal for how to treat actual people with their current holdings; and that the sequencing here is a moral not a temporal ordering.* Think of the positions in the distributive scheme as arrayed on a ladder, with the smallest share at the bottom, and shares getting larger as they ascend the ladder. Then, the lifetime share at the lowest rung must be the largest it can be, the share on the second rung must be the largest it can be without making the one below it yet smaller, the share on the third rung must be the largest it can be without making the two lower than it still smaller, and so on all the way to the top. This is precisely how Rawls understands the difference principle to work, in its lexical version (see Section 2.2).

In short, with people's shares measured in material goods, and inequalities measured in labor-time exchanged, the parties in the Marxian-Liberal original position agree to a standard equivalent to Rawls's *lexical difference principle*. People in the imaginary Marxian-Liberal original position, then, will consent to a right to property governed by the difference principle – with the proviso that workers can forego increases in their material standard of living in exchange for reduced labor-time compatible with efficient production.

This provides a deduction of the difference principle. Note that this argument does not require appeal to a maximin decision strategy. It results directly from the parties' ignorance of what position they will end up in, their inability to gamble on that, their understanding of economic distributions as exchanges of labor, their interest in maximizing their absolute material standard of living, and their interest in minimizing social subjugation, at whatever position they end up in, as a means to promoting their interest in exercising their liberty.

For Marxian Liberalism, the difference principle is more than a principle of distributive justice. It is a principle for making the structural coercion built into the property system such that it would be rational for people to consent to it. Thus it makes for a property system that, albeit coercive, is compatible with the natural right to liberty.

Since both the principle of equal basic liberties and the difference principle are needed to protect liberty, they are morally on the same level. Nonetheless, Marxian Liberalism holds the first principle to be lexically prior to the second, for reasons related to those that Rawls gives for the priority of liberty. As we saw in Section 2.2, Rawls gives priority to liberty because he takes people to have a "higher-order interest in how their other interests are shaped and regulated by social institutions" (*TJ*, 475). For Marxian Liberalism, this higher-order interest takes the form of people's need for a genuinely democratic state to protect against the coercion in the property system, and to make sure that that economic system works to maximize everyone's liberty. The lexical priority of the first principle is not limited to only the political liberties (though they are to be

181

maintained in their fair value), but covers as well the liberties of personal life, freedom of conscience, freedom to choose one's life-style, and so on, because these are necessary if the people are to have a rich personal life, filled with varied experiences on the basis of which they can determine how best to guide their political and economic life.[24] That the third principle prohibits unwanted coercion not necessary for protecting the basic liberties and for implementing the difference principle entails that the first two principles are lexically prior to the third.

Accordingly, the parties in the Marxian-Liberal original position will agree to the following three principles of justice in lexical order:

1 Each person is to have an equal right to the most extensive total system of equal basic liberties compatible with a similar system of liberty for all, with the fair value of political liberties guaranteed, in a democratic state.
2 Economic inequalities will be governed by the lexical difference principle understood in terms of the moral version of the labor theory of value – with the proviso that workers can trade increases in their material standard of living in exchange for reduced labor-time compatible with efficient production.
3 All coercion not necessary for implementing the first and second principles (as well as this third one) is prohibited.

A final note: The argument presented here for the difference principle gives us a Marxian-Liberal definition of *exploitation*. Marx understood exploitation as the capitalist's appropriation of unpaid (surplus) labor. This is fine enough for a technical definition, but,

[24]Rawls's lexical prioritization of protecting basic liberties over maximizing the worst-off's share of goods depends on the society having reached a level of civilization at which "the basic liberties can be effectively established" (*TJ*, 132). Until a society has reached that level, basic liberties may be restricted to increase material well-being, though such restrictions are "granted only to the extent that they are necessary to prepare the way for the time when they are no longer justified" (*TJ*, 132). A similar condition applies to the lexical priority of the basic liberties in Marxian Liberalism.

as some writers have pointed out, it does not correspond to the normal use of the term exploitation which conveys, rather, the *unjust* appropriation of labor.[25] Marxian Liberalism defines exploitation (in normal economic transactions) as any greater-than-equal forced labor contribution that is not necessary for maximizing the laborer's material standard of living. This is unjust social subjugation. This definition entails that a capitalist system that conforms to the difference principle is not exploitative.

6.5 The Difference Principle as a Historical Principle of Justice

Marxian Liberalism understands the difference principle as a historical principle of justice. Its demands change as historical conditions change. One way this happens is the following: Marxian Liberalism understands the goods that workers receive back for their labor under the difference principle as material means to freedom, and it seeks via the difference principle to maximize that freedom. It is, however, implausible to think that freedom will increase endlessly with endlessly increasing shares of material goods. If so, then there must be a point after which additional material goods will no longer increase freedom. As this point is reached, rational workers will opt for cutting back on work rather than for getting more stuff, or they will work for the pleasure of it. The difference principle still holds, but – given the proviso permitting workers to trade increases in their share of goods for decreases in time labored – the principle is, so to speak, applied in reverse, that

---

[25]I was convinced of this by John Roemer; though I do not agree with Roemer that a Marxian understanding of exploitation can do without the notion of force. See John Roemer, "What Is Exploitation? Reply to Jeffrey Reiman," *Philosophy & Public Affairs* 18 (1989), 90–97; and Jeffrey Reiman, "Why Worry about How Exploitation Is Defined?: Reply to John Roemer," *Social Theory and Practice* 16, no. 1 (Spring 1990), 101–113.

is, toward reducing the amount of labor required to provide people with sufficient goods for real freedom.

A relative version of this is always at work. Workers must choose how much work is worth doing for the goods that they can earn with it. Even before workers have all the goods necessary to live freely, they may have enough of what is available to prefer leisure to additional work. This already accounts for the general reduction in labor-time over the course of the twentieth century from ten- or twelve-hour days, to eight-hour days and sometimes less.

But Marxian Liberalism expects that one day an absolute limit will be reached on the material goods that will increase freedom, though this limit itself may change as technology makes new things possible, and as people's conception of what choices are truly worth acting on change. Thus, the limit will surely be difficult, controversial and maybe impossible to identify. So, in practice, the difference principle will still call for maximizing shares of goods for the worst-off on up, and we will have to leave it to workers to choose between more goods or less work. (Something analogous will apply to the difference principle considered simply as a principle of distributive justice, as it is in Rawls's theory: When additional goods are no longer attractive – that third dishwasher, that eighth TV – inequalities will not be justified by piling more goods onto workers, and rational workers will take their additional benefits in leisure, or work because it pleased them to do so.) As long as workers can stop laboring at the point at which they have goods sufficient for genuine freedom, work they choose to do beyond this is not coerced.[26]

More generally, the difference principle provides for moving from the capitalist standard of distribution to Marx's socialist principle, and from there to Marx's communist principle, as human nature changes in history. These principles have been enunciated by Marx in *Critique of the Gotha Program*. There, Marx introduced two standards of distribution, one for the first phase of communism (later called "socialism") as it emerges after capitalism and one for the

---

[26]I take it as obvious that, even in the advanced nations of the world, the point has not been reached at which everyone has goods sufficient for genuine freedom.

184

second, or higher phase (later called "communism," as such) that emerges when productivity is so great that scarcity is, for all intents and purposes, overcome.

Marx's distributive standard for socialism is identical to what we identified earlier as the baseline of equal exchanges of labor-time. At this stage, Marx wrote, the laborer "receives a certificate from society that he has furnished such and such an amount of labour . . . , and with this certificate he draws from the social stock of means of consumption as much as costs the same amount of labour. The same amount of labour which he has given society in one form he receives back in another" (*MER*, 530). Marx's distributive standard for communism is the famous slogan, "From each according to his ability, to each according to his needs" (*MER*, 531).

The difference principle allows deviation from equal exchanges of labor-time, when incentives are needed to draw forth the more productive labor of the more talented members of society so as to maximize the share of the rest. Since the calculation of labor-time includes time spent training and developing one's talents, such incentives in effect reward people for their possession of greater-than-average natural abilities. I say "in effect" because people are rewarded, not merely for possessing greater talents, but for using them in ways that improve the shares of others. Nevertheless, since this amounts to unequal rewards for equal amounts of labor, its resultant effect is to bestow greater rewards on those who happen to have greater talents. For reasons outside of their control, those with lesser abilities have no chance to receive these greater rewards. Rawls recognizes that fortune in the distribution of natural abilities is arbitrary and thus inappropriate as a ground for greater reward (*TJ*, 89). This is what led him to require that the incentives work to the benefit of the rest of society, not just the more talented ones. Nevertheless, since fortune in the distribution of natural abilities is an arbitrary ground, allowing such incentives must still be viewed as a necessary accommodation to human nature as it is.

If the difference principle justifies this accommodation to human nature when it is (practically) necessary to maximize the share of the worst off, it follows that the accommodation is no longer justified when no longer (practically) necessary. If history brought us to a point at which either production were so efficiently organized that what everyone would do in exchange for an equal share were enough to maximize the share of the worst off, or people were so unselfish as not to want or need unequal incentives for more productive work, inequalities would no longer be necessary to maximize the share of the worst off, and thus would no longer be allowed under the difference principle. What would remain as the standard of just distribution would be equal exchanges of labortime, Marx's socialist principle, Cohen's utopian egalitarianism. It follows that, under the difference principle, the question of when economic justice requires the socialist principle is answered by determining if the conditions obtain in which incentives are no longer (practically) necessary to maximize the share of the worst off.

Much the same can be said of the question of when economic justice requires the communist principle. Marx's communist principle is a more perfect principle of equality than his socialist principle. The socialist principle countenances inequalities that the communist principle does not. Since the difference principle requires reducing inequalities down to that point necessary to maximize the share of the worst off, it leads to socialism when unequal incentives are no longer necessary, and it leads from socialism to communism when socialist inequalities are no longer necessary. This is hard to see because the socialist principle appears to be a perfectly egalitarian principle, while the communist principle no longer requires equal shares at all. This has led some commentators to take Marx's move from the socialist to the communist principle to reflect his abandonment of egalitarianism.[27] Marx's reasons for the move from

---

[27]Wood, for example, writes that Marx criticizes equal right "by showing how it necessarily leads to a defective mode of distribution even in its socialist form. To do away with these defects [Marx] says one must 'wholly transcend the narrow horizon of bourgeois right' represented by all principles of equality. Marx alludes to Louis Blanc's slogan 'from each according to his abilities, to each according to his needs' precisely *because this is not in any sense a principle of 'equality.'*" Allen Wood, "Marx on Right and Justice: A Reply to Husami," *Philosophy & Public Affairs* 8, no. 3 (Spring 1979), 292 (emphasis mine).

the socialist to the communist principle, however, indicate that the reverse is the case. Since misinterpretations of this move are common, it will repay us to quote Marx's explanation of it at length. Having stated the socialist principle of equal reward for equal time labored, Marx wrote:

> This *equal right* is still stigmatized by a bourgeois limitation. The right of the producers is *proportional* to the labour they supply; the equality consists in the fact that measurement is made with an *equal standard*, labour.
>
> But one man is superior to another physically or mentally and so supplies more labour in the same time, or can labour for a longer time; and labour, to serve as a measure, must be defined by its duration or intensity, otherwise it ceases to be a standard of measurement. This *equal* right is an unequal right for unequal labour. It recognizes no class differences, because everyone is only a worker like everyone else; but it tacitly recognizes unequal individual endowment and thus productive capacity as natural privileges. *It is, therefore, a right of inequality in its content, like every right.* Right by its very nature can consist only in the application of an equal standard; but unequal individuals (and they would not be different individuals if they were not unequal) are measurable only by an equal standard in so far as they are brought under an equal point of view, are taken from one *definite* side only, for instance, in the present case, are regarded *only as workers* and nothing more is seen in them, everything else being ignored. Further, one worker is married, another not; one has more children than another, and so on and so forth. Thus, with an equal performance of labour, and hence an equal share in the social consumption fund, one will in fact receive more than another, one will be richer than another, and so on. To avoid all these defects, right instead of being equal would have to be unequal (*MER*, 530-31).

It is probably this last statement that has led commentators to think that Marx's move from the socialist to the communist principle is a move away from egalitarianism. But this overlooks the nature of the defects in the socialist principle that the communist principle is meant to avoid. As the quote indicates, those defects are the inequalities that result from measuring naturally unequal (that is, differently endowed) people by an equal standard. Interestingly enough, those are the same sort of defects that led from unequal incentives to the socialist principle, namely, rewarding people more because of their greater natural endowments or, as Marx has it, allowing these endowments to function as "natural privileges." The communist principle avoids those defects because it makes each person his own standard: each person's productive contribution is measured against his own abilities ("From each according to his ability"), and his share in consumption is measured against his own needs ("to each according to his needs"). Compared to this, the socialist principle is still a principle that allows inequalities.

For Marx, it is the effective conquest of scarcity that allows transcendence of the socialist principle, with its defects, and movement to the communist: When "all the springs of cooperative wealth flow more abundantly – only then can . . . society inscribe on its banner: From each according to his ability, to each according to his needs!" (*MER*, 531).[28] The substantial overcoming of scarcity makes this possible because, with abundance, it is no longer necessary to force people to labor by making how much they consume depend on how much they labor.[29] Once it is no longer necessary to do this, it is no longer necessary to measure people's contributions and rewards by a common measure. This is why the final phase of communism, unlike the socialist phase, no longer needs a state. The interest of individual and group coincide, and no one needs to be forced to work for the common good. Once this is no longer necessary, it is

---

[28] The "effective conquest of scarcity" does not mean the total elimination of scarcity or, for that matter, of work. It means the reduction of scarcity to that point at which the desire to labor is itself sufficient to motivate whatever work remains necessary for the satisfaction of everyone's needs. Thus it coincides, for Marx, with the point at which "labour has become not only a means of life but life's prime want."

[29] For this reason, and in light of the fact that Marx is talking about a time when "labour has become . . . life's prime want," it is a mistake to think that Marx's communist slogan means that people will be required to work as much as they are able. In any event, it should not be understood this way in the context of Marxian Liberalism. See *RJE*, 208–209, 225, 407 n. 85 and accompanying text.

possible to avoid the inequalities that result from measuring differently endowed people by an equal standard. For this reason, I said earlier (in Chapter 1) that the difference principle ultimately *gives way* to the communist principle. The latter is hardly a distributive standard at all, and so it should not be thought of as a form of the difference principle. Instead, people are equal in that each person is his or her own standard. The result will be that people no longer stand in conflictual relationships, and their natural generosity can flourish. Then justice will coincide with the complete equality that was, until this point, only an ideal.

7

As Free and as Just as Possible
Capitalism for Marxists, Communism for Liberals

Parties in the Marxian-Liberal original position have a natural right to liberty, and an interest in exercising their liberty. They agree to a principle guaranteeing equal basic liberties, and requiring that the political liberties are maintained at fair value. They agree to a right to private property limited by the constraints of the difference principle understood in light of the moral version of the labor theory of value. And they agree to a third principle prohibiting unwanted coercion not necessary for implementing the principle guaranteeing basic liberties and the difference principle. The principle of basic liberties is lexically prior to the difference principle, because real democratic control of the state is necessary to make the economy function to maximize liberty overall. And these two principles are lexically prior to the third principle. The parties agree to a state with the limited function of realizing these three principles.

As Free and as Just as Possible: The Theory of Marxian Liberalism, First Edition. Jeffrey Reiman.
© 2014 Jeffrey Reiman. Published 2014 by John Wiley & Sons, Ltd.

In this chapter, I will sketch out the nature of the just society – the state and the economy – that Marxian Liberalism calls for in the current historical era. That state will be limited in its authority as a liberal state should be. The economy will be a form of capitalism with the least social subjugation necessary for maximizing the material conditions of freedom from the bottom of society on up. I will suggest how a society made up of such a state and a capitalist economy can be thought of as a form of capitalism acceptable to Marxists, and a form of communism acceptable to liberals. And I shall show that a society of the sort that Rawls calls "property-owning democracy" constitutes the ideal society – at least now and for the foreseeable future – for Marxian Liberalism. It is as free and as just as possible.

My argument in this chapter proceeds as follows: In Section 7.1, "The Just State," I sketch the nature of the limited state required by Marxian Liberalism. In Section 7.2, "Capitalism for Marxists," I show how a form of capitalism constrained by the difference principle could be acceptable to Marxists because it maximally achieves the material conditions of freedom, while reducing social subjugation to the minimum necessary to achieve that goal. In Section 7.3, "The Marxian-Liberal Ideal: Property-Owning Democracy," I turn to the form of society that Rawls recommended in his last writings, and show how it represents the ideal society for Marxian Liberalism. In Section 7.4, "Communism for Liberals," I revert to the earliest meaning that communism had for Marx and show how a Marxian-Liberal society would be a form of communism acceptable to liberals because it is a society controlled by free individuals and dedicated to maximizing individual liberty.

7.1 The Just State

A state would be chosen in the Marxian-Liberal original position because it is necessary to specify and enforce the rights to liberty and property. The just state must protect the basic liberties for all, it must assure that the economy works in conformity with the difference principle, and it must otherwise protect every sane adult's natural negative right to be free from unwanted coercion. The state and the economy are here distinguished by their functions, roughly, creating and maintaining the basic ground rules of social interaction for the former, and production and commerce for the latter. Marxian Liberalism does not accept the distinction between the political and economic realms that Marx attacked in his essay "On the Jewish Question" (*MER*, 26–52). That distinction is ideological because it suggests that while the state is coercive, the economy is not. For Marxian Liberalism, the economy must be governed by the difference principle precisely because it is a realm of coercion. For this reason, unlike Rawls's theory of justice, the principle guaranteeing basic liberties, the difference principle, and the principle prohibiting unwanted coercion not needed for implementing the first two princples are – in their lexical ordering – constitutional requirements to be enforced by the equivalent of a Supreme Court (see *PL*, 230).

The just state is limited in its activity to enforcing these three principles, and providing the conditions necessary to their functioning. Under the first principle, the just state will protect the basic liberties, and assure that the political liberties are maintained at their fair value. Under the second principle, the government will assure that distributive outcomes conform to the difference principle, and that the conditions for the effective functioning of the economy are in place. Under the third principle, it will outlaw coercion in its common forms not already prohibited by the first principle, such as overt violence, and fraud as well, since fraud functions like coercion to undermine choice. And it will prohibit laws against the so-called "victimless crimes." The third principle also requires that public policies with less coercion be favored over policies with more. Thus, it dictates that preference be given to private – that is, voluntary – solutions to public problems. Because racism and sexism are forms of structural coercion, they are in violation of the third principle. Thus, the government will combat them and other (perhaps as yet unidentified) "isms" that are structurally coercive as well.[1] For this reason (plus the provision for education of children mentioned below), the difference principle need not be associated with a principle of fair opportunity, as it is in Rawls's version. Systematic denial of opportunity is a form of structural coercion prohibited by the right to liberty.

Decisions about how the just state will satisfy these requirements will be made democratically – based on the principle of one person, one vote. That assures that all people have equal ability to determine their society's conduct, and thus their own conduct as members of that society. For Marxian Liberalism, democracy is the collective expression of each person's natural right to liberty. Since the principle guaranteeing basic liberties includes provision for maintaining the fair value of the political liberties, the just state will make sure that private property does not undermine people's equal rights to shape their society's decisions. Since collective decisions must be reached, people cannot in this respect simply act on their individual choices. However, collective decisions can respect each person's equal natural liberty by granting each an equal right to influence those decisions. That requires democracy, that is, majority rule, since majority rule gives each individual's vote the same weight. Requiring a two-thirds majority, for example, would give the votes

[1]Note that I here agree with Cohen that the principles of justice are not limited to the legally enforced aspects of the basic structure, because the basic structure includes informal practices, such as racism or sexism, that are themselves coercive (they are patterns of action that systematically and profoundly restrict women's and nonwhites' range of options). Cohen reaches this conclusion in two steps. First, he argues that sexism and racism are injustices that are sustained by informal social processes, not (at least not anymore) by legal coercion (*RJE*, 132–138). Then, he realizes that even those aspects of society that are legally coerced are so only because of the acquiescence of large numbers of people, which acquiescence is not coerced (*RJE*, 145–146). Thus the distinction between what is legally enforced and what is due to informal habits of behavior is blurred. Marxian Liberalism reaches this conclusion from the opposite direction. It starts from the dereified view of social structure that both Rawls and Marx shared, and thus makes no essential distinction between the way law functions and the way sexism or racism do. It notes, rather, that both are coercive, and thus both must be kept from violating liberty. On this issue, see also Section 2.2 and Section 5.5.

of those against a decision twice the weight of those for. Requiring such a supermajority for changes in the constitution is appropriate precisely because constitutional provisions are meant to be difficult to alter, which means that votes against change should have more weight than votes for change.

By protecting liberty for all and implementing the difference principle, the just state is an *egalitarian* state. The right to liberty is possessed equally by all, and the difference principle is egalitarian because it calls for the greatest degree of equality that can be had without making the worst-off people even worse off (see *TJ*, 68). Compared to simply leaving the economy to exchanges undertaken without threat of force or fraud, the difference principle is a principle of redistribution. That redistribution is necessary to make the coercion built into property ownership such that all can freely consent to it. It is not redistribution in the sense of taking from anyone what they were justly entitled to; it is redistribution to get people the shares to which they are justly entitled. Nonetheless, the government of the just state will be more active than the minimal "nightwatchman state" preferred by libertarians. For the following reasons, it is, nonetheless, still truly a *liberal* state.

There will be no morals legislation, no victimless crime laws and the like. Moreover, the state will engage in public projects necessary for protection of liberty and conformity to the difference principle only when these cannot be assured privately.[2] The only paternalism in which the just state will engage is where paternalism is appropriate, namely, in the treatment of children and the severely handicapped. Since children are unable to provide for themselves, and unable to decide how to use freedom, the state will have to assure that they receive the care and education needed to develop into adults who can provide for themselves and decide how to exercise their liberty. Here too, if such care and education can be provided privately, then it will be. Decent provision will be made for the

[2]For example, some part of people's shares in the distributive scheme might take the form of health services that would be provided by the state if that were the best way to provide them efficiently and reliably.

194

severely handicapped along similar lines, so that they can exercise their right to liberty as far as is feasible.

More deeply, however, the just state is a liberal state because the state itself and its laws, including those constraining the economy to conform to the difference principle, *exist only to protect and promote liberty*. This is the significance of the fact that Marxian Liberalism is based only on one moral principle, the natural right to liberty. The just state appears to be doing more than this because of the general invisibility of structural coercion. Since the just state both protects the right to liberty and limits social subjugation in the economic system to the minimum needed to maximize people's shares in the material conditions of freedom, it is *as free and as just as possible*.

7.2 Capitalism for Marxists

The parties in the original position recognize, as did Marx, that capitalism brings unprecedented increases in material productivity, and that this is the material condition of increasing workers' real power to act on their choices, and ultimately of reducing the amount of unwanted toil that workers must do. They recognize as well that, after presiding over effective if brutal transitions from agrarian to industrial production, socialism and communism bogged down and produced economies with low and stagnant levels of productivity compared to capitalism.

Moreover, the parties in the Marxian Liberal original position believe both that private property is necessary for individual freedom, and that capitalist societies have generally protected individual freedom more effectively and more consistently than socialist or communist societies. On Marxian grounds, they refuse to place the enormous power to control means of production in the hands of any trans-individual authority, such as the state. They believe that, whatever its problems, capitalism leads to relatively decentralized control of means of production owned by people who are competing with one another, and thus who have an interest in limiting the power of other owners. Likewise, these owners have an interest in limiting the power of the state to interfere in the market, and thus they tend to support a limited state. In short, the parties understand that capitalism's historical record of support for individual liberty – though far from unblemished – rests on firm grounds. It rests not on the good will of the powerful, but on material conditions that capitalism itself sustains and promotes.

At the same time, the parties understand that private ownership of property – especially means of production – is coercive. It forces those who do not own means of production to work for those who do, and thus it forces them to do the work desired by owners rather than the work they might themselves desire to do. Moreover, this coercion is expressed in authority relations on the job, such that workers are subject to the authority of managers who are themselves subject to the authority of owners. It is ironic that, for all their undeniable protection of liberty, modern-day capitalist economies are nonetheless ones in which the vast majority of people take orders most of their waking life.

In short, the parties see that capitalism is both liberating and coercive. Because of that they opt for the difference principle. Understood in terms of the moral version of the labor theory of value, the difference principle aims to reduce the coerciveness of capitalism – what I have called social subjugation – to the least amount necessary to maximize the share of the worst off, which is to say, to maximize the availability to workers of the material conditions of freedom.

Since social subjugation occurs where there are forced unequal exchanges of labor-time, this means that the difference principle will insist on reducing distributive inequalities to the smallest necessary to maximize the share of the worst-off group and on up. For the most part, those distributive inequalities are matters of workers' pay, since it is that that gives them access to the material conditions of freedom. As was already recognized, it is also a matter of decreasing the amount of required work, which is to say decreasing the length of the workday, and decreasing the amount of undesirable (hard, unpleasant, repetitive) work. However, there is no reason to stop there. Authority relations on the job are also matters of unequal liberty, unequal freedom to decide how to spend one's worktime

– which makes up, after all, a large part of one's lifetime. Thus the difference principle will aim as well at reducing inequalities of authority on the job. Here Marxian Liberalism's difference principle joins up with Rawls's version in addressing not only economic inequalities, but social inequalities as well. And that will take the form of encouraging both widespread ownership of means of production, and democratization of the workplace.

Crucial, however, is that all of these forms in which the reduction of inequalities will occur are subject to the requirement of not interfering with the ability of capitalism to maximize the material standard of living of the entire society from the bottom up. This (as we saw in Section 6.4) is of great importance because it provides for increasing the material conditions of freedom for all members of society. The result will be a form of capitalism that is as little unequal in every respect – in income distribution, in allotment of workplace authority, and in people's ownership of means of production – as is compatible with raising the material standard of living of the whole society.

This is a capitalism that is as equal as is compatible with realizing what Marx identified as one of the civilizing aspects of capitalism: "it enforces [the extraction of] surplus-labour in a manner and under conditions which are more advantageous to the development of the productive forces, social relations, and the creation of the elements for a new and higher form than under the preceding forms of slavery and serfdom" (C, III, 819). I take it that, in the face of what history teaches about socialism and communism, and in light of the Marxian theory of the conditions of freedom (discussed in Section 6.3), this is a form of capitalism that Marxists can accept because it as free and as just as possible.

7.3   The Marxian-Liberal Ideal: Property-Owning Democracy

In *Justice as Fairness: A Restatement*, Rawls's last written work, he compares a property-owning democracy to a system of welfare-state capitalism that looks very much like what Rawls saw around him in the United States (*JF*, 137–140). Rawls held that welfare-state capitalism does not satisfy either of his two principles of justice. It provides for a safety net for the poor, "a social minimum covering basic needs," but it does not subject economic distributions to a principle of reciprocal benefit like the difference principle (*JF*, 137–138). And, while it provides legally for liberties, it does not assure the fair value of political liberties. Welfare-state capitalism "permits very large inequalities in the ownership of real property (productive assets and natural resources) so that the control of the economy and much of political life rests in few hands" (*JF*, 138).

By contrast, "the background institutions of property-owning democracy work to disperse the ownership of wealth and capital, and thus to prevent a small part of society from controlling the economy, and indirectly, political life as well" (*JF*, 139). No such dispersal characterizes welfare-state capitalism. It "permits a small class to have a near monopoly of the means of production" (*JF*, 139). Property-owning democracy aims to avoid this concentration of economic power, not so much by redistributing income *after* it has been earned, "but rather by ensuring widespread ownership of productive assets and human capital (that is, education and trained skills) *at the beginning*. . . . The intent is not simply to assist those who lose out through accident or misfortune (although that must be done), but rather to put all citizens in a position to manage their own affairs on a footing of a suitable degree of social and economic equality" (*JF*, 139; emphasis added).

Accordingly, writes Martin O'Neill, a property-owning democracy would

> entail the wide dispersal of the ownership of means of production, with individual citizens controlling productive capital (and perhaps with an opportunity to control their own working conditions). . . . [It] would also involve the enactment of significant estate, inheritance and gift taxes, acting to limit the largest inequalities of wealth, espe-

cially from one generation to the next. . . . [And it] would seek to limit the effects of private and corporate wealth on politics, through campaign finance reform, public funding of political parties, and other measures to block the influence of wealth on politics (perhaps including publicly funded elections).[3]

As O'Neill points out, guaranteeing the fair value of the political liberties can be achieved in welfare-state capitalism, even if it is not in fact achieved in most of the existing instances. Welfare-state capitalism is, as numerous European examples show, compatible with public funding of election campaigns, and other guarantees aimed at reducing the influence of private wealth on political outcomes. Thus, O'Neill contends that what is distinctive about property-owning democracy is its commitment to wide dispersal of ownership of means of production. And he argues that this is necessary for satisfying the difference principle, when that principle is viewed as applying not only to economic inequalities, but to social inequalities, such as inequalities in authority, as well.[4] Only by dispersing ownership of productive assets widely can we assure that people will have access to positions of power and authority that merely receiving welfare payments cannot provide.

These considerations reveal that the tie between Marxian Liberalism and property-owning democracy is stronger than the tie between Rawls's theory of justice and property-owning democracy. To see this, consider what we might call the perfect form of property-owning democracy. That would in fact be property-owning democracy in the form in which James Meade, from whom Rawls borrowed the concept (*TJ*, 242n; *JF*, 135n), first thought of it, namely, as a system in which "the ownership of property [was] equally

[3]Martin O'Neill, "Liberty, Equality and Property-Owning Democracy," *Journal of Social Philosophy* 40, no. 3 (Fall 2009), 382.
[4]O'Neill, "Liberty, Equality and Property-Owning Democracy," 385.

distributed over all the citizens in the community."[5] Rawls recognizes that Marx might object to property-owning democracy because wide dispersion of ownership of means of production does not itself assure "democracy in the workplace." To which Rawls responds by pointing out that "Mill's idea of worker-managed firms is fully compatible with property-owning democracy" (*JF*, 178).

For the perfect form of property-owning democracy, then, let us go all the way and insist that, in it, all firms are managed democratically by their workers. After all, as Nien-hē Hsieh points out:

> If ownership of productive assets is distributed equally, it is likely that any given enterprise will be owned by a large number of shareholders, each with a relatively small share of ownership in relation to the market capitalization of the enterprise. Under such circumstances, the share of ownership for any one worker is unlikely to be great enough to grant her . . . effective control.[6]

Hsieh argues that the importance of wide distribution of productive assets is that it makes people "less dependent on [their] labor as a source of earnings." And he holds that this is not enough unless it means that "workers are not in relations of servitude" on the job.[7] That, he argues, means at least that there must be "changes to the decision-making procedure within economic enterprises . . . to protect workers fully against . . . arbitrary interference" by managers, and these changes "*might* include a right for

---

[5]James E. Meade, *Efficiency, Equality, and the Ownership of Property* (Cambridge, MA: Harvard University Press, 1965), 71; cited in Amit Ron, "Visions of Democracy in 'Property-Owning Democracy': Skelton to Rawls and Beyond," *History of Political Thought*, 29, no. 1 (Spring 2008), 181.

[6]Nien-hē Hsieh, "Justice at Work: Arguing for Property-Owning Democracy," *Journal of Social Philosophy* 40, no. 3 (Fall 2009), 402. Waheed Hussein agrees: "What matters . . . is changing how decisions are made in economic life, and it is not clear that expanding the class of owners in a managerial economy will have much effect in this regard." Waheed Hussein, "The Most Stable Just Regime," *Journal of Social Philosophy* 40, no. 3 (Fall 2009), 415,

[7]Hsieh, "Justice at Work," 403.

workers to participate in the management and governance of economic enterprises."[8]

In the perfect case, at least, these changes *must* include a right for workers to participate in managing and governing economic enterprises, since relations of authority on the job are also matters of liberty, and workers have an interest in maximizing liberty. This interest also includes minimizing social subjugation in the economy while taking advantage of capitalism's ability to maximize the material standard of living. *Marxian Liberalism, then, takes as its ideal, a form of perfect property-owning democracy that is a capitalist society in which ownership of means of production is distributed equally, and firms are managed democratically by their workers.* Assuming that its state meets the Marxian-Liberal conditions of the just state set out earlier in this chapter, this perfect property-owning democracy is ideal from the standpoint of Marxian Liberalism – at least for now and the foreseeable future – because it is a capitalist economy with the least possible amount of social subjugation. With everyone an owner of means of production, no one is simply forced to work for others.

---

[8]Hsieh, "Justice at Work," 408. Hussein suggests that democratic corporatism would work better than democracy in the workplace. By democratic corporatism, he understands an arrangement in which "there would be a number of encompassing associations in each industry or sector of the economy to officially represent the perspectives of capital and labor, and these associations [that is, their democratically selected representatives] would meet regularly to establish the parameters for competition between firms" (Hussein, "The Most Stable Just Regime," 414). Hussein is particularly concerned with stability, the tendency of a just social order to generate supportive attitudes, and he argues that democratic corporatism would do this better than political democracy itself, due to the small minority of people who actively participate in electoral politics (Hussein, "The Most Stable Just Regime," 421–422); and he suggests (without quite arguing) that industry-wide democracy would do better than firm-wide democracy to foster interest in the justice of the social order as a whole (Hussein, "The Most Stable Just Regime," 422, 423, 428). This strikes me as an empirical matter. Firm-wide democracy would raise issues closer to the daily concerns of workers and thus attract more active participation on narrower issues than democratic corporatism. Democratic corporatism would address wider issues but might draw less active participation. In my view, we lack the data and historical experience to decide this issue.

And with every worker a democratic manager, no one is subjected to the unequal authority of others on the job.

For Marxian Liberalism, perfect property-owning democracy is the ideal of a society that most fully honors the natural right to liberty while satisfying the difference principle's requirement of minimizing social subjugation (understood as forced unequal exchanges of labor) while maximizing the material standard of living (understood as providing all members of society with the maximum share of the material means of freedom from the worst-off people on up). That is, if we held on to capitalism for its productivity, while minimizing social subjugation, we could do so by distributing the ownership of means of production equally to all members of society, and authority in the workplace to all workers. In such a society, everyone would be a capitalist. No one would be forced to work for others, since each would already own as much of the means of production as everyone else.[9]

However, Marxian Liberalism insists that a social system conform to the difference principle. And that requires that it maximize productivity so as to maximize people's access to the material conditions of freedom. The equalization of capitalism that property-owning democracy promises is only acceptable to Marxian Liberalism *as long as it is compatible with capitalism's ability to maximize productivity*. If it is, we would have the least possible forced unequal labor exchanges, and thus the least possible social subjugation, along with capitalism's maximization of the material conditions of freedom. It would be as free and as just as possible. Having not been tried, however, we do not know if this much equality is compatible with the ongoing maximization of the material conditions of freedom. For this reason, ideal property-owning democracy is an ideal for Marxian Liberalism in another way. It is

---

[9] It should be obvious that I am here sketching only the outlines of this sort of society, the details of which would have to be further worked out. For example, as capitalists, workers might lose the wealth they own, and some provision would have to be made for this, without eliminating the risks that give owners an interest in efficiently using their productive assets, along with the possible gains that give owners an interest in innovation.

a *regulative ideal* in the way that systematicness was a regulative ideal of science for Kant. It is the model of the society we should aim at, pushing as close to it as we can without compromising capitalism's ability to increase productivity.

In *The Critique of Pure Reason*, Kant contends that "reason quite uniquely prescribes and seeks to bring about concerning [our understanding] the systematic in cognition. . . . Accordingly, this idea postulates the complete unity of the understanding's cognition, through which this cognition comes to be not merely a contingent aggregate but a system cohering in accordance with necessary laws."[10] Kant takes this regulative idea to give rise to three principles of systemization, "the principles of *homogeneity, specification,* and *continuity*."[11] *Homogeneity* requires us to look for a single fundamental power underlying natural phenomena (as Einstein sought a unified field theory to account for both relativity theory and quantum mechanics, and modern-day physicists look for a unitary explanation of the variety of subatomic particles and forces), *specification* requires us to "bring our specific concepts ever closer to the full particularity of individual natural objects" (as modern-day ethologists strive to bring scientific explanations in line with the full diversity of species and subspecies), and *continuity* requires us to "strive to construct a continuum of concepts between the lowest- and the highest-order concepts . . . which will bring ever more order into our science" (in line with the scientific motto: *Natura non facit saltum*: Nature makes no leaps).[12]

Kant takes these to be regulative requirements on our judgment, not principles of objective knowledge. That "nature makes no leaps" does not assure us that there are no leaps in nature. It counsels us to keep looking for continuity when gaps appear. These requirements govern what scientists are to look for in nature; but only what

[10]Immanuel Kant, *The Critique of Pure Reason*, trans. Paul Guyer and Alan Wood (Cambridge: Cambridge University Press, 1998), A645, B673.
[11]Kant, *Critique of Pure Reason*, A658, B686.
[12]Paul Guyer, "Kant's Principles of Reflecting Judgment," in Paul Guyer, ed., *Kant's Critique of the Power of Judgment: Critical Essays* (Lanham, MD: Rowman and Littlefield, 2003), 7.

scientists find there is knowledge. Though Kant holds that we must seek this systematicness, and we must therefore believe that it is possible, we cannot really expect to achieve it completely. In short, a Kantian regulative idea holds out an ideal goal that we believe is possible even though we can at best approach it asymptotically,[13] *"as far as possible,"* says Kant.[14]

For our purposes, it is not necessary to be quite so pessimistic. Perhaps Marxian Liberalism's ideal of perfect property-owning democracy is possible. Perhaps it is possible to equalize ownership of means of production and authority in the workplace without sacrificing capitalism's ability to maximize material productivity. What is important for us is that this is the target, something a Marxian Liberal must aim for. How far it can be achieved can only be determined in practice.

7.4 Communism for Liberals

In his early writings, Marx took the notion of alienation as central to his analysis of capitalism. Marx derived his notion of alienation from Hegel's philosophy of knowledge. Following Kant, Hegel held that the secret to knowledge was that the conscious mind determined the nature of its objects. Since, in ordinary experience, it seems that the nature of objects is determined outside of mind, it is necessary to account for this illusion. For Hegel, this account took the form of attributing to the mind the tendency to project its concepts outward, so that it seems to confront objects at a distance from it, which it must come to know. Though Hegel used various terms for this projection (e.g., externalization, estrangement), its core is *alienation*, a making foreign of what is essentially one's own. In the *Phenomenology of Spirit*, Hegel tried to show that the mind determined the nature of its objects and alienated them from itself, suffered pains of doubt and skepticism because the seeming foreignness

[13]Guyer, "Kant's Principles of Reflecting Judgment," 4.
[14]Kant, *Critique of Pure Reason*, A665–666, B693–694; emphasis in the original.

of those objects made them appear out of reach of certain knowledge, and then in time learned to recognize those objects as its *own*.[15] Mind that finally has this recognition Hegel called "Spirit," which is more like *shared human culture* than like private individual subjectivity. This doctrine is called *absolute idealism*.

Among Hegel's followers, Ludwig Feuerbach tried to formulate a materialist alternative to Hegel's idealism. Most importantly, he took the notion of alienation and applied it critically to religion. In *The Essence of Christianity*, he contended that God was a product of human beings' self-alienation.[16] We create God by investing our idea of Him with the perfect form of all our own traits; then, failing to recognize that God is our own creation, He appears other than and distant from us. We then think of ourselves as weak and miserable pawns of a being that, in fact, embodies our own powers and virtues. Feuerbach's view of Christianity was enormously influential in nineteenth-century Europe. Marx's view of Hegel and of society was deeply influenced by it.

Marx generalized Feuerbach's critique of religion into a critique of all existing social institutions. Not only God and the Church, but the state and the law, as well as the wealth and property of capitalists, were produced by self-alienating human beings who lost sight of their creative role. Wealth and property are directly created by human laborers; and religion, state, law, and the rest, have power only because people treat them as having power. This is, as I have argued earlier, what is seen from Marx's dereified view of social reality. Instead of being masters, however, the vast majority of human beings are pawns of the social powers that they create. Moreover, Marx tried to develop a more sophisticated materialism than Feuerbach's, emphasizing, not merely material objects, but embodied practical activity in the physical world. Thus he

---

[15] Georg Wilhelm Friedrich Hegel, *The Phenomenology of Spirit* (Oxford: Oxford University Press, 1979; originally published 1807).
[16] Ludwig Feuerbach, *The Essence of Christianity* (New York: Harper, 1957; originally published 1841).

understood the process by which these alienated powers were created as a material process, a matter of labor not merely of knowledge: "The more man puts into God, the less he retains in himself. The worker puts his life into the object; but now his life no longer belongs to him but to the object."[17]

Against this backdrop, we can understand something that at first seems very puzzling in Marx's *Economic and Philosophical Manuscripts of 1844*. There Marx tells us that alienated labor is the source of the workers' oppression. Since he alienates his labor from himself, it must belong to someone else. By alienating his labor, the worker creates the capitalist: "Through *estranged, alienated labour*, then, the worker . . . engenders the relation to it of the capitalist."[18]

This seems backwards. It seems that, by privately owning the means of production, capitalists cause the workers' oppression, taking labor from them in the form of products and wealth, giving them back only enough to subsist on until the next day on the job. Based on Hegel and Feuerbach, Marx saw the workers as the agents of history, albeit creating society in alienated form and thus not realizing that it was their own creation: "though private property appears to be . . . the cause of alienated labour, it is really the consequence."[19] Since the workers create the social system that oppresses them by their labor and their cooperation, Marx believed they would eventually realize this, see in it their enormous power, and then take back as their own what they had created in alienated form.

Marx's view of the process of workers taking back the alienated powers they created and making them their own powers was modeled on Hegel's absolute idealism, transposed from the theory of knowledge to the realm of economics. It was as laborers – rather than as knowers – that human beings created the powers that dominated them, and it was as laborers that they had to take those

[17] Karl Marx, *The Economic and Philosophical Manuscripts of 1844* (Mineola, NY: Dover, 2007), 70.

[18] Marx, *Economic and Philosophical Manuscripts*, 79–80.

[19] Marx, *Economic and Philosophical Manuscripts*, 80.

powers back. Where Hegel's absolute idealism saw human minds gradually recognizing that they determined the nature of the world and, thus, making it their own, Marx saw human workers gradually recognizing that they created the world of material objects and social powers and, thus, making it their own, their common possession. Before being a form of society, then, *communism* was, for Marx, the material version of what absolute idealism was mentally – *the reappropriation by human beings of the world that they created in alienated form.*

Thus, Marx (and Engels) wrote in *The German Ideology*: "Communism is for us not a *state of affairs* which is to be established, an *ideal* to which reality [will] have to adjust itself. We call communism the *real* movement which abolishes the present state of things" (*MER*, 162). Marx is speaking here from his dereified view of society and its institutions. Rather than seeing institutions (laws, rights, markets, police, and so on) as hard fixed realities, Marx saw them as created by the activity of the vast majority of the society, and he saw that these institutions have power by the virtue of the fact that the vast majority of the society cooperates with them. If the vast majority of people stopped respecting the right of capitalists to own property, if the vast majority stopped respecting the rights of the courts to enforce laws, neither property nor law would exist. Thus the movement of history that Marx is here calling communism is the movement from a social world unknowingly created by all members of society to one in which all members of society recognize that the institutions of society are their ongoing creation – which, therefore, must rightly be judged by its service to those members. Thus, anticipating communism in *Capital*, Marx wrote: "The life-process of society, which is based on the process of material production, does not strip off its mystical veil until it is treated as production by freely associated men" (*C, I, 80*).

The form of capitalism and of the state that I have described in the sections prior to this one, and especially the ideal of perfect property-owning democracy, are compatible with the idea of seeing the whole society – the whole life-process of society, not just the process of economic production – as the ongoing creation of

207

freely associated people. This means that political and economic institutions would not be seen as rigid and unchangeable, but as continually created by the cooperation of all members of the society. People would see at all times that those institutions were valid only insofar as people continued to have good reason to create them. They are not valid because God-given, or because constitutionally prescribed. They are not valid because they match some preexisting right to property, though, for Marxian Liberalism, they must conform to a preexisting natural right of all to liberty.

I contend that any form of political and economic arrangement that the people could all see and treat as their joint creation would count as communism. Communism need not be thought of as a specific political or economic arrangement, "not a state of affairs to be established." What counts is that the people freely and knowingly create together the institutions that surround them. Then, the people would together truly and practically *own* those institutions.

Moreover, seeing that institutions that benefited them and treated them fairly and respectfully were being created by everyone for everyone else, their society could become a real community. Not an ethnically identified community, but a social life in which people constantly saw that their well-being was being served justly by the creative and cooperative activities of their fellows. Seeing our social arrangements as forms of human cooperation amounts to seeing them in a dereified way, that is, as continually created by the cooperative actions of all members of our society. It leads us to want to reciprocate, and to develop bonds of affection with them, as a result of moral psychological processes described by Rawls (*TJ*, 429–434). For example, Rawls holds that, for a person brought up in a normal loving family, "given that a social arrangement is just and publicly known by all to be just, then this person develops ties of friendly feeling and trust toward others in the association as they with evident intention comply with their duties and obligations" (*TJ*, 429). The result is a genuine affective community. As a genuine affective community of people truly and practically owning their social institutions, this would be a true communism.

If, then, people could all recognize that they were creating a state that protected their right to liberty and a capitalist economy that maximized their possession of the material conditions of freedom; if they could recognize this as their own free and rational creation aimed at their continuing and growing liberty; that would be a form of communism. And because it maximized liberty both by reducing social subjugation to a minimum and reducing material subjugation, it would be a form of communism that liberals could accept. It would be as free and as just as possible.

Conclusion
Marx's "Liberalism," Rawls's "Labor Theory of Justice"

With the full statement of Marxian Liberalism before us, it is worth pausing to ask what this merging of seemingly opposed doctrines tells us about those doctrines themselves, particularly as they have been formulated by Marx and Rawls. What is it about Marxism as it emerges in Marx's writings that makes it possible to join it to liberalism? What is it about liberalism as it emerges in Rawls's writing that makes it possible to join it to Marxism? Parts of the answers to these questions have already been stated in previous chapters. Here in the conclusion, I will try to bring those statements together and supplement them with more general observations that, I hope, will give the reader a fuller sense of Marxian Liberalism's ancestry.

Traditional liberalism, defended by John Stuart Mill in his classic *On Liberty*, effectively defines freedom as the absence of overt violence. This makes it, for Marx, an ideological notion. It hides the subtler structural coercion that occurs without the need for overt

As Free and as Just as Possible: The Theory of Marxian Liberalism, First Edition. Jeffrey Reiman.
© 2014 Jeffrey Reiman. Published 2014 by John Wiley & Sons, Ltd.

violence. We saw Marx recognize this, for example, when he announced both that the realm of exchange is a Garden of Eden of the rights of man, where freedom rules "because both buyer and seller of a commodity, say of labour-power, are constrained only by their free will" (C, I, 176), and that the worker "is compelled to sell himself of his own free will" (C, I, 766). That the worker's sale of his labor-power is free according to traditional liberalism's conception of freedom – the worker is not threatened with overt violence if he does not accept the capitalist's terms – hides the compulsion at work in that free sale. The effect for Marx is that capitalism is a system of "forced labour – no matter how much it may seem to result from free contractual agreement" (C, III, 819).

Note the two-edged nature of this statement. Yes, traditional liberalism's definition of freedom works ideologically to hide the coerciveness of capitalism. But ideology works to hide the ways a society goes wrong. What makes the coerciveness of capitalism bad, in need of an ideological mask? Marx's condemnation of capitalism for being coercive, while seeming free, is based on the notion that freedom is good and coercion bad. Thus, while traditional liberalism's definition of freedom works ideologically, Marx's pointing this out as part of a condemnation of capitalism's coerciveness is based on sharing traditional liberalism's insistence on the value of freedom. This freedom is individual freedom, because it is as individuals that workers are compelled to sell themselves of their own free will (even if it is as members of a class that they must set themselves free).

And so, it should not surprise us that, in his writings, Marx explicitly endorsed the individual freedom upon which traditional liberalism insists, even as he condemned liberalism's narrow way of defining freedom. We saw both these features – the endorsement of individual freedom and the need to broaden the definition of its nature and conditions – in Marx's (and Engel's) assertion in *The German Ideology* that "Only in community [with others has each] individual the means of cultivating his gifts in all directions; only in the community, therefore, is personal freedom possible" (*MER*, 197). And we saw as well, in Marx's essay "On the Jewish

Question," his recognition of the value of liberal individual rights alongside his critique of their limits (*MER*, 35, 40–44).

Marx was, then, a defender of individual freedom who discovered in the coerciveness of private property a new threat against which that freedom must be defended, and who discovered as well the need to broaden the definition of freedom to see more clearly what must be done to make it a reality. This is what I mean by Marx's "liberalism." I put it in quotation marks because it is surely not a label he would apply to himself.

In his early statements about morality, Marx endorsed a Kantian liberalism.[1] He emphasized the crucial importance of individual autonomy, freedom as self-legislation, rather than merely freedom as doing what one happens to desire. Marx's Kantian liberalism was transformed into Hegelian liberalism as a result of his early and profound encounter with Hegel's philosophy. Hegel adopted and transformed the Kantian notion of freedom as autonomy. In particular, Hegel filled out the idea of autonomy to encompass both rational self-legislation and identification with one's desires, thus making Kant's abstract notion of freedom more concrete and bringing it closer to experience. Hegel went on to argue that human history was the history of the coming into real, concrete, institutional existence of the idea of freedom.

Marx was deeply impressed by Hegel's account of history, but disappointed as well. Marx looked for the inevitably advancing individual liberty that Hegel argued characterized human history, especially in modernity. But he could not find it. Instead, Marx saw the vast majority of people living as workers subject to the harsh conditions of nineteenth-century capitalism. Most of their waking life was spent taking orders, and doing work that drained and

---

[1]See, for example, Marx's "Comments on the Latest Prussian Censorship Instruction," and "Religion, Free Press, and Philosophy," in L. D. Easton and K. H. Guddat, eds., *Writings of the Young Marx on Philosophy and Society* (Garden City, NY: Doubleday Anchor, 1967), 67–92, 109–130; and "Capital Punishment," in L. S, Feuer, ed., *Marx and Engels: Basic Writings on Politics and Philosophy* (Garden City, NY: Doubleday Anchor, 1959), 487.

weakened them. Their leisure time, what little there was of it, was spent recuperating from work or hiding from it in alcohol. When Marx called religion the opiate of the people, he was not thinking of opium as a recreational drug, but as a painkiller.

Marx's projection of a cure for the workers' miserable unfreedom was communism understood as workers taking control of the economic world that they created and making it their own. He saw this as a matter of free control of the workplace and of the economy as a whole. He wanted the "life-process of society, which is based on the process of material production" to be "treated as production by freely associated men, and . . . consciously regulated by them in accordance with a settled plan" (C, I, 80). Marx was confident that, without capitalism to set worker against worker in competition for jobs, workers would live and work according to conditions to which they freely agreed. Though Marx saw the economic liberalism of his time as ideological, there is here, in his view of the solution to capitalism's ills, the germ of a concrete liberalism – that is to say, a portrait of a society designed to make individual liberty real by giving workers real control over the economy that heretofore treated them as slaves. One can see Marx's belief in democracy, and even a foreshadowing of the original position, in Marx's confidence in the ability of "freely associated men" to regulate their productive activities in a mutually reasonable – and thus just – manner.

There are, then, in Marx the elements that could develop into Marxian Liberalism. There is the valuing of individual freedom versus coercion, the preference for democracy, and even a foreshadowing of the original position. Of course, to Marx's disappointment with nineteenth-century capitalism as a basis for genuine individual freedom, Marxian Liberalism adds the unhappy history of socialism and communism in the twentieth century. But, in so doing, Marxian Liberalism carries forth Marx's attempt to ground a concrete liberalism.

But what of Rawls? How is it possible to join Rawls's liberal theory of justice to Marxism? Though there are in Rawls also the elements that could develop into Marxian Liberalism, Rawls was not a closet Marxian Liberal anymore than Marx was. Rather, just as Marx saw his Marxism in ways that overlapped with the deep value commitments of liberalism, so Rawls recognized his own liberalism in terms that overlap with beliefs that are crucial to Marxism.

Chief among these is Rawls's dereified view of society, a view that he shared with Marx. Marx wrote, "capital is not a thing, but a social relation between persons" (*C*, I, 766). And Rawls wrote, "The social system is not an unchangeable order beyond human control but a pattern of human action" (*TJ*, 88). Both saw that social systems – the state, the economy, and so on – were just people acting in certain regular ways. And this plays a crucial role in Rawls's theory. It leads to his seeing justice as a matter of the mutual reasonableness of institutions – understood as patterns of human behavior – to the people whose behavior constituted those institutions. This in turn led Rawls to see economic justice as a matter not simply of the allocation of goods, but more importantly as a matter of mutually reasonable terms of cooperation. For example, when Rawls defends the difference principle, he writes that "the more advantaged, when they view the matter from a general perspective, recognize that the well-being of each depends on a scheme of social cooperation without which no one could have a satisfactory life; they recognize also that they can expect the willing cooperation of all only if the terms of the scheme are reasonable" (*TJ*, 88).

Economic justice is not in the first instance about the distribution of goods. It is about the mutual reasonableness to the cooperators of the terms of their cooperation. It is about, as Marx, said, "a social relation between persons." Both Rawls and Marx seem to have learned from Kant that property ownership is not a relation of a person to a thing, but "a relation of a person to persons" (*MM*, 55). This applies as much to freedom as to property. "Whether men are free," wrote Rawls, "is determined by the rights and duties established by the major institutions of society. Liberty is a certain pattern of social forms" (*TJ*, 55–56). What Rawls said about the social system being a pattern of human actions, applies as well to social forms. This means that rights and duties, and liberty itself, are relations between persons. They are products of their ongoing cooperation.

Then, since rights and duties, liberty and property, are the substance of justice, it follows that justice is a matter of the mutual reasonableness to the cooperators of the terms of the cooperation that produces their rights and the material means to exercise them.

Rawls recognized this. Rawls explicitly distanced himself from an allocative notion of justice, in which justice is a matter of simply allocating a stock of benefits, be they rights or liberties or goods. He held, instead, that his "justice as fairness" aspires to a kind of "pure procedural justice," in which, not merely the shares with which people end up matter, but more importantly what people have done to produce the benefits to be distributed. Writes Rawls, "in this kind of procedural justice the correctness of the distribution is founded on the justice of the scheme of cooperation from which it arises and on answering the claims of the individuals engaged in it. A distribution cannot be judged in isolation from the system of which it is the outcome or from what individuals have done in good faith in light of established expectations" (*TJ*, 76).

Moreover, like Marx, Rawls sees that, since social arrangements are simply patterns of human behavior, they can be mechanisms by which individuals coerce their fellows. Thus, Rawls writes that "unjust social arrangements are themselves a kind of extortion, even violence" (*TJ*, 302). This extortion and violence are built into the social arrangements themselves and thus can exist without resort to overt force. Though he does not speak of it in those terms, Rawls sees, as Marx does, the possibility of structural coercion.

Rawls's theory of justice is, then, a theory of the mutual reasonableness of the scheme of cooperation that produces a social system. It calls upon us to own up to our actions that do this and make sure that they are fair in the sense that they would be reasonable for all to accept them. The original position, then, is a bit like Marx's projection of a future in which society is openly created by the freely associated producers. Where Marx calls upon us to project that future and compare the present to it, Rawls calls upon us to imagine people openly deciding on the principles to govern the society that their cooperation will produce, and to compare the present to that. In both these ideas we can see descendants of Kant's notion of the *kingdom of ends* – a just society whose rules are agreed to unanimously by people who treat one another as free and independent beings of intrinsic value – a notion which both Marx and Rawls knew well.

In Marx implicitly, and Rawls explicitly, the standard of justice is the mutual reasonableness of the scheme of cooperation by which people produce their society. How, then, do we determine the mutual reasonableness of a scheme of cooperation? A scheme of cooperation is an ongoing exchange of "operations," that is, of actions, of doing things from which others benefit in some way (including doing nothing when one might prefer to do something). Thus, to determine if the scheme of cooperation is mutually reasonable to the cooperators, we need a measure of cooperation, that is, a measure of the actions which each does that benefit others. Such a measure cannot assume the validity of any system of ownership, since systems of ownership are themselves schemes of cooperation in need of being tested for their mutual reasonableness. Then, we must measure the actions that each contributes in the scheme of cooperation in terms of the time and energy they expend, since that is what any individual's action costs that individual in any social system.

But time and energy are the substance of labor. Thus, if we broaden our notion of labor, stretch it beyond the workplace to refer to all the ways in which we work to make a society together, justice is a matter of what it is reasonable for each to give in terms of labor for the benefits he or she receives from the labors of others. This is not to say that Rawls implicitly accepts Marx's labor theory of value. What he accepts, at least implicitly, is a *labor theory of the moral value of justice*. I call this Rawls's "labor theory of justice," put in quotation marks for the same reason as was Marx's "liberalism."

In this book, I have argued that thinking of economic distributions as distributions of labor enables a stronger defense of the difference principle than Rawls was able to give. I have argued that these considerations lead to a deduction of the difference principle that Rawls hoped for but did not achieve. And I have argued that Marxian Liberalism gives a stronger defense of property-owning democracy than Rawls did. Could it be that these are the results of making explicit and working out the implications of the labor theory of justice that was implicit in Rawls's work?

Instead of answering this question, I offer an example of how looking at Rawls's theory as a labor theory of justice illuminates an aspect of his theory that has often been the object of criticism. Numerous philosophers have objected to *A Theory of Justice* because, to them, Rawls seems to ignore people's desert – by which I here mean strictly their economic desert (not, for example, desert of punishment, which, for reasons mentioned below, is quite a different matter). These philosophers have argued that in submitting the question of economic rewards to what people would agree to in the original position – ignorant of what they may have done to deserve (or not to deserve) some reward – Rawls has disregarded the natural way in which people's desert attaches to their actions and abilities. He has treated this as derivative from the rules of good institutions – that is, the institutions that would be chosen in the original position – when he should have first figured out what people deserve and then designed institutions to match those deserts.

Rawls seems to deny that people who exert efforts in an economic system do already, naturally, deserve something for their efforts. For example, George Sher writes:

> In his major work, *A Theory of Justice*, Rawls argues that desert of reward or recompense are . . . artifacts of social institutions which are in turn justified in quite different ways. Instead of imposing constraints upon our choice of social institutions, personal desert is only established within and by such institutions.[2]

Sher goes on to criticize this, writing: "If desert-claims do reflect only the demands of institutions . . . , persons . . . will not deserve

---

[2]George Sher, *Desert* (Princeton: Princeton University Press, 1987), 14. Sher applies his criticism to both economic desert and desert of punishment, which I think, for reasons that I will state presently, are quite different matters. Accordingly, I set aside Sher's objection regarding desert of punishment.

wages that are not dictated by our economic system." And, further, "if desert *is* determined by the demands of institutions, then it will be unintelligible to criticize institutions on the grounds that they themselves are insensitive to desert."[3] These assertions do make Rawls's approach to economic desert seem counterintuitive, but the notion that his theory is a labor theory of justice shows how what Rawls is doing is appropriate after all.

The response to the objection is a simple, but easily overlooked point, namely, that what one person deserves as an economic reward for his services *is produced by the labor of others*. Thus, the determination of just economic rewards is derivative from the justice of economic institutions in the sense that it depends on first determining what constitutes just recompense for goods and services in an economy. This is one crucial way in which economic desert is different from desert of punishment. The fairness of a punishment given to a criminal is not a matter of exchanging the labor that goes into punishing for the labor the criminal put into his crime. In this sense, desert of punishment may have a natural – noninstitutional – basis that economic desert cannot have.

But there is a deeper theoretical point worth noting here. Viewing Rawls's theory as a labor theory of justice enables us to see that economic desert is not just a matter of goods, but – as Marx said of capitalism, and Kant said of property – *a social relation between persons*. It is a matter of the proportions in which people should work for one another. And thus it must be mutually reasonable to all concerned. Thus no argument for a natural noninstitutional economic desert can be satisfactory.

Finally, some may oppose the joining of Rawls's and Marx's views because they take Marx's ideal for society to be more of a communal ideal than an ideal of justice. Some elements of the reply to this objection were given in Section 2.4 and Section 2.5; and other elements were given at the end of Chapter 7. But I also think that viewing Rawls as putting forth a labor theory of justice enables us

---

[3]Sher, *Desert*, 15.

to understand in a deep way the kind of community that a society governed by Rawlsian principles would be.

A labor theory of justice is based on seeing the society as the ongoing product of its members' efforts. If society is just because modeled on a labor theory of justice, and if its citizens know this, then we can expect this to lead them to generalized affection for their fellow citizens. People would see that the justice from which they benefited was created, not by buildings or law books, but by the ongoing cooperative actions of their fellows. Seeing this would naturally prompt gratitude. That gratitude would naturally lead to affection.

Rawls holds that, when the principles of justice "are satisfied, each person's basic liberties are secured and there is a sense defined by the difference principle in which everyone is benefited by social cooperation. Therefore we can explain the acceptance of the social system and the principles it satisfies by the psychological law that persons tend to love, cherish, and support whatever affirms their own good" (*TJ*, 154–155). But, since the social system is just a pattern of action, it is the people themselves whose cooperation produces that social system who will be loved, cherished, and supported.

Such friendly feeling would make of the just society a community. By this, I do not mean a community in the sense of one sharing a specific conception of the good life, which Rawls held to be an inappropriate model for the modern democratic state.[4] I mean, rather, a community characterized, as Rawls says, by "civic friendship" (*TJ*, 470), an *affective* community.

Since such a society would be one in which all people saw themselves as producing their society together, they would be like those freely associated producers whose knowledge Marx thought would

---

[4]Rawls writes: "justice as fairness does indeed abandon the ideal of political community if by that ideal is meant a political society united on one (partially or fully) comprehensive religious, philosophical, or moral doctrine. That conception of social unity is excluded by the fact of reasonable pluralism" (*JF*, 198–199). Jürgen Habermas essentially agrees with Rawls on this point. See Jürgen Habermas, *Between Facts and Norms: Contributions to a Discourse Theory of Law and Democracy* (Cambridge, MA: MIT Press, 1996), 278–279.

strip away the veil of ideology. Such a society would equally be like one whose members had, so to speak, one foot in the shared real world, and one foot in the imaginary original position from which they determined together the nature of their interaction. This then is what Marxian Liberals hope for: a capitalism that Marxists can accept because in it freely associated producers maximally produce the material conditions of freedom for one another, a communism that liberals can accept because it is recognized as truly and effectively their own by all members, a society that is as free and as just as possible, in which all citizens can feel friendship and affection for their fellows, even those whose names they do not know.

Index

As Free and as Just as Possible: The Theory of Marxian Liberalism, First Edition. Jeffrey Reiman.
© 2014 Jeffrey Reiman. Published 2014 by John Wiley & Sons, Ltd.

Index

Blanc, Louis 186 n. 27
Buddhism 86

campaign finance reform 199
Capital (Marx) xi, 16, 57, 176
capitalism
  acceptable to Marxists 191,
    195–197, 220
  adoption by free people 16
  adoption by People's Republic
    of China 19, 20
  and alienation 21, 59, 204
  and coercion 23, 31–32, 37, 38,
    111, 119–121, 196, 211
  and decentralized ownership
    of property 15, 16, 174, 175,
    195
  and extraction of surplus labor
    197
  and freedom/liberty xi, xii,
    15–16, 21, 23, 196
  and human nature 157
  and inequality 151
  and justice 56, 60, 66, 157, 186
  and liberalism 14
  and Marxian Liberalism 5–6,
    21–22, 56–57, 175–177, 191
  and Nozick's version of the
    Lockean proviso 101
  and ownership of means of
    production xii, 5–6, 13, 15,
    16
  and power xi, 198
  and productivity xi, 17, 18, 21,
    65, 150, 156, 175, 176, 177,
    195, 202, 204
  and property-owning democracy
    207
  and rights xii, 52–53

  and self-interest 151
  and standard of living xi, 17–20,
    197, 201
  and surplus labor 197
  and the difference principle 23,
    157, 183, 196
  and the state 173 n. 20, 175 n.
    21, 196
  as liberating xi, 196
  as system of exploitation 53
  as system of forced labor 30, 31,
    55, 111, 112, 210
  as system of free exchanges
    120
  definition 22
  dissolution of feudalism by xi
  ideology of 37, 39
  invisibility of structural
    coercion in 24, 112, 121,
    161, 162
  libertarian defenses of 24,
    100–102, 106–111
  Marx's condemnations of xi, 59,
    112, 211
  Marx's theory of xi, 13, 16, 17,
    18, 20–21, 26, 30–39,
    111–121, 169
  material conditions of 175 n. 21
  neutrality of the state under 33,
    120
  socialism as Marx's remedy for
    xi
  treatment of workers under
    20–21
  welfare-state 198
categorical imperative, in Kant's
  ethics 102–103
charity 7 n. 6
children 11, 76, 82, 194

222

Index

and ownership of means of
    production 200
and property 9, 27, 90, 158, 159,
    181–182, 190
and redistribution 129, 131,
    194
and self-interest, *see* legitimate
    personal prerogative
and social subjugation 25, 55,
    202
and standard of living 47–48
and talents 51, 145
and the communist principle
    189
and the just state 192
and the labor theory of
    value 55
and the moral version of the
    labor theory 27, 123–147,
    158
and the principle of fair
    opportunity 193
as a principle of distributive
    justice 128, 184
as a principle of mutual benefit
    or reciprocity 27, 52, 129,
    142, 144
as distributing labor-time 27
as limit to property rights 2
bias in favor of the least
    advantaged 132, 141–147
Cohen on 48
deduction of 9, 178–81, 216
definition 9
egalitarianism of 9
labor theory of 122–157
lexical version of 47–48, 147,
    180–182
Nozick on 131 n. 5

Rawls on 2, 9, 27, 122, 128–130,
    143, 144, 147, 160, 180, 181,
    184
distribution, economic
    and justice 124, 133–141, 151
    and structural coercion 159
    and the difference principle 9,
        46–48, 50–52, 122–157, 198
    and the principle of reciprocal
        benefit 198
    and liberty 25, 160–162, 181–182,
        191–192, 194, 195
    as distributions of labor 132,
        142, 145, 147, 162, 216
    as distributions of money 146
    capitalist standard of 184
    definition 131, 134
    marginal productivity theory of
        54
    Marx on 14, 58–60
    measures of 176
    of labor 122–147
    of privileges 42–43
    of the means of production
        58–9
    social dimension of 126–127,
        145
    standards of 184–185, 189
doctrine of right, Kant's 102, 103
dominium 165
drug use, recreational 174

easements 164, 165–166
Eastern bloc states *see* socialist
    states
*Economic and Philosophical
    Manuscripts of 1844* (Marx)
    206
education 50, 194, 198

Index

Index

Index

state, the
  and capitalism 173 n. 20, 175 n.
    21, 196
  and coercion 160, 192
  and consent 100
  and justice 191–195
  and liberalism 12, 15–16
  and liberty 209
  and Marxian Liberalism 10, 159,
    191–195
  and ownership of means of
    production xii, 15
  and the right to property 104
  and the social contract 6, 88–93,
    113–114
  as whole people organized
    politically 114
  democratic 15–16, 173, 182, 190
  distinguished from civil society
    160, 161
  in the final phase of communism
    188
  involvement in economy 22
  Kant on 113–114
  Locke on 100, 113–114
  neutrality of in Marxian theory
    33, 120
  "nightwatchman" 12, 194
  power of 173 n. 20
  see also just state
state of nature 39, 41, 71–72, 88,
    97, 98, 103
Stillman, Peter 13
structural coercion 1, 32, 95,
    111–121, 123, 132, 171, 173,
    181, 192, 193, 195, 215
  and consent 181
  and economic distributions 159
  and inequality 176

definition 23–24
invisibility of 24, 112, 121, 161,
    162, 168, 176
property as a form of 26,
    111–121
subjective illusion 35, 36
subjugation 25, 55, 160–163, 168,
    169, 171, 177, 178, 179, 180,
    181, 183, 191, 196, 201, 209
substantive rationality 82
suffrage 173 n. 20
supermajorities 194
Supreme Court 192
surplus labor 31, 54, 56, 169, 183,
    197
surplus value 31
systematicness, for Kant 203, 204

talents 51, 124, 125, 130, 131, 132,
    133, 134, 145, 146, 150, 151,
    185
Tawney, R. H. 163
taxation 22, 47, 141, 147, 152, 164,
    198
technology 22, 184
terrorists 85
theoretical consent 1–2, 6, 7, 89–93,
    182
thought (or mental) experiments
    7–8, 42, 71, 125, 158
time labored 134, 135, 136, 183,
    187
training 134–135, 185, 198
transfer payments 48, 141
Treatise of Human Nature, A (Hume)
    61

unemployment 12
universal ownership 95, 99, 101